AMRYL JOHNSON was born in Trinidad and came to England when she was eleven. A poet who works in schools, she combines this with an attachment to the University of Warwick as writing fellow and junior lecturer in arts education. Her poetry has appeared in *News for Babylon*, *With a Poet's Eye*, *Watchers and Seekers*, and many other anthologies. Her prose has been published in several publications including *Facing the Sea*, *Spare Rib* and *Ambit*. Her highly acclaimed collection of poems, *Long Road to Nowhere*, was published by Virago in 1985. She has recently completed another volume of poetry as well as a book of short stories set around her childhood in the Caribbean. She is currently working on a novel.

AMRYL JOHNSON

Sequins for a Ragged Hem

Published by VIRAGO PRESS Limited 1988
Centro House, 20–23 Mandela Street, London NW1 0HQ

British Library Cataloguing in Publication Data
Johnson, Amryl
Sequins for a ragged hem.
1. Caribbean Area —— Description and
travel —— 1981–
I. Title
910'.091821   F2171.3
ISBN 0–86068–971–9

Typeset by J&L Composition Ltd of Filey, North Yorkshire
Printed in Finland by Werner Söderström Oy

I acknowledge the use of extracts from the following calypsos: 'Pirates' and 'Ah Come out tuh Party' by the calypsonian Shadow; 'Adam and Eve' by the calypsonian Lord Fluke; 'Hot hot hot' by the calypsonian Arrow.

INTRODUCTION

Sequins for a Ragged Hem came in response to experiences which begged for posterity. The ghosts would not leave me alone. They kept coming back to tease. An expression here, a gesture there. Something someone said.

Had I gone to the Caribbean with the intention of writing this book, I do not think I would have been as receptive to spiritual influences or as sensitive to vibrations as I was. I now believe the presence I sometimes sensed to be an ancestral figure – I do not know how many times removed. It seemed as if I was being drawn towards some greater understanding, forced to reassess my values. Again and again, these seven words stabbed at my brain: 'Where do you stand in all this?' Every incident was of importance. None was isolated. Pieces of a jigsaw. They would come together in the end, drawing me to a conclusion.

In 1982, I returned to Trinidad for four weeks. It had been many years since I previously visited the island of my birth. I had been postponing the trip. I had been putting it off because I was afraid. Had I been away too long? My mother had returned several years earlier but I had not thought of Trinidad of being anything more than the place where I was born.

During those four weeks, I felt very much an outsider, almost 'foreign' to my own culture. Stilted and inhibited, too many things gave me away. They betrayed me as someone who had, indeed, been away for too long. The question of identity was a very powerful and disturbing one. Every day became part of a complex learning process. Yet every day left me with a deeper hunger. I would return. At the earliest opportunity I would go back and this time I would be better prepared.

Sequins for a Ragged Hem tells of my return visit the following year. Still an outsider but I was no longer afraid. I had never seen any of the other islands. I visited them because I wanted to know what life was like there. But *Sequins for a Ragged Hem* is not a travelogue nor is it a guide for those who wish to visit. I am writing about my own experiences on the islands.

The 'ragged hem' of the book's title refers to the rape of slavery and all this had done to my people. 'Sequins' are the colour and sparkle they have woven into the state of being in exile.

Memories demanded that I complete this book. If what I experienced was, in effect, a haunting, I believe I have now laid these ghosts to rest in a style which I hope will satisfy even the most determined ones.

Amryl Johnson
Oxford, August 1987

'Girl, when you get off the plane, run!'

I stepped off the plane into Carnival fever. Even before my feet had touched the ground, I could feel the hot, pulsating beat of calypso music shoot like a bolt up the well which enthusiasm had pierced in my right leg. I was standing on the tarmac almost dancing on one foot. We were two weeks away from Carnival. Only two weeks before it exploded on the streets of Port of Spain.

The pilot had told us to keep our safety belts fastened until we were advised to the contrary. When the plane stopped, we would be towed the rest of the way. Regulations, he assured us. But we didn't remain seated until advised to the contrary.

'Girl, when you get off the plane, run!'

Word had got around that the immigration officers at Piarco airport were very thorough, a highly efficient group of employees who do not cut corners. If you found yourself near the end of the queue – more fool you. You could be there for hours. Ours was a full flight. Revellers would be flying in from all over the world in their thousands to enjoy the celebrations which have been dubbed the greatest show on earth. Unless you were holding a Trinidadian passport the officials wanted to know all about you. It could be a very long and drawn-out affair. The word had got around. So despite the pleas of the flight captain and crew, we were on our feet, hand luggage and coats over our arms before the caution light had gone out. I heard afterwards that the

3

sight of passengers rushing down the steps and running towards immigration was really something to behold. I was one of the first off the plane but somehow the minute my feet touched Trinidadian soil, I forgot the warning.

'Girl, when you get off the plane, run!'

I mean, what do you expect? Well, what I expected was something more than cramp and backache when the initial reaction subsided. When the initial reaction had subsided, I almost hobbled to immigration. While I was doing my dance on the tarmac, the other passengers swept past.

An hour later I seemed to have made little progress. There were two officials dealing with passports. But since our queue was at least three times the length of the nationals, we wanted to believe help would be coming. At the very least, when all the holders of Trinidadian passports had been dealt with, he would come over to give us a hand. The air conditioning was not working, so the hall was like a torture chamber. We are talking of an island where the temperature is invariably in the eighties. The thought that they may have been attempting psychology on us passed like a slow train. Some sort of appetizer for the interrogation to follow. Beads of perspiration were running down my face and body. I felt as if I was going to faint. I wasn't sure I could take much more. Some relief came when thoughts suddenly took me back to much cooler times.

That Sunday marked the first day of snow. I took it as an omen. Good for me. Bad for them. While struggling with the lock on a suitcase I heard whimpering coming from a corner of the room. It synchronized with two sets of groans being emitted from somewhere near the window. The friends taking me to the airport didn't much relish a journey from Oxford to Heathrow in weather like that. I offered a few words of sympathy. Genuine sympathy.

4

They are good friends. It wasn't going to be any joke. There was I flying off to soak in the Caribbean sunshine for six months, leaving them behind to battle with the elements. Tough. Really tough. But, well, that's the way things are. So we moved carefully through the snow. We had hoped for better that Sunday. It had been bright up to the previous day. They were glum and silent. I was silent also but my thoughts were naturally on other things. A car-load of people wrapped in thoughts which could not keep us warm. I should have been cosy, snug and smug but I really could not believe it was going to be so easy. Was it really that easy? You tick off the days on a calendar, pack your things and leave. The gods may yet demand to be appeased. So how come my passport was in order, ticket in order, baggage allowance inside the limit and flight scheduled to leave on time? Too easy. I still would not believe it was happening until I was strapped into my seat, watching Heathrow getting smaller and smaller as I moved swiftly and sweetly but not too discreetly towards a brighter sun. I rose slowly but unsteadily as a voice over the loud-speaker asked passengers on my flight to make their way to the final departure lounge. Standing there about to step forward, I was in the right attitude to have an arm flung around my neck. The gesture almost knocked me off balance. Two more friends had made their way through the white drift to see me off. I stayed until the final call became imperative.

'We wish we were going with you.'

I believed them. I knew they meant it. I waved a last goodbye, wishing I could leave enough affection behind to warm them through the rest of the winter. They huddled together, shivering inside the same brave smile. I turned quickly, trying to take little more than my overcoat with me. It would be another six months before I saw them again.

5

There is some reassurance to be gained after you have manoeuvred your way through security and overspent at the duty-free shop. Only then did I feel able to remove my overcoat. I was stepping out of one garment which would eventually be replaced by some other layer. But for the time being, I was freeing up. Freeing up under the loss of restriction and getting freer yet with a spring in my step as I lightly tripped the long journey from the final departure lounge to gate whatever-it-is. When I stepped inside the plane, I was walking on a cloud of air. By the time I fastened my safety belt, little remained of my recent past. I had been selective without realising it. Despite myself, I had taken this and that. The odd smile. A gesture. They clung for a while. It wasn't easy to shrug off the cloak of close friendships without some shivers of regret if only because I wished I could have taken at least one or two of them with me. The smiles and gestures remained for a while. They disappeared when a voice broke into my reverie. The spectres slid away to lose themselves among the melting white being reduced under the retracting wheels of the aeroplane. The voice at my side did not belong to the stewardess. I should be so lucky! It would take all my powers of persuasion to attract her attention when needed. There was no way she was going to volunteer her assistance.

The pleasant middle-aged Englishwoman sitting next to me was attempting to draw my attention to something or other. You would need to be of a particularly anti-social breed or a very fixed determination not to strike up some sort of acquaintance with the person at your elbow until the plane landed. We got into light conversation. That, the movie and lunch helped to while away the time. In what seemed a good deal less than eight hours, we were fastening our safety belts again. An hour earlier, we started peeling off sweaters as the tropical sun invaded. Time was on our side. I put my watch back five hours to synchronize with Caribbean time. Rays of sunlight filtered through the windows. We came down from the skies hesitantly, falling from level to level until the turquoise, sometimes blue-grey, sometimes bright blue Caribbean sea lay below us. Waves like tiny sails left even white trails in their wake. A shadow on the surface of the water followed us. This transparent black bird mimicked our every manoeuvre as it skimmed across the sea. Could the shadow the plane cast really be that minuscule? A land mass appeared below us. We were gliding down to meet lush vegetation. No longer minimized against the vast Caribbean or sandwiched between it and the sun, the gigantic iron bird swooped down on Barbados. There was a strong wind coming in also. It combed the coconut palms. It was so unreal yet I had to believe it. I was almost there. Everything was happening so quickly. We were unbuckling our safety belts. Passengers were disembarking.

This was as far as my companion was going. She had come to Barbados on holiday to visit her son who lived and worked there. Some of the passengers going on to Trinidad did not bother getting off. It was a brief stop. I needed to sample Caribbean sunshine again. The Barbadian air was exquisite. It was like being stroked by a warm, gold, silken glove of benevolence. I was in a daze, a state of euphoria. In my mind I kissed the ground several times. Perhaps that was my undoing. It put me in good stead for my arrival at Piarco. The people milling around the airport were out of a colourful play. I saw them in reds and pinks. I saw them in blue jeans drawn tight across ample bottoms. I saw them through a haze. I am not sure what I saw and what I imagined I saw. I wandered through the airport taking in everything. The easy, nonchalant movements of the Barbadians in civilian clothes, the khaki abruptness of the officials.

7

A voice told us it was time to board. There were a number of new faces. My new companion was a Trinidadian. Very friendly, very chatty. He began talking about this and that as soon as he sat down. When he wasn't chatting, he turned his head to exhange a few words with three other men who had boarded at the same time. He told me a gang of them were doing some construction work in Barbados and were returning home for a few days.

I watched Grantley Adams airport ebbing in the background. The runway was still plainly visible below us. It lay stretched out at my feet. Planes dotted at random were no bigger than toy models. I kept them in view until we were too high and there was nothing to see. I watched until the clouds we harnessed were too thick and dense to see the ground below. We were less than an hour from Trinidad.

I am not sure how it happened but my companion and I found ourselves exchanging recipes. He informed me he was an excellent cook and gave me a few hints on the use of herbs. He also gave me his address, assuring me he lived on his own. Would I like to drop in sometime to sample a little something? I was about to request a more specific definition when the pilot's voice came over the intercom.

'If the passengers sitting on the left of the aircraft would care to look out of the window, they will see Tobago below.'

Unfortunately, my seat was on the right. I had to wait another ten minutes or so before I could see land. Trinidad was in sight. We were told to fasten our safety belts. The descent commenced. We were going through grey clouds and approaching Trinidad from the south, coming in over lush green hills. We went down over the ominous rivulets of the Caroni swamp. A strange foreboding crept over me at the thought of having to crash land there.

'See over there?'

My companion gave me an eagle's eye lesson in the geography of the island of my birth.

' ... And that's Port of Spain.'

We were coming in quickly.

'Over there is – '

Less than ten hours flying time held a bubble, intact, untarnished, safe. The island was always somewhere out there. Largely oblivious to my presence, untouched by my absence. I wanted to puncture the bubble and yet hold it intact. I was none the wiser for my dilemma.

We were being towed. Nose pressed close to the glass, I searched faces in the crowd. Their faces were pressed against the wire fence which separated the runway from the outside world. It would be some time before I was on their side of the wall.

And what miracle was this, my Lord? Another immigration officer joined the section for holders of non-Trinidadian passports. He seated himself comfortably in the centre booth but there was no space for a third queue so he would deal with passengers from the other queue as well as ours. Under the gruelling conditions of the immigration hall, the inmates soon got the hang of things. And it had nothing to do with the everyday, run-of-the-mill concept of who was next in line. Under normal circumstances, one might suppose the person at the head of the queue to be next. But it was how quickly you could shove or elbow your way from six places behind. People came through like torpedoes. Never mind about him! He only *thinks* he's next in line! The idea was to get there before he did. All done with a great deal of exquisite timing, no one actually came to blows. I decided to chance my luck. There was a space I could manoeuvre through. I plotted my route. Just as the person at the third immigration desk was about to walk away, I moved in, beating someone else to it by a whisker.

He read my immigration card then went through my passport, carefully. Trinidad was the richest island in the Caribbean. Oil had seen to that. Its wealth, naturally, made it an attraction to the people from the poorer islands, not to mention the European who saw himself as a modern day buccaneer.

He glanced up at me.

'You born here but you hold a British passport?'

I ignored the accusation in his voice.

'The address on my immigration card? That's my mother's. That's right, I'll be staying with my mother.'

I told him I wanted to stay for six months, making Trinidad my base as I came and went among the islands. He stamped my passport with a permit which allowed me to stay for two months. If I wanted to remain after that date I would have to go to the immigration office in Port of Spain to have it renewed.

'And don't forget you go have to get a tax exemption certificate if you want to start travelling round the place.'

The reminder was just as sharp as the crease on the sleeves of his freshly laundered khaki jacket, impenetrable with starch. I thanked him because I did not know what else I was supposed to do. I was now free to go and collect my luggage.

There was a strange apparatus at Piarco airport which fascinated and stupefied even the most seasoned of travellers. In the baggage hall you came face to face with it. It was a conveyor belt which moved as if in the throes of a nervous breakdown. The luggage was going round at a pace which would make any snail look like a sprinter. A highly nervous, careful piece of apparatus, the advance moves were as careful as if it was a game of chess. Its energy level rose. A quick spurt. It stopped. Two quick spurts before resting for five minutes. I was in for another long wait. We were all in for another long wait. A number of people had formed a semi-circle, watching as if hypnotized. No gently swaying reptile movements lulling you into complacency here. This one didn't even have a brain. You stood rigid, fists clenched in disgust. Only your eyes moved as you followed the line of luggage going round. Every now and then, someone sprang into action, jerked forward as if worked by a puppeteer. The traveller then turned like an automaton to head towards customs at full speed. Another person and then another in the crowd came to life. Soon, mercifully, it was my turn. I saw my cases coming in at the sort of speed which for a moment had me wondering if they were going backwards.

The customs officer looked weary and fed-up. He asked all the expected questions, went through the motions of flicking through the contents of my cases then slapped labels on them to let the officer guarding the exit know he had completed his part. This gentleman was showing enough aggression to make up for his colleague's lethargy.

'Put them down so I can mark them!'

The cross he made with his enthusiastic marker extended beyond the bounds of duty. It slipped off the customs label on to the fabric of my brand new canvas bag. I suspected the mark would not wash out. I tried to tell myself it could be worse but my eyes stayed riveted on the broad black ink lines soaking into the beige fabric. I opened my mouth to tell him about it but thought better of it. The fact remained I was finally free to leave.

I stepped out into the clean, sweet air towards a throng of happy, anxious people bathed in sunshine. I was scanning the faces when I heard my name. A woman strangely familiar. A stranger yet not a stranger. Familiar. Totally.

Yes. One hundred per cent familiar. A woman is showering me with affection. All layers of recognition were peeled away in the space of two seconds when I saw my mother. Two other relatives were present. And someone else. Her presence came to overwhelm me. Only I could feel her kiss. The roughness of her eager embrace. For the time being I shrugged her aside. I left her there as we drove away from the airport. Or so I thought. Coherent, yet in a dream-state. My lips formed words of joy and excitement. They were responded to with happiness and affection. The road took us through Tunapuna. Tunapuna where I was born, to Curepe, the town some short distance away where my mother now lives.

A year earlier I had made tentative steps along the stepping stones to my formative years only to find myself marooned on unfamiliar territory. Only three days earlier, they had demolished the house where I was born. They had stripped the flesh. Only its shell remained. Nothing but time would bring me home from that despair. Heel to toe within every footprint, matching the outlines until I was back on that one road. The same I had travelled. The only road I really knew. When I moved onward in time, this time, I would be better prepared. No longer looking through rose-tinted glasses, I would see the ruts and gradients quite clearly.

The scenery was one of palms and fruit trees. Coconut, banana and mango among others. Shacks, exotic houses, cars, bicycles, half-naked children playing in the road, sophisticated ladies walking along the streets in what looked like designer clothes. And the smells. The odours wafting in through the window were of food, fruit and the island's own fertility. Colours rose out of the steamy heat to mingle with the languid sights and sounds. They came with intensity. They filled my senses, making them alive to the touch and smell of everything I saw. Conversation was as relaxed and easy as the life outside. My eyes were closed in acknowledgement of the sightless images still piling into the car, begging for recognition. I accepted, welcoming them all. I rejected none.

No longer floundering, every forward step had me feeling the ground beneath my feet for subsidence. Pot holes may come in pairs. Eyes which stare back from the asphalt where it has been sucked into the funnels of irregularities bear witness to the shifting nature of pitch in the mid-day sun. It can barely resist the feet which have trampled in the hysteria of centuries. But never mind – I was back now! And as confident as a tightrope walker.

I opened my eyes, again, to the housing complex with its neatly manicured lawns. The shacks and simple houses of the poor had given way to the more substantial dwellings of the well off. Past industrial estates until we were once again driving towards shacks and simple houses of the poor. I shut my eyes to try and check the sight and sightless image which came to play under my nose. The image of need. The car swung to the right, and the odour of want gradually ebbed, receding once again to the smell of fruit trees when we stopped outside my mother's neat bungalow. There were more relatives waiting. The greetings and conversation went on until my eyes were like slits and my lips merely moving to form the right words.

Evening comes quickly and dramatically in the Caribbean. I have likened it to a bird of prey which descends out of the sky, wings outstretched, covering the land. I slipped away to walk through my mother's garden among her avocado, mango, banana, cane and corn stalks. I wanted to watch the sun go down. It set slowly. Someone came to call me at the very instant it was out of sight. I took with me an impression of embers which rose to scatter a fine, grey dust over the island.

I closed the gate still waving goodbye. We had taken our relatives home. The moon hung bright and full. It and a cloudless ink-blue sky were the background. In the foreground, a coconut tree which almost leaned on the front gate reached up, branches like arms extended in supplication. Perfectly still. There was hardly a breeze. The moon, the sky, the palm. I took them all.

> 'Killing me
> Killing me softly
> Killing me
> Killing me softly'

The words and the driving bass which motivates the calypso beat were like a red hot pin stabbing at my brain. The throbbing was causing some discomfort but the insistence of the calypsonian's plight had me listening intently.

> 'My friend who loves me
> wants my record free
> But he already have a cassette
> which he brought from a pirate –'

After a while, Shadow, the calypsonian singing about the illegal taping of his music, the loss of royalties through it and what he thinks of the people recording and selling these tapes, comes back with the refrain.

> 'These big time bandits
> Just ripping off my music
> Killing me
> Killing me softly

Killing me
Killing me softly – '

I sympathised. I felt I knew what it would be like to have someone killing you softly. My first morning in Trinidad. Was I suffering from jet lag? Was I suffering from culture shock? Or what? I came to the conclusion it was a combination of both plus a little of the 'or what' brought on by the frantic two weeks before leaving England. Hot calypso favourites being belted out from radios, record players and what I suspected was a ghetto blaster from the street gradually got louder to boom at me.

'Ah come out tuh party'

The sound faded to mingle with everything else, crashing into my bedroom. The door creaked open. My mother stood in the doorway, bathed in smiling daylight.
'I woke you?'
I shook my head, returning her smile. She answered mine. My mother and I exchanged miles upon miles of smiles. She was the first to break the spell.
'I am going out. I have to go into town. If anyone comes tell them –'
I glanced at my watch. Seven-thirty. Buses into Port of Spain would be packed. She left me lying there, still smiling. The smile faded to a grimace extending from ear to ear. Calypso music was still going full blast. The throbbing wasn't only in my head. I could feel it right through my body. Each throb was like a cut. Spaced out, it soon felt as if I had been dissected by an army of knives. I did not dare move. If I did, I would leave backbone, midriff, hands and thighs behind.
A force once again came to overwhelm me. I could sense

a presence in the room. Was it this which took me down beneath the surface? I could understand and recognise the purpose and form of the initiation. Lying at the bottom of the well, sounds came like pendants of water. The knives kept their pale grey hue but softened before melting to drops of water. Forced to retract and retrace, I found myself once again in harmony with the rhythm of acceptance.

I could be blind and still function normally. Guided by my aural sense, I closed my eyes and turned over in the peace and tranquillity of a single bed.

The woman next door was doing her laundry. She was washing her clothes in the large concrete sink at the side of the house. The muffled monotony of her labour as she forced the clothes against a washing board made a dull irregular thud. A loud animated conversation was punctuated by peals of laughter. Once heard, never forgotten. Raucous and uninhibited, it was also warm and vibrant. Above all, the woman's laughter contained a tinge of maliciousness. It left you feeling you had just missed out on a really juicy piece of gossip. My vision of recall entered the space where a woman stood, hands on hips, head thrown back in laughter. The woman slowly turned, her chuckles now more subdued. Her smile faded. The eyes darkened as iris and pupil became one, huge and deep. Features were melting like pitch with the eyes getting deeper and larger like holes in the road.

I started. What the hell–? I was on my own again, breathing clear above the surface of the water. My eyes were open and staring long before I heard the klaxoning. It has been said that Trinidadians drive on their car horns. Plenty of Trinidadian impatience had been reaching me from the road for some time. This one, however, was coming from no further than our front gate. Mothers should know or at least remember to remind you. I had to leap out of bed as the day's agenda came back to me.

For the rest of the week, I as good as lived on the beach. Any and every invitation for any time of day or evening was gratefully accepted. Carenage, Maracas, Blanchisseuse, Toco, Manzanilla. Any of the other bays, and there were many, would do just fine. To feel the sand between my toes just before I hit that wonderful, wonderful cool water and lie cradled in the arms of the rippling sea was, basically, all I wanted from life. 'Pots' and iceboxes were the next stage. You eat, drink, then fall slowly backwards, prostrate against one of a row of coconut palms. At twenty feet or more above the sands with their branches fanning downwards in a gentle breeze, it always felt as if they were on my side.

'I come because I have a dream 'bout all you. I know the child here.'

The voice had come, unannounced. A tall, mysterious figure stood in the living room. My thoughts did somersaults when I saw the woman. Elderly and erect, she was as black as coal.

'Child, I know you before you was born.'

But I did not know the voice.

'Aunt Ruby!'

My mother's recognition of the woman caught me completely off balance. I had never met her before but my mother had talked of her. Crouched among the misshapen shadows spawned by those derelict walls is the history of a woman who, though not a blood relative, had insinuated herself into the family so long ago that no one could remember where she came from. She simply arrived on the doorstep from time to time, bringing gifts of mangoes, avocados, oranges, guavas, tamarinds or whatever happened to be in season. She would walk straight into the house without knocking and announce her presence with the words, 'I come because I had a dream 'bout all you.' She would spend the rest of the day domineering, disrupting, interfering, before disappearing – until the next time. My mother told me later that prior to her visit that morning she had not seen her in five years. Aunt Ruby proceeded to put me through the third degree. I was obliged to answer a barrage of questions.

'No, you can't spend all your time on the beach. It have other things you must do. And tomorrow you going to town. You get up early, you dress and you try and get yourself into town before ten o'clock. Now listen to what I telling you. It real, real simple. When you leave the bus station, you cross the street and –'

My mother meanwhile had made a very discreet exit to the garden to potter among her okras and beans. I caught sight of her face from the window, she was still chuckling to herself.

Day begins as dramatically as it ends. By six o'clock life was already starting to stir. By seven it had long erupted. Cocks were still crowing, water running, people speaking, laughing, singing and calypso detonating your ear drums. The Caribbean morning began too damn early for my taste. I opened the door of my mother's bedroom.

'I woke you?'

'As if you didn't know.'

She smiled at me. I returned her smile. My mother and I were once again exchanging miles of smiles. I was the first to break the spell.

'I am going out. I have to go into town. If anyone comes tell them – '

I glanced at my watch. It was nine forty-five. No matter how hard I tried it was the earliest I could manage. Having been up since six o'clock, my mother was taking a mid-morning rest.

The world is put to rights, people are converted, some lose their faith on the buses which run from Tunapuna to Port of Spain. I caught a 'limited stop' at the last pick-up point in Curepe before it went non-stop into the capital. In addition to a fast, efficient service, complex political and cultural problems are unravelled and sorted. Solutions are offered. This occasional service was held at a particular time of day. Generally speaking, between the hours of nine and ten-thirty. Prior to these surgery hours, travelling companions were of a less receptive, more preoccupied genre. Those less privileged travellers wore dour faces. I never did find out the ruling on standing restrictions. There appeared to be none. Packed like sardines, it was all they could do to breathe, least of all attempt anything too profound. With the conductor squeezing them in tightly, there was really no space for thoughts and inspiration to evolve into words which would flourish to bear fruit. Those early morning travellers were on their way into the capital to work or on business. Any business which took you into Port of Spain should have you stepping out of the bus or taxi at eight o'clock. That was the time when almost all the worthy establishments opened their doors. You should have it concluded by twelve o'clock. You did so in order to avoid the dry, dusty, relentless heat of the midday sun. Should you, by need, find yourself in its clutches, you would get little solace from shade you might draw from passing walls.

I boarded the bus taking the last seat and made myself comfortable. For a few minutes, all was fairly peaceful.

'Ecclesiastes two, verse fourteen say, "the wise man's eyes are ... "'

The man's voice was loud enough to be heard by everyone on board. He was seated at the back with an open bible in his hand.

A young man in a navy blue string vest and wide-brimmed hat began to heckle.

'What you know 'bout Ecclesiastes two? You could read bible? You don't look as if you ever even learn your ABC.'

The young man's companion took up the chorus.

'Pa, who you think you fooling? Your bible upside down!' Loud guffaws.

A woman's voice brought even more raucous laughter as she jumped on the bandwagon.

'Bible? He? He look like all he know 'bout is rum shop.' Someone else chipped in.

'Why you don't leave the man alone? He harming all you?'

A new voice.

'All you people should keep quiet and listen to the word of God. It go do all you good. None of all you look as if you see the inside of a church since you was baptise.'

Someone made sure she didn't get away with it.

'Who ain't see the inside of a church since they baptise? You know 'bout me? You passing your mouth on me, a God-fearing woman who does get down on she knees in church four times a week and every morning and evening in she bedroom? You playing in your arse. What you know 'bout me? What you think you know 'bout me? Is cuff you want me cuff you in your mouth or what?'

Three passengers were now on their feet as the temperature inside the bus began to rise. The conductor tried to make himself heard above the din.

'Why all you people don't shut your blasted mouth?'

He didn't really expect to be heard. The bus was not scheduled to stop again until it reached the terminus in

Port of Spain. He would not be making any emergency stops to deflate the situation or throw anyone off the bus. He would not be doing anything about it. And the reason why he would not be doing anything about it is because that was the way things were. Everyone enjoys a good argument. So we were speeding along the 'Priority route' where only buses run and the only respite was the occasional traffic signal. A busload of passengers speeding and swaying towards the capital.

Trinidadians know their bible. Churches are packed on Sundays. No chance of pulling the wool over their eyes. The argument folded back on itself with half the bus soon involved in the true interpretation of Ecclesiastes two, verse fourteen. I sat quietly, not only because I was overwhelmed by the spontaneous nature of it all but also because I knew nothing about Ecclesiastes two. The temperature inside the bus was still rising. I sat quietly in my seat as did the lady sitting next to me. A quiet, bespectacled soul of about fifty and ten. Our eyes were fixed firmly on the road ahead. I drew solace from the peaceful aura of her company while passion around me raged. The rest of the passengers, if not joining in verbally, were responding in some way. Loud laughter at some of the ribald, 'clever' comments or facial expressions. Suddenly, like a bolt of lightning, the thin, fragile frame next to me leapt to her feet.

'All you blasted people!'

Her voice was of the quality which consumed mountains, dragons, fire and all. She had gobbled up all other voices with her resonance, far stronger and louder than I would have imagined.

'All you blasted people put me through this shit every time I travel on this kiss-me-arse bus. A poor woman can't even have a minute peace and quiet. Why the arse you can't keep your blasted mouth shut for even five seconds?

But, no, all you loud mouth vulgarness brought up in the l'abasse who don't even know how to wear shoes does save all your pennies to come out and ride bus with decent people and you does bring all your dirty nasty habits with you. Why the arse you don't keep your tail at home until you know how to behave? Why the arse they don't stop the kiss-me-arse bus so all you can get off at the shanty town where all you come from? You worthless, idle, good-for-nothing people who does – '

Once or twice, someone had tried to interrupt her flow but it was of the essence and fluency which severs, annihilates all competition. She held centre stage, the others were now nothing more than supporting actors. Bit performers. A jolt brought her to a halt. The easy sliding of the door as it opened signalled our arrival at the terminus. As they streamed out, a few threw words at her the way a losing fighter throws in his towel.

'Woman, hush up your mouth!'

'You blasted tell me I from some damn l'abasse?!!'

'You lucky I don't buss up your mouth!'

'You need man. That what wrong with you!'

'Grandma, get off the blasted bus!'

She stood her ground and saw them off like a guard dog you know will sink its teeth into your ankle if you make a wrong move. Or, more likely, she would knee you in the groin or beat you over the head with the leather shopping bag she was brandishing. Not one of them would have been a match for her. Not one of them was. She held the stage until all the passengers were off the bus. The driver and conductor looked on with interest. The floor show would not have been entirely new to them.

The heat generated on the inside was matched by the eighty-two degrees on the outside. I didn't stand a chance. Less than half an hour since I left the house, I wasn't just hot, I was hot and sticky.

I stood back in awe as my erstwhile companion, still fuming, bustled out of the terminus. She steamed past me, moving quickly through the busy terminus as she went about her business.

It cost just fifteen cents to make the trip into Port of Spain. A fraction of the taxi fare. And Trinidadians will leap into a taxi with as much zeal as they do everything else. Petrol was cheap. If you don't have a car then you use the taxis. It was the way of life. Trinidadians travel everywhere by taxi. It was only when the government introduced a priority route used only by buses and which ran from Arima in the north to the capital that people started to take public transport seriously. There are those who feel it would be bad for their image to be seen travelling on buses but if you wanted to get from Arima or, more conveniently, Tunapuna, to anywhere on the route into Port of Spain then you waited at one of the sheltered bus stops for a 'non-stop', 'limited stop' or 'all stops', depending on where you board and your destination. And so I never used a taxi if I could help it. Always the bus.

Outside the bus terminus, Port of Spain was waiting. Noisy, dirty and awful, waiting in all its magical, terrible, unique beauty. Before I had even left the shelter and coolness of the terminus, I was being enticed. Smiling young men with cane baskets containing packets of roasted nuts serenaded me. Two of them followed for a few yards, one on either side.

'Doo doo, darling. You looking nice, nice, nice. Why you don't stop and talk to me. Let me tell you how much I does love you.' I walked on.

'Girl, how come you look so nice? I like the way you does look in your green dress.'

My sunglasses were shielding more than the sun's glare.

'Nuts! Nuts! Get your roasted nuts! Sweet and fresh!'

Their commercial instinct prevailed as a throng of passengers came towards the exit. Trinidadian men appear to have a favourite occupation which begins, more or less, when they are boys. They do not grow out of it on reaching manhood. They simply become selective and subtle. It seems as if from the time they are old enough to realize what there may in one form or another be in it for them, they start 'troubling' girls. A friend explained the predicament.

'We take our womanizing seriously.'

And there is a good reason for this. The island is the most cosmopolitan in the Caribbean. The peoples of Europe, Africa, China and India have mixed to produce complexions which range from the palest tan to the deepest ebony. The women are among the most beautiful and sophisticated in the world. Faced with the dilemma this choice brings it is not surprising that the men take it so seriously and tackle it with such dedication.

So when peanut vendors or anyone else for that matter approach you with sweet, wooing words, you do not turn round and 'cuss' them out any more than you take them seriously. They are only doing what comes naturally.

Back in the open air, the heat enveloped me. It was too hot to be soothing or of comfort. It was oppressive.

The layout of Port of Spain is strikingly symmetrical. An aerial view would give streets going horizontally from the port to Dry River and streets running vertically from Queens Park Savannah to South Quay. The streets are like straight lines which intersect to form oblong boxes. We have the Spaniards of the eighteenth century to thank for this monotony. I walked up Independence Square and tried to remember what Aunt Ruby had told me. Simpler than struggling with a map.

'It real, real simple. When you leave the bus station, cross the street and go so.'

Her hand indicated the direction. Straight ahead.

'You in Nelson Street. When you get to the corner, you go so.' A left turn.

'The streets go be George, Charlotte, Henry, Frederick, Chacon.' She chimed a memory aid.

'Abercromby, St Vincent, Edward. Going straight up Frederick Street to the savannah, you go meet seven more going across.'

She had stopped to take breath before launching into another memory aid.

'Queen, Prince, Duke, Park, Oxford, New then Gordon. You hear what I telling you?'

I had been enjoying this city by night, taking in the odd calypso tent and show after a late evening on the beach. I would now need to learn to love her by day, also.

The people I met on my way up Independence Square to Frederick Street were out of a magnificent technicolour dream. The people 'liming' on street corners didn't need to work at being individuals. They were. There was a man perched on a bicycle, wearing baseball boots without laces. His orange pants were cut off at the knees where raw edges still frayed hard. The 'Carnival 82' teeshirt had suffered the same fate. Some indiscriminating scissors had removed the sleeves. So he was now quite sleeveless as well as knee to ankleless. A soft, green felt was pulled low over his eyes.

I had no idea they made jeans in that size. He was chatting to a woman with an unbelievably generous bottom held momentarily inactive by the severity of blue denim. Her top half was of the same generous proportions. It had undergone a similar fate. It, also, had been straight-jacketed into submission, tamed and pacified by a controlling influence which held her rigid. She had squeezed herself into a pink stretch top. I could only hope she would be around and congenial if it started to rain and I was without an umbrella.

The conversation came to meet me while I was yet a little distance from them. Strolling leisurely, I didn't need to eavesdrop.

'But Mavis, I telling you. I walk into we own house and catch she there on the bed with she sweet man.'

'Well, boy, you real unlucky, yes. I don't know how you does have so much bad luck with your women and them. Must be somebody do you something.'

She lowered her voice as she gave him the next piece of advice. By then I had drawn level so what she had to say reached me anyway.

'Look, Snakie, boy. I heard 'bout this man in Siparia. This friend I have say he good, good. Why you don't go and see if he can't – '

There was a sudden screeching of tyres at my elbow. A second later I could feel the heat from a car wheel as it singed the hairs on my leg.

'Is blind you blind or what? If you take off your damn sunglasses like you some blasted tourist, you go see the cars and them coming up the road. And if you –'

All this was meant for me. Pedestrians, street vendors, limers, all turned to look in the direction of an incensed taxi driver. Everyone but me. I put my nose in the air to look as disdainful as I could while I continued crossing the street. In truth, I was shaking like a leaf. The wheel was like an iron about to be branded into my flesh. The memory of it was still searing. And where the devil had he sprung from? He sure as hell wasn't there when I first stepped into the street.

'They should put an L-plate on all you before they let you out. That way we go know –'

The rest of what he had to say was drowned by the

klaxoning of horns from the traffic behind him. And where had they suddenly come from? Traffic seemed to appear as if by magic.

There was so much happening on Frederick Street. Commerce, shops, vendors, pedestrians, cars. Frederick Street, as always, busy, teeming with people. Noise ripened in the high temperature to become bolder, louder. People, cars, shops – and Lord Fluke. The refrain from his calypso about the creation reached me.

> 'Naked they come
> Naked they go
> Naked they come
> Naked they go'

The rest of his song was sucked into the vacuum which consumes all energy not moored by gravity, distorting sound. The wind toying with discarded paper made an almost indecipherable rustle.

My sunglasses had a pinkish tint. Perhaps that was the reason why I could no longer tell the difference between reality and what I imagined I saw. But if I took them off I would be blinded by the glare. In that dry, dusty heat, I found myself choking on a desert of mirages. Images coming towards me seemed to seep out of cracks in the pavement. Heat waves transposed shapes, melted movement, absorbed colour. Ghost-like figures wafted upwards as if seeking light, reaching for substance. Somewhere between the two aspirations they were cut down. Bullet holes like wounds on their cloaks. They bled yellow, purple, orange, red, blue, green. The colours merged, one into the other then fading back to nothing, waned to the level of the gutter to be pulled back beneath the surface. The funnel of sound was now chewing on Lord Fluke's words.

' – they come
Naked they go
– they come
Naked they go'

Later, I would need to ask myself if I had not had a premonition of things which were to come.

I would need to learn to love this terrible city by day. And learning was the lesson of the day. There was a right and a wrong way of doing things. It went beyond mannerisms and speech. There were specific ways of going about things. After two hours shopping in Port of Spain, I learnt to economise on my 'please' and 'thank you'. I also learnt you could well be wasting your breath by saying 'sorry'. I tripped on someone's heel and the look she gave me when I tried to apologise made it clear I was wasting my time. I should have done what everyone else did, pretended it hadn't happened.

Determined to survive that part of the initiation, I wandered through Port of Spain, observing. I put my bag over my shoulder and my hands behind my back. There was a painful throb which ran from quick to wrist where I had burnt my fingers so I tried to keep them still.

There are many areas in Trinidad more accessible by taxi than bus. It took a while to decipher the semaphore being used by some travellers. It was used when hailing a taxi. The arm would be extended at some point within a hundred and eighty degree angle from the hip upwards to the side of the head. The taxi driver would know the passenger's destination by the angle of the arm and if there was still space in the taxi he would stop. When you saw a car with an H-plate travelling along a street which led to your destination, you could try calling to the driver.

'St James?'

28

'Gonzales?'
'Belmont?'
'Cascade?'
There were also specific pick-up points.

It was part of a distinct order, a pattern, something peculiar to them and them alone – a Trinidadianism. I also noticed the passengers coming into town, the way they asked to be let out at their destination and the way they paid the driver. I would need to remember all of it.

'They does cross the street as if they in their bedroom.'

Another day-time trip to Port of Spain. This time in a friend's car. The indignant exclamation had been provoked by a pedestrian stepping out in front of our car and sauntering nonchalantly across the street. Under normal circumstances, I would have taken little notice. There was something almost suicidal about the way he had stepped out in front of the car. But that wasn't it. He wanted to cross the street so he crossed, knowing the cars would have to stop for him. Far more practical than running him over to teach him a lesson. The laws on homicide are taken as seriously in Trinidad as they are anywhere else.

I watched and made mental notes. There was a rapport between driver and pedestrian. It was like a game being acted out. I would see it between clerks and customers, between audiences and performers. It had everything to do with action and response or clever repartees. Parrying with words.

I saw pedestrians react to drivers in a second way. There was indignation from one middle-aged gentleman when a car's bumper touched the crease in his trousers.

'Bounce me down! Bounce me, nah! You go see what I go do you.'

The note of dare in his voice was matched by the action

of rolling up his sleeve. The hand closed into a fist. The driver put on a mask of remote preoccupation and waited for the man to move away from his windscreen.

And yet it became so imperative, I found myself having to retreat even further than a few initial steps I had taken to become objective. The day I watched a car accelerate as it approached a pedestrian crossing just to watch the children scatter with me, myself, caught in mid-stride, I stormed back to the crossroads, tore up the highway code and fell to my knees. I would need to crawl before I could walk again.

There are no rules being broken. How can there be? You are making them as you go along. When you are behind the wheel, drive with your foot on the brakes and your hand on the horn. You beep every few minutes just in case and you keep a wary eye on taxis. They will screech to a halt in the middle of the road if there is a fare in the offing. You anticipate the other driver's movements. He probably won't bother to indicate. You learn that all drivers expect to be let in and given right of way. When you pull out, you do so at the most hazardous time. You keep a look-out for the canines. Their approach to life is as laid-back as their masters'. They will cross as leisurely, ignoring the horn. When they are taking the sun, paws sometimes come dangerously close to the road. The number of dogs with limps are a fair indication of those who got their timing wrong. You do not forget to yell abuses at fellow-motorists, pedestrians and any two-wheeler which gets in the way.

When you are on the other side of the fence, you take your heart in your hand. At the very least, bite your lip and wait for your blood pressure to go up. You are given no priorities. You are not safe at pedestrian crossings any more than you are safe on an empty road. Within a second, some maniac is sure to come hurtling round the corner at breakneck speed. Your best bet would be to stand in the shadow of one of the brazen young men who will actually signal the traffic to stop so he can amble across at his own leisurely pace. Having gained the pavement on the other side and dusted yourself off, you are now ready to come to terms with the other hazard you are sure to encounter.

'I here waiting and all you chatting 'bout what you boyfriend do you last night? But what the arse is this?!!'

In a crouching posture, halfway between crawl and walk, I could think of no good reason why anyone paid to serve and to smile should, necessarily, be expected to do so.

You go have to wait until we finish we business!

It is not said. Merely implied.

The customer stood, hands on her hips, waiting. Next in line, I waited also.

One of the salesgirls came over. The expression and manner made it quite clear: she was doing us a favour.

'Yes, madam. Is cloth you want?'

As we happened to be in a dress fabric shop the answer would undoubtedly be – yes.

I would need to get used to the power which clerks at various levels exert over their customers.

'But they're so rude.'

The friend I was complaining to thought it over for a while. It was perhaps the first time she had ever needed to distance herself from it.

'Is apathy. They don't care 'bout we.'

It wasn't always like that. A few were pleasant. But not enough of them to make up for the inefficiency, the aggression and the number of times I had to listen to the change from my purchase being slammed on the counter.

I turned uneasy, beneath the surface, blowing bubbles as I came up for air.

*

If anyone had told me I could do it, I would have called that person a liar. Six in the morning. I was already up and dressed. My mother was fretting. We should have left much earlier. It was Saturday. I insisted on going with her to the market in San Juan, just a few miles away. All I succeeded in doing was keeping her back.

When we got there I understood why she was so insistent. The market was already crowded. I was greeted by a wonderful melange of fruit, herbs and other smells.

And mothers should know or at least remember to remind you.

In headscarf, flip-flops and print dress she blended totally with her surroundings, the throng and atmosphere of early morning chaos. I, in my normal day clothes and heeled sandals, looked distinctly over-dressed.

Had it not been for my mother I would have had to make my way back along the now well-worn trail. She stopped me a couple of times as I was about to over-reach my threshold.

We were confronted with a cycle of prices. Tomatoes $5.99, bananas $1, salt fish $4.80, cucumbers $1, oranges at three for $1 and so on. A number of stalls were carrying the same price but the quality of goods of one or two of them were better than the others. Further into the market, we found stalls which were cheaper. Either way, you shop around. When you have decided which stall you would like to buy from, you have to temper your approach. I was doing some shopping of my own. You do not interrupt the vendor when she is taking the customer's money or, more importantly, giving change. Chances are she will turn round and give you a mouthful. My mother's hand went out to stop me from making myself the centre of attraction. Timing is of the essence. The stall which carried some nice grapefruit did not display a price. I was about to ask, when my mother stopped me once again. She took her time about asking and her intonation and language were different from that which I would have used.

'How much your grapefruit, darling?'

That would do for the time being. Flippers and goggles in position, I came out of the water surfacing only marginally above my self-consciousness. I can pull away and look at this strange creature which rose out of the sea, shrugging water like a mountain. Leaving amphibian footprints which came dangerously close to the edge. Nevertheless, they betrayed no human traits. I could go undetected. When I turned to look over my shoulder, I felt oddly detached, strangely apathetic. The water was still and calm, calmer than it had been in a long time. So still, so calm, so deceptive. Waiting. I looked back only once and I had not seen a beach in days, nor did I have any inclination to do so. But I would need to return, discard the footprints which leave no trace, peel off the black seal skin and mask of the subterranean refuge and walk barefoot in just the white of my gown and head tie. The reflections from the waves which distort the image also distress the lines beyond recognition. Soon I will lose all memory, cut from the womb by a razor-sharp curve of the mirror. I would go down three times. Before long I would be baptised in the waters of six islands.

> 'and I'm going to shout
>> party!
> and I'm going to scream
>> party!'

A group of young men on a street corner were singing along with the chorus, arms pumping in appreciation.

Even before the last strains had died, the opening bars of another calypso had them moving their bodies, leading the calypsonian into his song. I had been partying non-stop for days until my eyes were fixed in a glazed stare and my feet ached. Any steel band or calypso beat had us absorbing more of this fever of body and mind. There would be no let up. Just two days away from Carnival and Trinidad was on fire.

> 'How you feeling?
>> Hot hot hot!
> How you feeling?
>> Hot hot hot!'

And the temperature was still going up. Soon it would explode – on the streets of Port of Spain.

It is no joking matter. Trinidadians start getting into training from a good month before Carnival. Some take the ability to wring as much as they can out of the festive season seriously enough to take up jogging. You do not see them running around Queens Park Savannah at any other time of the year. You certainly do not see them piling on the pressure in trainers and shorts to the same extent. If you don't jog, you may need to attend keep-fit classes because if you are truly dedicated, as it gets closer to the big Monday, you may find yourself going for as long as three nights on the trot with little sleep. If you are truly dedicated there will be a new pattern to your life. From work, you go home to get a couple of hours sleep, get up, shower, go out partying, get home in time to get a couple of hours sleep before going off to work. It is an exercise in stamina. And I was not doing very well. Hence the glazed expression. My reflex action had become very acute. Any calypso or steel band beat had me twitching head, shoulders, midriff and feet. I do believe I was on overdrive.

The various competitions are held in Queens Park Savannah. I had seen the Children's Carnival, Carnival King and Queen preliminaries and Panorama preliminaries, the first round of the national steel band competition. It showed the delirium of support which steel orchestras such as Desperadoes, the band based in Laventille, one of the most deprived areas of Port of Spain, could inspire. I sat in the Grand Stand. I was there for one reason and one reason only, I could not get into the North Stand. The North Stand is where you go to enjoy yourself and have a good time with your friends, as opposed to sitting reasonably quietly to enjoy the music as you are expected to do when in the Grand Stand.

Catelli All Stars from Duke Street, Port of Spain, took the stage. The average Trinidadian is a pan critic. He can pick up the nuances between the different arrangements and innovations of the same tune when it is played by several bands. Catelli was playing the same tune as Desperadoes. A particular subtlety or brilliance of arrangement caused the gentleman who had been sitting quietly in the row in front of mine to leap to his feet, pull off his teeshirt and wave it in the air in appreciation. The gesture had been a spontaneous one. As soon as he realised what he was doing, he sheepishly put it on again and took his seat. I had not picked up the ingenuity which had warranted such a response but others in the audience reacted with the same appreciation, albeit on a less visual level. I watched the raucous appreciation of revellers on the opposite side of the stage, the North Stand. I was frustrated by the truth that I could only come mid-way to what I wanted to achieve. Although thrilled and excited by the music, I did not know enough about steel band music to recognise the finer strands of the various arrangements.

On the Sunday before Ash Wednesday, the Children's

Carnival takes to the streets. Prior to that, costumes are confined to the stage of Queens Park Savannah. I had seen some of the kings and queens the previous day at the Red Cross Children's Carnival. Seeing them in Independence Square with the other members of the band gave me a more accurate idea of just how tiny some masqueraders were. One of the queens looked no more than seven and there were two who looked even younger.

Her face had been painted gold and silver. The head-dress was almost as tall as she. It was made of fringes of pearl beads, ostrich feathers, beaten gold encrusted with jewels. The costume was even more stunning. Her body suit of gold and silver motifs was completed by a shock of gold feathers. These spanned such a wide circle that it dwarfed her already tiny frame. There is an expression 'dancing your costume'. It means swaying your body in such a way that your costume takes on a life of its own. This little professional already knew about 'dancing your costume'. She responded to the pulse of the steel band by stepping in time to the music. Whatever she was doing with her body at the same time caused the feathers to move as if an enormous bird was shaking its entire body of soft feathers. She was the 'Golden Fledgling of Paradise'.

There is a great deal of devotion and valour attached to the wearing of these costumes. Authenticity is the order of the day. If the band's theme is around European mythology then the Norse gods will be dressed in a costume which consists of copper helmet, leather, fur cape and anything else you may have expected them to wear. Hardly Caribbean wear but, like their parents, the little troupers will carry their art through the streets under the eighty degrees of a merciless sun for hours. Aspects of martyrdom played a strange irony behind the fun, frivolity and excesses of Carnival when my thoughts went to the headpieces which

36

had to be removed from time to time to ease the pressure and give the little stalwarts a break.

On another occasion, I witnessed what some would see as the antithesis of all that Carnival represents take to the stage during the preliminary round of the Queen of Carnival competition. From the moment she appeared on stage I was hooked. There was an orchestra in the pits playing calypso music for the competitors. When Washer-woman, the queen of the band River, came on stage, there was no music for her. She danced dressed in white, pure, stark against the silence. The only props were her washing blowing on the line and her clothes basket. Alone on stage, not a single note accompanied her. She went through her routine and then danced off. From the moment Washer-woman came on stage, she played havoc with my senses. It wasn't just what she stood for, purity and simplicity. When she turned to dance towards our section of the audience I had a strange feeling as if she and I had been removed from that environment to a different setting. There was just the two of us on a dirt road which had canefields on either side. Still some way off, she was moving towards me in brilliant sunshine. The heat waves cut, fragmenting the clothes lines, her body, the basket under her arm. And yet she kept coming. Slowly advancing against the steamy heat which fractured her image. Coming forward against the odds. Coming forward against convention.

The experience was shattered by a voice announcing the next contestant. And we were back to the explosion of feathers and glitter. But I would meet her again soon. A woman in white cotton simple and plain, her washing blowing in a Caribbean breeze.

Every Trinidadian is a potential artist. With the scope and ingenuity to sew sequins on to a costume with the same flair embroidered into his everyday speech. It is a miracle of delicate reasoning which wafts, leaps or performs on the stage. Has the masquerader succeeded in portraying the essence of his theme? It is for the judges to decide and, as is sometimes the case, the public to disagree with. It would be decided during Dimanche Gras, the final show at Queens Park Savannah before the two big days of celebrating on the streets.

It was a very intense, nail-biting evening in which drama was everywhere. Little pockets of it hovered, waiting to be released. Dimanche Gras was, in a sense, one pinnacle of the week's activities. The drama began when we attempted to find our seats for the show. There was much confusion, despite the ticket system. We were eventually told where to sit. Eventually, because although the rows were numbered, the seats were not. We got a feeling the usherette was working by guess.

'Well, this row is KK so your seat must be 'round here, somewhere.'

What she was obviously saying was work it out for yourself. These things had a way of righting themselves. If we were in the wrong seats, when the ticket holders arrived we would be asked to move. The drama began before we were even seated. It continued with the final judging of the Carnival kings and queens plus the calypso monarch competitions.

Art at its most inventive was on stage, off stage, side stage. When kings and queens go forth, they do so under their own volition, interpreting the calypso music they have chosen or which has been chosen for them. On stage they weave their own specific variations into the theme. A vibrant personality goes a long way. One by one, the eight queens in the final round came on stage. The breathtaking display of colour, fashioned and formed around feathers, net, sequins, beads, precious stones, metals, plus a wealth of other materials leapt, shimmied, bobbed in unbelievable splendour. The unexpected happened when the queen of the band Carnival Was erupted on stage. Carnival in all its splendour, complete with wheels, flags and everything else. Happy, bouncing with zest, she overdid the enthusiasm. She fell. A queen like a dying swan, fluttering, struggled to get to her feet. It took a couple of minutes for us to realise that the twitching, trembling bundle of extravaganza was going to stay there unless someone came to her rescue. Two attendants rushed on stage to help her to her feet. Once lost, the moment can never be regained. Her smile became fixed, more of a grimace. She stood no chance of winning or coming within the first three, the fall had lost her valuable points.

Washerwoman, purity of body, spirit and mind, was not among them. She had not got any further than the first round of the competition. I did not know it, at the time, but on the following day her image would be transmitted to me by alternate waves.

Her male counterpart, Mancrab, dominated and won the kings' section. The mechanical crab, a robot with contrivances, acted his part with foreboding and sleight of hand. Only the unique concept of a giant red ant bearing a leaf of marijuana, called Bacchac Pushing Ganja, came close to having the same effect on me.

Almost two in the morning. It was silent in our street as, once again, I alighted from a car in the dead of night. I very quietly opened and closed the gate behind me. My friends would not drive off until they had satisfied themselves they had brought me home safe and sound. Too many incidents of lurking men for them to take any chances. The house was deadly silent. It took all my time to tiptoe to my room.

'Girl, the music sweet, sweet. All the big shot and them does jump with the band.'

I was dead on my feet which under the circumstances was perhaps not very surprising. I had two hours to kill before making my way back to Port of Spain for the J'Ouvert celebrations. I would need to get there by four-thirty if I didn't want to miss out on anything. Shattered. The past three days had been hectic. Now, I could chance a lie-down. Or could I? I certainly didn't want a cat-nap turning into anything more profound.

I had been told Invaders was the band to jump with on J'Ouvert morning. When I got into Port of Spain, I would walk down the Tragerette road to their camp. I looked at my feet. You do not wear anything which will expose your toes to this dawn revelling. Comfort, cushioned comfort, was what was needed for when fourteen stone comes crunching down before you can get your feet out of the way. I reached in a drawer for some socks and under the bed for some trainers. When things started getting too hot, I could always peel them off. The rest of me asked for something less practical. J'Ouvert demands freedom of body as well as mind. I checked the patched khaki shorts I was going to wear for a pocket. Even though the early morning air would be a little chilly, the rising sun and all those bodies would find me needing to cool off. A halter top with a shirt over it. When things got urgent, the first layer could go. The friction of bodies like sardines in the same can would nurture the right amount of excess oil one could easily do without. Before long, we might be swimming in it. I grabbed a large handkerchief. With all the dancing I planned on doing, I would be soaked to the skin within a couple of hours of my first gyration to the steel pulse.

I checked myself in the mirror. Conservative by J'Ouvert standards. There are no holds barred. So if you see your bank manager among the throng, in fishnet tights, jockey shorts and some broken-down tennis shoes, you don't act too surprised.

I cocked my ears. How extraordinary. Barely more than the normal level of sound for that time of night. I didn't exactly expect to hear the whole street prancing against the cool, early morning tarmac drawn by pied piper resonances. But I certainly expected more noise.

I closed the front door quietly behind me. Walking out into the quiet dark added to the excitement I was already feeling. I made excuses to everyone who tried to rope me into their own arrangements for J'Ouvert. I needed to experience it on my own. I wanted to do it under my own steam. That part of the initiation was too important to allow myself to be hampered or to share with anyone. I was the only person waiting at the bus stop. When the bus came it was already packed.

In Port of Spain walking up to Independence Square, to Queen Street, I got a better idea of what was going on. I walked straight into a nest. People like ants. And it wasn't only the bus and carloads which got there just ahead of me. I suspected most of the people didn't bother going home after Dimanche Gras or whatever fête or all-night party they had been attending. I had missed Old Mas, the 'pre-freedom' celebration and competition held after Dimanche Gras and before J'Ouvert.

I had to push my way through the throng to get to where I was going, up St Vincent Street and then along the Tragerette Road. I did not need to go far. I met them coming up. There is always a big all-night fête at Queens Park Oval not far from their tent, and many had come straight from that. I was standing on the pavement with a number of other early morning revellers, waiting for the dancing throng of steel band and followers to draw level. As they came alongside, some of us were peeled off the pavement to gyrate along the periphery. I was a little self-conscious, at first. Aware that I was on my own and not with someone, or with a group as everyone else seemed to be. Not everyone had come straight from a fête. They would not have left the house dressed as carefully for anything but J'Ouvert. I did not take time to analyse what it was all about. Someone once said that had it not been for J'Ouvert and Carnival, in general, more psychiatrists would be in business on the island.

We were on the right side of morning. In the eerie darkness we were dancing towards the coming dawn. For the coming dawn? The incantation which draws the sun above the horizon and keeps the echoes of our serenade safe for the next three hundred and sixty-five days? Until the next J'Ouvert?

The band was playing 'Mathilda', one of the old-time calypso classics about a woman who steals her lover's money and runs away to Venezuela.

There was a freedom which went beyond the wherewithal to express your liberty by putting on whatever you choose to wear.

An arm was slipped around my waist. I did not turn. Nor did I shrug it away. It was part of the camaraderie, the temporary state of euphoria, limitless, unabandoned pleasure. The gentleman – at least, I believe it was a male hand I was wearing around my waist – and I had not met face to face. Nevertheless, we were sharing precious moments.

And the steel band was still playing 'Mathilda'. I had long since forgotten my self-consciousness. No longer a tourist, I was being drawn towards the heart of the ex-perience. We were moving onwards in time to the music and singing the words, raucously.

'Mathilda, yuh tek meh money an' run Venezuela.
Mathilda. Mathilda.
Mathilda, yuh tek meh money an' run Venezuela.'

Small bands of Jab Molassi slipped out of pockets of darkness to reverberate through street lights. They stayed just long enough to brandish tridents and beat tin drums at the spectators before being swallowed back into the darkness. Their cries of 'Jab Molassi, pay the devil! Jab Molassi, pay the devil!' made indentations in our music. There was so much going on around me, I could only glimpse some of the other activities. Our band was moving forward at a leisurely pace. We passed other steel bands and groups of marauders. If the Jab Jabs had kept to tradition, they would be covered in red or black grease wearing horns and a tail. This was not always the case. The only thing the various groups seemed to have in common was that all were scantily dressed. There were also groups of people who looked as if they had been rolling in mud. The mud bands. These revellers probably comprise Trinidadians from the pinnacle of the island's society. They were carrying buckets of mud to smear you with if you got in the way. By the same token the more mischievous Jab Molassi will not only try and frighten you but also rub their heavily greased bodies against yours. It was all part of J'Ouvert. The hand around my waist had gone. I was on my own again.

'–hundred dollars in de bank
Mathilda tek dem every one.
Mathilda yuh tek meh money an' run Venezuela.'

We were stepping in time to the music, shoulders twitching, hips swaying, interpreting the beat with our own

43

individual sense of timing. Despite other tunes in the band's repertoire we kept coming back to this calypso hit of the forties. I had visions of the classic being played by Invaders every J'Ouvert since it was composed. The concept of a link which fused past with present in a strong, irrevocable bond excited me.

The musicians and their instruments were on a low platform mounted on wheels. I had graduated to pushing the steel frame. There were several of us to each section of the band, pushing it through the streets. It took some doing when wheels got caught in potholes or when it slid over uneven patches of ground to get jammed in the gutter. Luckily, there were a number of very strong men, willing and able to put their backs to it. I put my back to it as the importance of my role became apparent. There were as many people on the pavements as there were on the streets. Port of Spain was packed to capacity. I made the mistake of looking down at my feet. Already far from perfect when I put them on, my trainers were soon almost unrecognisable beneath the mud from other people's footprints. The more people in the band, the more difficult it became to control the steel orchestra. I was pushing against one of the metal bars to keep upright and to stop the wheel from swinging too far to the right. There were now so many people leaning on it, it went forward too quickly or swerved threateningly towards onlookers.

I made the mistake of looking down at my feet a second time. It was by looking down, not up at the sky, that I realised morning was breaking. Obviously, if I had noticed the dirt of my trainers it was light enough the first time. Once dawn began to break, it was like wafer-thin layers of grey being rapidly peeled away, accelerating all the while. I could not recall when the barriers became weak enough for the sun to make its own perforations. I could only remember being suddenly aware of details and colour. I had been dancing through the streets and 'pushing pan' for hours. Revellers left, wanting a few hours sleep before coming out again in their Carnival Monday band costume. Spectators leapt into the band to replace them. It was like a tag match.

As the sun began to bathe us, we continued to sweat, body rubbing against body generating heat. Only now we were doing so more profusely. I realised what I should have taken with me and had not. Some of the revellers were wearing hand towels around their necks. Others were mopping their faces with face flannels. I was doing the best I could with a handkerchief. It was a man's kerchief but no cotton square was sufficient to mop perspiration which leaves your body and clothes soaked. The square of white cotton was soon useless. Sodden. We moved in a circle, following the same four angles. So that at one time we faced the savannah, another the port and so on. There is a great difference between being veiled and masked by night and being unmasked by the full glare of day. I found myself turning my head like a worried vampire to avoid its rays, and moving away from the perimeter where the clean, fresh, street-wise, newly arrived spectators stood on the pavements watching. My face was oily and shiny. My body soaked. I could feel beads of perspiration still running down my chin. I was conscious of my inability to do any more than wipe the back of a hand across my forehead. I felt sure I looked a ghastly sight and I became over-aware of it. The sun continued its unmasking effect to suddenly come full force. Perhaps the macabre, unnatural effect of daylight was something we could all have done without. There were those busy leaping and flinging their arms around who had just come in on the tail of the bird. We had been on its back since "fore day morning'. You cannot arrive at eight o'clock and tell yourself you have come to enjoy J'Ouvert.

Full sunrise. We had accomplished what we set out to do. The sun was in full flight. Brilliance of sunrise now covered everything. The band was dispersing. Other gentlemen who had had their arms around my waist were now disentangling themselves from my interest. No one actually said goodbye. It was in their eyes as they turned to go on their way. Those who had been with us from the beginning had been dancing through the streets of Port of Spain for a good four hours in abandoned, uninhibited pleasure. For a few this was where we paused for a while. For many more, it was just the beginning. Invaders were now returning to their base on the Tragerette Road. There had been bands of revellers wearing old Carnival costumes. There were also bands wearing costumes which had been especially designed for J'Ouvert. I had been on the march like some avid warrior, doing battle with the forces who would prevent day from breaking. I was now a foot-sore conqueror limping home from the fight.

Port of Spain was still packed with revellers and spectators. It would stay that way until nightfall. There would be J'Ouvert bands moving through the streets enticing people to join them for a jump-up for some time yet. The celebration would merge with the Carnival Monday bands so no time was wasted, no effort unrewarded. Morning had come. The sun would remain with us until the bitter end.

I dragged my tortured body to the bus station. On the way I met people streaming up Nelson Street. Mentally and physically exhausted, I took a seat. The buses into Port of Spain were packed. The one I was on, going away from the capital, was only half-full. I was, despite extreme fatigue, still feeling very excited. Looking out of the window at a

46

Monday which had begun unlike any other, I wondered if I could, if I should, try to analyse that 'what it is' which circulated like an invisible net binding everyone, each to the other in blind ecstasy. One could talk of magic wands. One could talk of magnetism but the fact remained that the fever, and there was no other word for it, was there. It did most definitely exist. The exhilaration I felt was a complete and utter one going beyond the concept of mere pleasure or sharing a common experience.

'Well, you certainly look as if you enjoyed yourself. Good, was it?'

I was standing in the doorway, in a daze. My mother gave me a long amused look before going back to her sewing. It seemed strange to be walking into the house at a time when I would normally be stepping out of it. I wiped a hand across my dirty, sweaty face.

'Unbelievable.'

It was almost three hours since I returned from J'Ouvert. A long, cool shower took care of the grimier memories. Too many hours without sleep and the energy spent had taken its toll. I was in bed, almost dead to the world. Lying there like a zombie, I was racked with disappointment. I should have been turning my thoughts towards returning to Port of Spain to see the Carnival Monday bands but I did not even have the energy to get up and get dressed. Tuesday is the big day. It is when the complete bands, in full costumes, are on the road. On the Monday there will only be a limited number of people in each band and they may not necessarily be in full costume.

On Carnival Monday of the previous year, the top band, Papillon, was on the streets largely without their wings. Not until the following day were we able to get a glimpse of the four thousand pairs of life-size wings, representing so many different species. The beauty of their brilliant colours in the sunshine was breathtaking, as were the costumes of the main individuals in the band with their huge, sequined wings portraying famous characters.

The mas' leader who brought out Papillon was also responsible for the band whose queen had put my thoughts in turmoil.

The newspapers and television had had a lot to say about Peter Minshall's River. Some critics hailed him as a prophet. Traditionalists saw him as being controversial to the extent where he was not only destroying old values but mocking the true concept of Carnival by being too avant-garde. Minshall had described Carnival as 'theatre in the streets'. He had set out to illustrate this in River. The king and queen of his band, Mancrab and Washerwoman, were adversaries. He, evil. She, goodness. They represented Corruption and Purity. Had I been able to get to Queens Park Savannah that afternoon, I would have seen the drama take the shape of a fight between Mancrab and Washer-woman for possession of the river. Washerwoman was the conqueror on that first day. Act one.

From the advance publicity, I already knew the drama would be taken from the pure white costumes and accessories of the first act to the violation and murder of Washerwoman by Mancrab in the second act. The white costumes of the first day would be splashed with the colours of the rainbow.

Listening to the enthused commentator praising the purity of Minshall's band, I could feel myself sinking into a depression. I was left in no doubt as to the magnificence of the clothes and accessories which covered such a wide range of styles. The only thing they had in common was all were in pure white.

I translated the commentator's words into shapes and

contours. Any description he may have left out, my memory filled in.

I concentrated on putting her together piece by piece until she again danced white, pure, stark into the silence of that dirt road where rows of corn blew against the sky. As before, she came towards me in brilliant sunshine. I don't know how it happened but when she was the same distance as before, my concentration slipped. Impatience and disgust had me hissing through clenched teeth. The steam from my anger diffused the vision. It melted to a circular blob which sank without trace.

'Even if you have to crawl there, woman. Tomorrow, you are going to go and see for yourself.'

Later, friends came by to rub it in.

'Girl, where you was? We looking all over town for you. Minshall leave them standing. You should see he and he River. Every stream and river in Trinidad and Tobago was there. If the judges and them don't give he first prize, we giving all of them a cut-arse.'

That night, while half of Trinidad was out partying, I remained horizontal, conserving my energy for a full Tuesday. I was going to make an early start and get there in good time.

Nevertheless, by the time I got to Queens Park Savannah, the bands had already started their parade across the stage. I watched from a vantage point in the commentators' box. They danced across the stage in their thousands. They were fine. They were tremendous. They were colourful. They portrayed their themes and personalities to the hilt. While it was all very well and good to sit there watching, I was impatient for the event I was there specifically to witness. If the buzz of excitement which went round the stands as they approached the stage was anything to go by, I was far from alone in this. We had been waiting a long time. It was now almost six o'clock.

The drama of the previous day was taken a step further. Bareback drummers beat their tassa drums. Washerwoman's victory of the previous day was reversed. The virgins emptied the calabash of blood over their white clothes and burst into a frenzy of joy at the sight of the colour. Her lifeless body was carried on stage. Ravaged by the mechanical crab, the technological vampire, Mancrab, her washing brought on stage was now covered in blood. Her people had deserted her. He had corrupted them by showing them the rainbow. Prior to that, they had only known purity. In act one, eight hundred metres of white chiffon had been held aloft to depict the purity of their rivers. The chiffon they now carried bore the colours of the rainbow.

The triumph of evil over good was brought to a conclusion. Hoses containing dyes the colours of the rainbow showered them as they danced on stage. Costumes, headwear, faces and any exposed parts were sprayed with the different colours. The effect was absolutely unbelievable. Some revellers came through with the white of their costumes unrecognisable beneath the colours of the rainbow. Others, mere splashes of colour. The extent to which the colours had dyed their costumes spanned the spectrum.

The photographs I took were lousy. I had been given permission to sit at the front of the stage in an enclosure especially reserved for press and publicity people. The bottom half of all my pictures consisted of the heads, shoulders and cameras which surged forward when River was about to mount the stage. I did not stand a chance.

Two voices were carrying on an animated conversation about Minshall's art.

'The boy good.'

'This is why they 'fraid he so much. You think any of them could think of something like this?'

'They talking 'bout white not Carnival. White not

Carnival. You can't have no whole band and your queen in white and call that Carnival. But wait 'til next year. You go see how many of them go try the same thing.'

The rainbow River flowed on stage. Ticker tape, like confetti, wafted down. They crossed the stage delirious with happiness, singing, 'By the waters of Babylon'. Bands came through the streets of Port of Spain to the judging point at Queens Park Savannah. They had to wait their turn to cross the stage. There were a number of bands with over three thousand members. Like River, they had taken over an hour to cross the stage. You simply have to wait your turn. It can be a very hot and frustrating experience but once you get up there, you make the moment last. That is what it is all about. Every now and then it gets to the point where band members are enjoying themselves so much on stage, they are told to get off so the next band can come on.

> 'By the waters of Babylon,
> we sat and wept
> when we remembered Zion'

I heard later that when the tassa drummers began playing, a few people in the audience of the Baptist persuasion were physically moved by the spirit. I believe that what I experienced when those words reached me was not far short of what they must have felt. Waves of exhilaration shot through me with such force I could feel myself trembling. The strength of the theme turned me inside out. Those joyful warriors were far more ecstatic than any of the other bands I had seen that day. The rainbow had poisoned their waters. They were going to die. I waited and watched in a hypnotic trance until the pull became too strong, until the hunger became so deep I felt as if it was gnawing at my bones. I grabbed my things and ran to join them. The River had come down thick and fast, stripping our senses. The deluge had swept convention in its wake. And even though the judges put them at the bottom of the list, tenth and last, the people voted them their band of the year. They were *The People's Choice.* It had passed now and ebbed to almost nothing. Just the stragglers and a myriad of spectators with the same idea as myself in mind. Ahead of me, the River flowed, thick and fast. The revellers were still having a wonderful time. I joined them in their song. I joined in their exuberance.

> 'Carried us away in captivity
> demanding of us a song
> Now how can we sing the Lord's song
> in a strange land.'

I pushed my way forward, serpenting through the revellers, just looking and singing until I was in the centre, until I reached what seemed to be the heart from where all tributaries flowed. In the distance I could see the blood-stained line of washing hanging limp in the breeze. I had not glimpsed her since her lifeless body was brought on stage. I would not see her again. I was sure of that. The transience of the experience would take care of that. Washerwoman was gone and gone for good. But she had come. That other woman. I felt her presence barely seconds before I was once again taken down. This time it could be death by drowning. No. I came up again. Once. Twice. Three times the weight was lifted from my shoulders. I came struggling to the surface for air.

It was baptism of a specific kind. I was taken down again. This time I stayed beneath the water, willingly. Easy in my tomb. It was death with resurrection. When I finally came up again, the explosion in my ears was deafening. And I was cold. So cold. The centre did not hold. I must have set my own time fuse. I had lost all concept of time. There was a hole in my memory. It was getting dark and I was getting colder. Colder and colder. There was no longer the warm, consoling pulse of the River people. They were dispersing, going their separate ways, moving nonchalantly away like tributaries ebbing under their own volition.

But it was not the end for me. I could not let go. I could not let this thing go. Clenching my fists I stormed back to Queens Park.

The previous Friday, I had stood on Edward Street and watched things coming together. Seamstresses who sew for the bands had been kept very busy, working long hours. From the Thursday, band members had been collecting their costumes. I watched them trying to manoeuvre pieces of costumes like wings, breast-plates and plumed helmets into cars. On my way back to Curepe that Friday evening, I saw them speeding out of Port of Spain. Cars and taxis alike. Flags, standards and tridents hanging out of windows while exotic pieces like sequined wings and anything else too big to be manoeuvred into the vehicle was strapped to the roof rack.

That was four days earlier. And now, as far as they were concerned, it was over. I saw that same strange fruit which flourished from car windows and roof racks leaving the capital in droves. They had staggered their arrival by coming in from early morning until noon. When they left, they left in a hurry.

What strange world was this? A group of Aztec warriors passed me. Two fancy sailors. A limping she-devil still carrying her trident. The River people were easily distinguishable. I could not help but turn as each one passed. The hunger and longing was far from extinguished. They were all moving away from the savannah, going back to where they had parked their vehicles. Others lived within walking distance. A few masqueraders had come in on public transport and would go back the same way.

As I got closer, I met pockets of resistance. Groups of masqueraders still in Carnival spirit. The tune being blasted out was 'Rebecca'. It was the year's road march. The tune which had been played the most and proved to be the most popular among the Carnival bands. The calypso was about a woman who got so excited about Carnival she ripped off her clothes and those of the man she was with. I could understand and sympathise with the emotion. But while her exuberance knew no bounds, being yet a novice I was governed by restraint and inhibition. Nevertheless, I endeavoured to do the best I could. I leapt in behind three water-lilies with their arms around each other. They were singing the words with fervour, their bodies moving almost in unison. The water-lilies were from Rain Forest. The rest was made up of members from various sections of the same band. The judges had voted it their band of the year. When they came on stage earlier, they had done so in a particular sequence. Ahead of me I now saw the torrid silver fringes of the hurricane side by side with the emerald green, paling to white, chiffon squares of two masqueraders from the morning mist section. Palmanetto fans rubbed shoulders with flamboyants. They were a rain forest in chaos as if the day had been turned upside down. The natural sequence of nature destroyed, put in confusion by some impending disaster.

And to confuse matters even further, I now joined them. Arms flaying, my feet hardly touched the ground. My ode to Rebecca was rendered louder than anyone else's. The pink petalled heads of the lilies sat side by side, merging into the same quivering ecstasy. The delicate pink blush of their modesty now lost beneath the intoxication of reality. Their pond had been sucked into a larger world. It had pooled its resources with the river when it came down and their pads had been grounded. The music was coming from somewhere up front. The tempo changed. I heard the strains of Relator, another of our top calypsonians. This time, it was 'Don't touch meh Mas'. I passed familiar territory with a band of stalwarts edging their way slowly but raucously onward. Spectators going in the same direction joined us. We had our arms around each other. Some were in costume, some were not. It was 'las lap'. You join a band going in your direction and dance your way home. We were going in the opposite direction to Curepe. Some strong miles separated me from where I was from where I would need to get to. I would worry about it later. I was enjoying myself too much. We were coming into St James. 'Las lap' had ended for some.

'Goodnight.'

'Goodnight.'

Within half an hour, I was alone. It may well have been coming on to midnight. Yet I could not leave. It would soon be Ash Wednesday. Sometime between then and when Port of Spain woke, the refuse collectors would have combed the streets. Reams of litter now clogging the pavement and gutter would have been swept away. It would be clean but passive. Unaware, they would gather and dispose of all evidence, indiscriminately. Evidence of the kind I would far rather they left behind. If the first glint of sunrise found me skulking from the wide open glare of J'Ouvert morning then those last few strands before Ash Wednesday found me acting out a role which bore witness to my own endangered metamorphosis. I found myself tearing feverishly through town like an anxious vampire. The hunger I was feeling left me faint. I passed a few bodies. Some were inert in the gutter. Those still vertical came out of the darkness as if conjured by the street lamps. They curved out of a spiral of light, eyes glazed, faces covered with glitter. In full costume, still clutching standards, head pieces and flags, they came forward like zombies, unseeing, to get sucked into one street light after another, feet almost noiseless against the pavement. They reappeared further and further along the road until they were out of sight.

What strange world was this where I felt no fear? I could walk the streets all night until it receded before the face of light. I was looking for something and for a while was side-tracked. Ash Wednesday brings the remnants, the debris of the fire. Some of the ashes of Carnival Tuesday were in my hands. I found some among the litter in the gutter. I found some on railings. I was a scavenger, delirious for a flicker of life inside the eyes of death. I searched along the inner rim of sockets grabbing at debris from the fire. I collected as I went.

I am not sure how I found the taxi. Maybe it found me. The driver took me to Curepe. I climbed out of the car clutching an armful of treasures. The porch light was still on. I was close to tears when I opened the gate of my mother's house. In my trembling fingers, the key grated along the lock as I tried to find a way in. It scraped with the dull familiar of steel against steel. As my hand searched for the light switch, I became more rational.

What would she think? What would my mother say when she found the assorted pieces of fans, feathers, silk, chiffon and cotton cloths, gold, sequined belt and a broken helmet?

I had to make a choice. Selecting one item, I made a bundle of the rest and threw it into the bushes.

When I closed the door, I was on the inside. I opened the stretch of cloth. Footprints wore along its length where dirt and grime clung. Under that surface of wear were two other layers. The foundation was a bland, regular weave where erratic patches of colour stabbed through and blotted, creating their own design. Recognition ripped my thoughts. In my hands I held the blood of memory. The cloth lay across my open, outstretched palms. Her sudden presence overwhelmed me. Like a raging storm, impatience came to claw my brain.

Go on! Go on!
I lifted my arms higher. Higher.
Go on! Go on!
But I had no memory of it.
I had no memory at all.
I could find no altar to lay it.
I lowered my arms.
And the ritual remained incomplete ...

'Are you sure?'

   'It will be okay.'

   'She won't mind?'

   'She will be happy to have you.'

   'I don't know what to say. I – '

   'You don't have to say anything.'

   'How much should I offer her?'

   'Offer her what you want.'

   'Yes, but how – '

   'Are you a Christian?'

I hesitated.

   'Yes.'

   'Then give her whatever you want to.'

   'But I don't know what the usual – '

   'Don't worry about it, just give what you can afford.'

   'Give me some idea what – '

   'God is good. Tell her I will write her soon. Have a good stay.'

   The line went dead and I was left looking at the receiver.

   I went into the kitchen and found my mother, up to her wrists in flour.

   'I have just told a terrible lie.'

   The spluttering fat from the frying pan hissed at the very instant she placed the fish in the oil. She remained silent, turning from the dish of floured fish to the frying pan, the dish to the frying pan. I knew she was waiting for me to continue but I wasn't sure if I could make myself heard above the noise from the hot oil. I raised my voice.

'I just told someone I was a Christian.'

Her dead-pan expression cracked in several places.

'Well, your sins will find you out.'

My mother is devout. So why on earth was I making confessions to her at nine in the morning? Your sins will find you out, the lady had said. I made a point of remembering to pack a bible and my little pill-box number in case the method of devotion demanded your head be covered.

I had determined to spend Easter in Tobago. However, my spirit of adventure did not leave me blind to the fact that I did not know anyone on the island, any more than I had somewhere to stay when I got there. Hotels and guest houses were too expensive for my pocket. One of my mother's sisters in worship had a friend whose mother was a member of the Tobago church and who, she assured me, would be delighted to have me. She wasn't on the phone but no need, just turn up, it would be okay. Good Christian that she was, there would be no problem. When I got to the airport I should look up Mr Maynard who worked at the meteorological office. A good friend of her mother's and yes, a member of the church also. He would take me to her home.

Well, I could have taken the boat at five and a half hours more travelling time but less than a quarter the price it cost to fly. I took the plane. The departure lounge for the Trin–Tobago flights was packed. Any excuse and Trinidadians are on the next boat or flight across to the sister island. Tobago has the best beaches so when you want to 'chill out' and relax that is where you go. On a long weekend like this one, the world and his family would be making the trip across. There would be six flights to Tobago that day.

With the mass exodus by boat as well as plane, not to mention the ones flying to Barbados and other islands, one might imagine Trinidad to be little short of a ghost town. There are, however, thousands happy to remain behind, taking their families, 'pots' and iceboxes to the beach, Sunday and Monday fêtes and parties, and a not inconsiderable amount could be spending most of the next four days in Church. A thought crossed my mind along the lines of whether or not, as the guest of what's-her-name's mother, I would actually get a chance to see Tobago as opposed to spending the majority of my time in church atoning for years of transgression.

So many people turned up on spec that they put all the passengers who were booked on my flight together with the ones who were due to go on the previous flight, threw in those who were standing around with their fingers crossed and shipped us all out on one of the big planes. You've no sooner fastened your safety belts than you've arrived. It seemed odd to have to take a flight across and yet not need to produce your passport at the other end or satisfy a customs officer's curiosity. Crown Point is tiny, contained and the sort of place you may want to go and spend the day if you had absolutely nothing better to do. There were people sitting on benches outside, drinking beer and chatting. No doubt there would be Tobagonians who live in Trinidad flying home for the holiday. You get the impression that if you hang around long enough, there's sure to be one or two people you know stepping off the plane. There is a bar just a few yards away. It will keep you cool, quench your thirst during the wait. There is none of the hustle and bustle of the main airport. You've come to relax and it starts at Crown Point.

'Can you tell me if Mr Gilbert Maynard is on duty please?'

I had just climbed a flight of stairs to the meteorological office. Standing in the doorway, puffing a little, I waited for the two men in the room to finish scrutinizing me. One was looking at me with interest, the other with suspicion. When I had put my head round the door seconds earlier, they had been carrying on a conversation. One of them was relaxing in a chair. The other was leaning on a table, both hands in his pockets. Neither altered his posture. The conversation stopped, they turned their heads, but that was all.

'Who want him?'

The man with the screwed-up eyes, lolling in the chair, was the first to speak.

'My name is – '

I went through the whole rigmarole, switching or attempting to switch on the charm. I felt it might hold me in good stead. By the time I had finished telling them all about it, giving names, references, I was bored to distraction but still smiling. And I was still smiling sweetly because I already suspected that one of them was the person I was looking for and even if I was wrong, nevertheless, one of them was going to chauffeur me to where I wanted to go. An idle inquiry of the taxi driver who had propositioned me earlier confirmed my worst fears: it was going to cost a fortune.

'So you want to get to Mrs Ellison?'

I was not sure if he actually expected an answer or if he was reshuffling information I had already offered. He suddenly sat bolt upright as if whipped into action by some decision.

'Joinie, take the lady to Mrs Ellison.'

Joinie's hands came out of his pockets, slowly. They came out of his pockets so he could lift them in a gesture which implied that he didn't know how to get there.

'But, man, you must know Mrs Ellison. You go down past the hill where – '

Explicit instructions followed.

We went down past the hill where Alfred has his rum shop and took a left turn. It is wide open country, flat and somehow identical to roads which would be leading me from other airports to where I would be heading. The proportion of shops to houses, coconut palms to groups of boys somewhere along the route, just watching the traffic and the people go by, would be the same. The amount of dust stirred by the wheels of a vehicle taking you towards something new would become familiar.

But while the road in would always look the same, each island would offer its own unique experience.

As we came over another steep hill, Joinie manoeuvred the car around a sharp bend and skidded to a halt.

We walked up the path to a house which though unfinished was obviously being lived in. Bricks sandwiched by cement had been devoid of the solace of plaster. It was not a new house. The walls had been naked for a long time. Bricks carried the worn look of constant exposure to wind and rain. Cement pillars supporting the house were now grey. We walked up the stairs and knocked on the door. It took a while before we got any response. An apparition like a ghost eventually wafted towards us from behind the pane of frosted glass. The door was opened by a woman in a white blouse and white skirt. Her feet were bare. By the tape measure around her neck, I assumed she had been dressmaking.

'Hello, Mrs Ellison. I'm – '

I went on to tell her I had made contact with her daughter in Trinidad who felt certain she would be happy to have me as her guest while I was on the island. The woman looked at me in blank astonishment. For a period of two minutes all we did was look at each other. Her expression deepened to one of shock.

'How she could do me that? How she could do me such

a thing?' Her voice was full of disbelief. 'I have my plans for the next few days. I have things to do. How she could do this? I have – '

'I'm sorry, I'm so sorry. She assured me it would be – '

She left no doubt in my mind that I was most definitely not welcome. My presence in her home would thwart her plans. Rather than prolong the embarrassment, I told her not to worry. I would find alternative accommodation. I looked to Joinie for assistance. Luckily, he hadn't simply deposited me and driven off.

'Is okay. I know somewhere she could stay.'

'Well, I sorry. But I feel sure you understand. The girl didn't even give me warning. She didn't even write to let me know. She didn't – '

'It's all right. It's all right.'

Her next words nailed me to the ground as I was retracing my footsteps.

'If you don't find anywhere, you could always come back.'

The sentence was low. The last words almost inaudible.

I turned to take a good look. There was something very sinewy about her. It wasn't just muscular arms inside a short-sleeved blouse or even the taut, wide, high-cheekboned features. My experience of the past few minutes would surely have given me another dimension from which to evaulate her. From my distance I was able to view her in retrospect. And she didn't mean it, so why say it? I smiled, automatically, in reply to her last words.

'I doubt it will come to that, Mrs Ellison.'

She went back indoors and closed the door. I strained my eyes to see what the inside of her house could possibly look like. Outline of furniture, nothing too specific. A stranger on her doorsteep and not even the offer of a glass of water to quench my thirst? The rejection had cut me to the quick. When I turned to walk away I took with me the blurred image of a white figure becoming more and more distant behind the sharp relief on her frosted door.

'Will it cost much?'

Joinie was driving along a motorway where coconut palms stood like sentinels guarding a new gateway and where workmen continued to labour. We were on the Claude Noel Highway, still being built. The Christian lady offered little solace in the name of her faith or what other label it may go by. Since leaving her portal, I had been avidly taking in everything I saw for fear that something vital might escape my attention. I had, in consequence, come to the independent conclusion that everyone was right. Tobago is a very beautiful island. Reputedly where Robinson Crusoe was shipwrecked, it has all the classical features of a tropical island. Only in Toco, in the north of Trinidad, can you find beaches where the sand is clean, pale and fine enough to compare with any you may find in Tobago.

'It won't cost you anything. I have friends, good, good friends. They go be happy just to have you stay with them.'

Had we been in Trinidad, I doubt if I would have trusted so implicitly. But then, had we been in Trinidad the problem would not have arisen. I soon became aware of a specific neatness and order. A lot of the houses were beautifully finished, neat little bungalows with compact, well-tended gardens. Driving through Scarborough, however, you could not help but notice debris which banked the sea close to the waterfront. There are always children willing to brave a beach of shingles. Waste sifted on to it, greeted corrugated tin cans, old tyres and bottles. Yet, as always, coconut trees flourished. In addition to the usual sea craft, there was the boat from Trinidad which comes and goes twice a day. It was in the harbour. From the car I watched the huge black vessel which brought passengers and cargo being off-loaded.

The road twisted to the left, up past the market place and the street vendors. We stopped outside a house situated at the end of a lane just off the main road. It was half-shaded by a sapodilla tree. Hanging baskets lined the verandah. Steps and verandah were painted a dark red, contrasting with the cream of the outside. A neat and attractive bungalow. Fairly new. Certainly a good deal larger than I would have expected for the two people Joinie assured me lived there. Both gate and front door were open. I hung back while he mounted the stairs and walked into the house.

'Hey, Rita! You there, girl?'

He beckoned me to follow. I walked up to the front door admiring the garden which stretched out of sight. As well as sapodillas, there was an orange and a plum. The lane continued past the house, forking to the right before twisting again to curve around the garden and disappear. There were three dogs in the garden. The two big alsations, mercifully tethered, had stopped barking. The third, little more than a puppy, sat on its haunches, looking up at me, eyes attentive, waiting to offer a tentative bark. The house on the opposite side, a little lower down the lane, had flowering climbers curling around each other to frame large windows fitted with blue-tinted glass. Jacaranda, bougainvilleas and begonias grew prolifically in the garden.

I did not arrive on the island pre-warned or even pre-armed. All I knew about Tobagonians was what I had been told. They did not like Trinidadians and became incensed when people confused the two. Retracing my footsteps to look more closely at what I knew before arriving, I remembered and understood a feeling which I could not at first describe or really understand. I had from the moment I set foot on the island felt a sort of hush, a quiet unlike anything I had left behind in Trinidad. I felt it, sensed it there under the surface but could not hold it. It kept eluding me. Only later did I come to recognize it. The rippling turmoil was like Soufrière before she vomits. The hush before the hurricane. Metaphorically or literally, it was the lull before the backlash and Tobago was not happy about being governed by Trinidad. She wanted to secede. She wanted self-government. Time and time again, it was impressed upon me that they were very weary of Trinidadians.

'But you go be all right. You been away too long. You not really Trinidadian.'

I looked in on people's lives not out of the morbid curiosity which generally underlies such an action but because I wanted to know, needed to learn. And how else could I do that but through observing? Looking and seeing is learning.

'Hey, Rita, girl. I bring a friend to stay with you for a few days.'

And was it really so easy? In their lives, were things really as simple as that? 'I bring a friend to stay with you for a few days.'

Rita was a very attractive, plump woman. She was wearing a loose fitting printed cotton dress and her hair in cane rows. But it was her eyes I noticed first of all. They were a rich mahogany, shades lighter than her ebony skin. I took her to be in her mid-twenties.

She greeted me formally. The handshake and the standard English were something I would get used to. My own voice and manner may have been responsible for that. It was a natural response from some strangers on meeting me for the first time.

'You're very welcome. Pleased to meet you.'

66

She held out her hand, a little shyly, when Joinie introduced us.

'You was lying down then, girl?'

She relaxed.

'Yes, man, I was taking a little five minutes before he come home.'

Her mood had changed from coy hostess, languid, waking beauty, to preoccupation with straightening the modest but tastefully furnished living room.

'I ain't cook, yet.'

She emphasized the last word, still arranging things.

'You know how he does get when he come home and his food not ready. What all you want to drink?'

She moved towards what I supposed was the kitchen.

'Just bring some ice. We go do the rest. Don't worry yourself.' The wooden floor had been stained and varnished as in so many other homes I had visited. A large circular rug covered the centre. With one foot on the oyster-coloured pile, I ran the sole of the other sandal along one of the slats, admiring the deep, smooth polish.

'All you sure is just ice you want?'

Her voice came from the kitchen. We could hear her busying herself.

'Everything under control. Just ice.'

Through the cream lace curtains blowing outwards in a breeze, the living room window gave access to the view which had ended on the verandah. The house was standing in about half an acre of ground. There were two varieties of mangoes and a cashew before the land sloped gently down to where dasheen leaves, corn, okras, lettuce, peas and other vegetables grew. On the far left was a hedge which I took to mark the perimeter. The dogs began barking again.

'Good morning, Miss Rita.'

From my vantage point, leaning on the sill looking out at the rear of the house, I could see the girl's head as she came bobbing past balancing a basket of shopping.

'Right-o, Jackie. Give your mother howdy, you hear?'

She disappeared through the gap in the hedge and down the path on the other side, making her way towards a cluster of timber and corrugated iron houses. During my stay I would need to get used to the sight of adults and children alike using the grounds as a short cut between the valley and main road.

Rita came out of the kitchen carrying the ice and wearing her hostess expression, again. This time it was more of a reserved shyness. She handed Joinie the ice bucket.

'I am so sorry. Let me show you where to put your case.'

Taking my bag, she turned to Joinie.

'And you know where it is, why you didn't take she and show she?'

She took me into a room, overlooking the front of the house. It had a double bed and other pieces of furniture one would expect to find.

'Do you eat salt fish and dumpling?'

'Love it.'

'What you want drink?'

Joinie was standing in front of the open drinks cabinet, unscrewing a bottle of rum.

'Put some coke in mine, please.'

Rita disappeared to the fridge to get the coke.

I was straddling two worlds. One was reality, the other dream state. I was not too sure which was which. Everything was in motion, yet turning out radically different from how it was supposed to. I realized that I had been tremendously lucky. And when your luck turned up was it really that simple? This was the flip side of the same coin. Was there a mirror response where all things are reversed, just waiting for the right conditions in which to manifest itself? I strongly suspected that my bible and pillbox would remain fast to the bottom of my bag. I tried hard to push the almost overwhelming sense of reprieve and relief to the back of my mind.

'Let we go up home. I have some things to do. Bring you back later.'

Joinie wanted to take me to Castara where he lived. Dinner would not be ready for a while, Rita assured me.

'Go off and enjoy yourself.'

I had a quick shower and jumped into a pair of shorts. The feeling of being somewhere vast and panoramic came over me again as soon as we hit the open road. The facts I knew ran through my head as if on a teleprinter. Tobago wanted to secede. She wanted self-government. Felt she could survive without Trinidad. The histories of the two islands were by no means parallel. Tobago has been linked with Trinidad for less than a century. This was originally done solely for administrative purposes. Trinidad has its natural resources and Carnival. Tobago is the island with the beaches. It could, perhaps, succeed on just the holiday trade alone. But they would need Trinidad's oil, gas and asphalt. Tobago wanted to secede. She wanted self-government. I closed my eyes and cocked an ear to hear the clear-cut reasoning. The groan and strain of the hard and bitter rope was fraying with every twist and agony of fate. I turned back from the road we had just left and fixed my eyes firmly on the one ahead.

The journey from Scarborough to Castara was longer than I would have thought. What you're used to certainly doesn't bother you. Joinie worked in Scarborough making the journey in both directions sometimes three times a day for one reason or another. His family owned a business in Castara. I met brother after brother. No sisters, just five brothers. As the eldest it was his responsibility to ensure that things ran smoothly. The brothers helped in the shop and there was also a haulage concern.

It was a shop not unlike countless others I would see on the islands. A myriad of goods could be obtained in addition to the ones you would naturally suppose to find. In Grenada, I would meet an old woman who had never visited the capital, St George's, only a few miles from where she lived. And there would be others like her. The men as a rule were not subject to this restriction. They guarded their freedom and space as if there was no other option. The women, sometimes locked into a cycle of childbearing or because of the pattern of restriction which was imposed on them or for some other reason, were the ones in danger of this state of inertia. So even within a more flexible framework, I could imagine what a boon it must be to have everything you could possibly need for your livelihood right there within easy reach. The crowded shelves stocked everything from corned beef to candles, soap to salted pork, lentils to light bulbs, hairnets to haricot, butter to batteries.

'Joinie, all you could trust my ma quarter pound of split peas, please?'

I have always been fascinated by the quantity which customers buy.

'A small piece of salt fish, please.'

Business was brisk. Money and goods exchanged hands across the counter. Space could be a problem. Queueing is a phenomenon not natural to the Caribbean. Sacks of flour, sugar and rice, barrels of smoked herrings, salt fish, pig tails, stood in strategic places. Some smells served to cancel others. There was an overriding though not unpleasant smell of carbolic soap with everything else hovering on the periphery. One single naked bulb hanging from the ceiling later attempted to throw light on all this.

I went down to the sea. It wasn't far. I crossed the road and stepped directly on to the beach. A track at the side of the shop led to the two houses where Joinie and his family lived. They were two of several houses built on the hill at the rear of the shop. To get there, I had to hang on to him while he manoeuvred his way up the steep track. It would be a mistake to suppose there is some aesthetic quality attached to building your home on a spot which allows a view of white sands with coconut palms and the sea breaking against the rocks. There are two types of people who build their nests in trees. Many rich Europeans live in the Caribbean if not all year then certainly the winter months. The climate and privacy of hills shaded by trees which afford breathtaking access to the bay can be very supportive therapy. The poor sometimes build their houses among the hills on their part of the island because the land is cheaper or they may be able to claim squatters' rights. In the case of Joinie's parents, building a house which overlooks your business could be a sensible ploy for security reasons. As a rule, you do not find the rich and the poor on the same hill.

The sea came frothing up to my feet, binding my ankles, swaying me towards the water. It was a busy beach. There were far more children than adults in the sea. Peals of laughter and screams filled the bay. I particularly noticed a teenage girl and an older woman. They came stumbling out of the sea, holding skirts up to their knees. The younger of the two was falling about with laughter. Her skirt was soaked. There was something which singled them out as strangers, as not belonging. A look, a way of turning, a regard, a movement which does not quite synchronize, betrays you. In a word, attitude. I never quite got away with it. Not even when I was at my most relaxed was I ever able to pass for an islander.

'Where you from, Miss? America?'

I shrank back into my skin. It came out of the blue one day. A stranger who had been watching, observing me, asked the question. The thought running through my head barely seconds before he had asked the question was, I believe I may be close to coming home. No matter how sharp the blade, there was a thin sliver which the plane could not quite remove.

'Not far. Only Trinidad.'

I had asked the women where they were from. The younger came to Tobago on vacation every Easter to stay with friends in the village. The older woman was a friend she had brought with her. I went in up to the turn-ups of my shorts. They went back to their house to change. The water rocked me with a steady backwards and forwards movement but I thought, it doesn't matter. My feet were securely moored in the sand. A wave came in. It did little more than cover the beach for a few seconds before sifting back out to sea. Another followed with the sort of vengeance which sent me forward into the water. Not just the turn-ups but all my shorts and the lower half of my teeshirt got wet. I hoped there would be enough warmth left to dry them. Partially at least. The sunset was a bright orange scream across the sky. Like bright ink on blotting paper, it relaxed, spreading across the sky. Lying easy, it surrendered itself totally to the universe. I flapped around the beach watching the sun as it went through its various phases.

Joinie looked ridiculous. A whimsical gesture on his part to relate to me in a specific way. At least, I think that's what it was. He had changed from the jeans he was wearing earlier to the briefest pair of khaki shorts I had ever seen on a man.

He was a gaunt, terracotta-complexioned man with

teeth which were too large for his mouth. The first thing I had noticed about him was the way he walked. It was as if the lower half of his legs had been joined at an awkward angle to his knees. He was extremely knock-kneed. What would otherwise have been a good pair of slim, hairy legs had been marred by this major defect. I was amazed that he even had the nerve. I looked away to stop myself from laughing. He had been very kind to me and I would have hated to think I was showing ingratitude at such an early stage. His teeshirt had nice green and white horizontal stripes. So we were both wearing shorts as we got into his car for the drive back to Scarborough.

'Hey, Joinie. Like is suntan you looking for, boy.'

'All right! All right!'

A girl came along and tweaked his bottom.

'Joinie, what you doing dressed like that?'

'Okay Jean? How do and thing?'

We were standing on Main Street, near the junction where it takes the pull from traffic going both up and down its own busy road as well as the flow coming down from Fore Street.

Joinie was still in his short shorts. I was still in a pair of a more respectable length. We were not waiting for Joinie's friends and acquaintances to come past and admire his legs. That was definitely not why we were there. The suggestion that if you live on a small island you'll probably get to know all the other islanders became plausible the longer we stood there. At any rate, they certainly knew Joinie. Hardly a pedestrian or car went past without some comment being made about his shorts.

We were standing with eyes peeled towards where the passengers on the boat from Trinidad would be disembarking. Our wait was finally rewarded. They come pouring through the exit, on to the streets like an invading army.

Cars can be taken across also. And they certainly brought them. With them, they also brought great-grandmothers to babes-in-arms. Was this the promised land? No, just Trinis getting away for a holiday weekend. And Tobago is where the beaches are. There was now only one pair of thighs and knees on display. Joinie had gone forward against the tide. Battling his way through the throng to find the people we were waiting on. The wife and two children of a good friend should have been on the boat. Cars just disembarked drove off at top speed. It was the sort of speed reserved for people who knew exactly where they were going. The Trinidadians did not have it all their own way. Other passengers were met with cars and kisses. Many Tobagonians who live and work in Trinidad return home for the holidays.

'Hey, Joinie, boy! We reach!'

I don't know how the devil I heard it above all the din but I did. He was still within view. I saw him go forward to greet a woman with two small children in tow and —

'I bring a couple of friends to see all you.'

— two adults, as well.

There was a lot of coming and going that night. I was persuaded to go back to the village. When the children had settled in for the night under the supervision of Joinie's parents, all five of us travelled back to Scarborough.

I was a little apprehensive about meeting Kelvin. As the man of the house, I wasn't too sure, despite the reassurances, whether he would approve of my presence. In view of what Rita had said regarding his being difficult when his meal wasn't ready, I felt it would make sense to be well prepared for any unforeseen response on his part when we met. Kelvin turned out to be one of those big, handsome African men I swear it was worth going back to the Caribbean for. Despite her geniality, Rita was one woman I certainly did not want to get on the wrong side of. It never occurred to me to flirt with him but I made a mental note not to show too much partiality, particularly in her presence. Something about her warned that she was not the sort of person to trifle with. He was just as welcoming as Rita. And if that wasn't enough, he was a generous, unassuming man always ready to make a joke. It did not take me long to realise that it suited Rita to project an image of Kelvin as someone who would get difficult if his meal was not ready. He worked at the docks, about five minutes from the house by car. Indeed, a number of men I met were working or had worked there. I never knew his meal not to be ready.

That first evening in Tobago I met Fus Man, Moses, Gingo, Stylas, Hoop Head and a host of others introduced by their nicknames. During those unforgettable days which went far too quickly, they would become running partners and escorts.

I was about to witness goat racing. A little later, there would be crab racing. Easter Monday in Buccoo Village. I was fighting my way through ice cream vans, hoards of people, food stalls and hot music singeing my eardrums. Even though the general movement was towards the racecourse, I elbowed my way through the crowds in an effort to get a good pitch. An area had been cordoned off to make a course for competitors. Not quite on a par with the traditional racing scale but on a parallel assumption that spectators were to line either side of a stretch of ground along which the participants would travel.

I was not too sure who I was with. Neither Rita nor Kelvin were with me.

'Girl, I stopped going two years ago. If you see it once you see it a million time.'

Joinie took me to Buccoo Village before going back to work. Gingo and Stylas performed a sort of tag match. They were in an all-male group nearby, drinking and playing cards. I had been walking around the site, soaking in the atmosphere and enjoying being on my own. They would find me from time to time to phrase a variation of the same question.

'You want anything? You want ice cream, sweet bread, roti, a plate of stewed beef and rice, souse, black pudding, sugar cake, beer, mauby?'

A faraway look of concentration on their faces as hands delved into pockets to fish out coins or peel off a note which they felt corresponded to my culinary requirements. I told them yes to the first question and no to the rest. Rita was an excellent cook. I had had more than my fair share of breakfast that morning. Salt fish cooked with tomatoes and onions, washed down with a big cup of real chocolate was a heavier breakfast than I was used to. However, I was quickly getting accustomed to the change.

Some people take this event very seriously. I have been told that money changes hands. 'The goats are looking frisky'. I wish I could have used that expression to describe what I saw. The glazed preoccupation of the goats as they stood chewing their cuds made them look anything but frisky.' You will not find jockeys seated on their mounts here. Good job too! Feel sure they would have the Tobagonian equivalent of the RSPCA down on them like a ton of bricks. An attempt was being made to keep a handful of select goats in order. No mean achievement when dealing with an animal fabled to eat almost anything it can lay its mouth to. Around each animal's neck was a rope. At the end of each rope was a man holding a stick. Part of the uniform looked authentic. The trousers were white, near white, off white, and looked the sort of clothes you would expect to be worn by anyone taking part in an exercise of that nature. In that respect one could call the men minders. Bare feet, teeshirt or vest, identification number completed the ensemble.

And they were off! I soon got the idea. It was how quickly you and your quadruped could race the other men and theirs to the finishing line. Bare feet and hooves pounded stones further into the ground. The humans were moving as if their lives depended on it. The goats were probably certain their lives did. Curried goat is a delicacy on the islands. First one across the line got cooked? Or was it the last one to cross who went into the pot? Either way, it would be best to play safe and stay close to the middle. The tension on the rope was nail-biting. There is always one. There is always one soul who remains oblivious to ruin. The hooves of one billy were thudding on the quaking earth as if his life would begin when he reached the finishing line. His minder looked a worried man. He had reason. His feet had hardly touched the ground since the race began. He was hanging on to the end of the rope with both hands – must be some sort of life raft – and being tugged to the finishing line. He was declared the winner. Rumour had it the goat ended up in the pot, anyway. They had to throttle it to get it to stop running. The minder responded to everyone who congratulated him with the same surprised, bewildered smile.

Crab racing turned out to be even more of an inspiration. I don't know how long it had been since the creatures left their natural habitat but they looked as if they had resigned themselves to their fate. Even if the barrel they had just been taken from contained sea water or, alternatively, mud from their very own swamp, all memory of home had now gone. They languished in the afternoon sun as if they hadn't a care in the world. Since ropes would be ridiculous on creatures that size, a sturdy piece of string was attached to the anatomy of each crustacean. The minders spent much time in examining claws and paying attention to details. In addition to the string, there was a second prop. It was one which could be described as the urging and steering mechanism – a stick.

When the race began I tried not to rationalize or demand too much logic from what was taking place. But it was madness to the nth degree. A number of male adults were holding a piece of string. At the other end of the string was a crab. The men were endeavouring to urge the creatures forward at a satisfactory pace with the aid of the stick. One crab was going backwards and continued to do so regardless of any attempts to the contrary. Three of them appeared to be moving diagonally. Two others seemed to be dancing a quadrille. As always, there was a maverick. Slowly but surely he was inching forward. The crab was moving slowly but surely towards the finishing line. It was not so much a race as an exercise in patience. Not far removed from taking your pet snail for a walk. There was no longer any reason to scuttle. When you scuttle, you move with some intent to escape. If you are tethered by a string and the radius of your movement is governed by its length, then what's the point? These crustaceans, in any case, looked as if they no longer knew the meaning of the word scuttle. Even worse, some seemed to be experiencing difficulty in moving a claw forward. I didn't know the rules of the race. Were there any? Was it my imagination or did I notice some tugging on the string? It would obviously serve to pull the crab forward at a speed not of its own volition. My eyes were riveted on the maverick some short distance from the finishing line.

The spectators were better behaved than the ones in Trinidad. However, one or two began voicing their doubts about the precise physical condition of the winner.

'You damn cheat!'

'The crab dead! All you can't see the crab dead?!!'

I felt the protestors had a point. The only movement from the crab was the involuntary one made by any motion of the string.

'How all you people so blasted stupid? All you can't see the crab already dead when he haul it across the line?!'

This was very interesting. The crab went into a series of jerks as the minder worked the string to demonstrate it was still in the land of the living. Alternatively, it could indeed have been involuntary. Death throes.

'How man in he right mind go want pin medal on dead crab?!'

Howls of laughter from the spectators. The winner sat unconcerned. Surely rigor mortis had now set in. At any rate, no attempt was being made to lift a claw in triumphant acclamation of victory.

'And I say it dead before it cross the line!'

A number of people formed a circle around the winner. There was much close inspection going on.

'He move! I see he move!'

It was confirmed by another person in the circle. There was much jubilation. Everyone seemed happy. Everyone, that is, except the crab. And while we settled down to enjoy the rest of the afternoon, I was left with my doubts. Was there life in that body when the first claw slithered across the line?

My next encounter with them was the following day.

'Well, you just miss something.'

I walked into the house to be greeted by Joinie full of smiles. After the shock of that first evening, I was always very interested in what he wore. Mercifully, nothing came close to rivalling those shorts.

'If you did come half hour sooner you would have really see something.'

79

Rita came out of the kitchen, hands on hips.

'Girl, if you know what now, now happen to me.'

Moses came out of the kitchen sucking on a mango. He took his lips from the pulp long enough to set the scene.

'We walk in here to find a crab chasing she round the kitchen.'

Rita held one hand at a distance from the other in what might, at first, suggest an angler's tale. She narrowed the distance.

'And if you see the size of the thing.'

She grabbed my arm.

'Come, let me show you.'

I put my head round the kitchen to find Moses now almost down to the seed and still assaulting the mango with relish. On the draining board lay a mangled crab. The claws and back were indeed enormous.

'Moses had to kill the bitch.'

She became thoughtful for a few seconds.

'I feel is the same one that did do for Kelvin.'

They caught the crabs in the swamps. The men would shine torches on them late at night. The light would make the crabs active. As they scuttled to get out of the artificial sunshine, the men would grab and put them in the sack. Kelvin lost his grip on one. Trying to retrieve it, the claws sank into his shoulder cutting through the teeshirt. All this had happened the night before. I did not see the gash. I heard the next morning. Moses and Joinie were laughing and joking about the sight of the mother and father of all crabs chasing Rita round the kitchen. I never got to the bottom of it but it seemed as if the sack they were in was not properly tied or else there was a hole in it.

'Girl, I suddenly hear this noise. When I look down I see this thing coming. I never see a thing that size in my life. I start to run. How you mean? You think I so stupid I going to stand still?'

'He was coming for you, was he?'

'How you mean? The thing coming, coming.'

I tried to keep a straight face.

'Well, he probably wanted revenge. He must have heard of all the things you've been doing to his grandchildren in the name of sport.'

Someone was hammering nails into what was once a sweet dream.

'Get up! Get up! Get up all you!'

If all was to be believed, I should have been up and dressed long since.

'All you dead?! All you deaf or what?! Get up!'

The person was now banging loudly on the other bedroom doors. Rita's shock-awakened voice called back.

'Where the fire? You know yourself?!'

'We going beach for the day, girl. Get up and make a pot and thing. I coming back for all you now now.'

The dogs were still protesting loudly as the front door slammed. Rita called from the next bedroom.

'Moses mad. If he think I getting up to start any one set of cooking and it not even 'fore day morning, he lying to heself.'

Minutes later, I could hear her gentle snoring. I must have dozed off myself because the next thing I remember was jumping awake to heavy knuckles once again making repeated, impatient contact with my door. It moved on to Rita's.

'All you not ready, YET?!!'

I was sitting in the front seat of the Range Rover between Moses and Rita. His wife, their son, daughter, her boyfriend were in the back. As we were settling in, Kelvin came in from work. Back from an early morning shift. Moses made a suggestion.

'Sleep when you get back. Come go beach with we.'

He went indoors to come back with a pair of trunks, towel and a bottle of whisky. He pulled the door to behind him and came down the steps.

'Kelvin! You forgot to lock the door.'

He laughed.

'Lock? Lock what?'

Moses joined in.

'You must think you still in Trinidad with them thieving people you have out there. The only time we does have trouble like that is when they come.'

Rita nudged him.

'He don't mean you. None of we see you as one of them.'

Friends of Moses', standing on street corners, sitting on their porches, are given an invitation.

'Come go beach for the day.'

The back of the Rover already full when we started out soon had people hanging on the sides. We stopped en route to get the drinks.

'Here.'

As always I offered money towards my share.

'Girl, behave yourself.'

So it had been from the start and so it continued to be. The generosity was total. They gave a lot but they also demanded a lot. For that reason it was not unusual to have someone like Moses walking into your house early in the morning, screaming at you to get up so he could take you to the beach for the day. The people of the Caribbean love having guests, love being able to take you out, show you around and give you a good time. It was part of their nature. It was in my nature not to be too dependent on anyone. After a while, I learnt to handle the situation better. I would fold the money into the person's palm.

'No, *you* behave yourself. What happen now? Like you take out shares in the bank or what?'

And so it continued. I had to more or less fight for the chance to pay my own way.

We turned off the highway on to a track which only the type of vehicle we were travelling in could handle. The Rover trundled on, riding the rough ground with a motion which had us hanging on so as not to bounce our heads on the roof. We stopped a few yards from the sea near one of the most unusual beaches I had ever visited. Ours was the only vehicle. It would remain so during our stay there. The coconut palms were thick along the stretch of clean white sands. Some grew at a strange angle with the trunks at forty-five degrees to the ground. Other palms were lower still, growing almost parallel to the beach before turning upwards to the sky. They grew in the shape of an L. Apart from the aesthetic quality, and it was an extraordinary sight, it also proved to be practical. Moses always kept his machete close to the driving wheel. Later in the day, one swoop would bring a bunch down without too much effort. It was like having coconut water on tap.

The sea fell dramatically from one shelf to the next. It was a strange experience to be walking in water which reached mid-calf and suddenly find yourself falling to a depth where it reached your waist. I continued wading through the water, wondering at which point I might just as suddenly find myself falling again. The idea mesmerized and fascinated me. When it happened, my mind went blank. Decapitated. Just head and neck on a shimmering silver platter. Decapitated. Just head an neck. When I inclined my head I could find no reflection. That was when I panicked. An almost instinctive reaction seemed to be for me to try and find myself. I dived and pushed forward, cutting through the water as far as I could go. I closed my eyes so I didn't have to look at or think about this strange world which now seemed to hold my breath as well as my reason. When I came up, it was like crashing through a transparent dome. I could hear glass breaking. Splinters sucked into the funnel were revolving through a grinder in my brain. My feet now touched the bottom. I had reclaimed the top half of my body but my legs were like jelly. When I was finally able to steady myself and think clearly, I froze inside a feeling of being in no man's land. I turned to find I was the only one there. Everyone else was still on the beach and although I wasn't really all that far their voices seemed years away. Rita was holding up a paper cup and calling to me. When I didn't move, she started swimming towards me, the paper cup in one hand. Her head bobbing up and down, she kept the one hand aloft. She gradually narrowed the distance between us.

'Like you can't even tear yourself away from the water for five minutes.'

She turned and swam back. She had brought me a neat whisky. I made my way out of the water, slowly. The brooding shadow followed, aware that every movement which took my feet onward was not necessarily a forward step.

The feeling of nothingness which had me counting the waves as they broke against the rocks also had me contemplating the enormous expanse of shifting depth. When I looked to where it filled all space, I felt as lost as a grain of sand in the desert.

The others were now in the water. I found a pool where the sand was shallow enough for the water to barely cover me and sank into it. It was warm. It was comforting. It was calm. It did not seem to belong to the sea. The water was so clear when I stood up I could see the sand like pale pink ripples between my toes. Sunlight seemed to bend, reflecting a curved, jagged spotlight as if one of the sun's rays had fallen to sink into the sea. It now rested across my feet.

'Come, get some food!'

Lunchtime already. As Rita had stuck to her guns, the cooking had been left to Claudia, Moses' wife. They had driven up with her clutching a big pot of food. I had never seen anything the size of it. There must have been enough pelau in it to feed an army. She piled food on to my plate with a worn expression. Moses, an older infinitely more candid, grey-bearded, broader version of Kelvin was perfectly charming but one glance could tell he was a rogue. Being married to Moses would be no picnic. When they came to the house on my first evening he had wasted no time in chatting me up. Claudia had taken it in her stride. I felt sure she was well used to it. Rita had taken me to one side and given me some advice.

'If he invite you to go to the beach and is only you and he, don't go.'

When he invited me to the beach the next day, I told him I already had something planned. Later, Rita told me more about Moses.

'He does treat Claudia bad, bad, bad. And the man have children all over the place.'

Claudia handed the plate without looking at me. I took it from her, glancing down at her averted face wondering how she saw me. Was I just another tourist? Did she see me as some sort of threat? Moses and the other men were playing cricket on the beach, using the broad end of a dried coconut branch as a bat and pieces of wood as the wicket. Kelvin ran up to the wicket with an overarm action and sent the ball spinning. Moses drew his arm back, pacing the ball as it fell. He hit it hard then began to run. His stomach wobbled as his heels came into contact with the sand, kicking up jets as he fought with every step to make the next. I glanced back at Claudia before going to join Rita and the others.

I'm not sure where the day went. Part of it was taken up with frolicking on the beach and in the water. Someone had brought a guitar so we made a point of catching up on the latest calypsos. Yet, every now and then, the sound of glass grinding in my head would send the froth of memory rising to the surface. I would, despite myself, turn to look to where I had stood earlier that morning. It was now as still and as calm as if all memories had been drowned.

As still and as calm as it had always been.

I was on the Main Street, close to where Joinie and I had stood on my first evening on the island. Then, as now, I was looking on.

I may need to redefine the word 'overspill'. Had always thought it referred to members of a specific group who were obliged to take up residence elsewhere because there was no room in their natural environment. I very much doubt if the vendors on either side of the street had anything to do with an overspill from the market. It was a vantage point. They sold cooked food, provisions, and there was also a wet fish stall. Mercifully, he sold out early. The hands which reached across to brush away the flies were the same hands which wrapped your merchandise, took your money and gave you your purchase as you slowed down to buy. I saw it in action so many times. Some people prefer to handle what they are buying, turn it over two or three times, then examine it carefully to ensure that they are buying what they think they are before handing over their money. I suppose that if you are pushed for time or do not have a market shopper's mentality then this is an easy way out. When you build up a relationship through habit, there is nothing to be gained through bad service, At the least, being slapped across the head by a handful of wet fish which have turned out to be less fresh than the customer was led to believe. At the worst, you lose a regular customer. 'Slow down and buy' works best with cooked foods or commodities not governed by the vendors' wiliness.

'Two coconut water!'

The vendor selected two nuts at random from the bunch. A downward movement of his cutlass severed them from the cluster. The expert wielding of the blade and turning of the nut on its axis pared the pointed end of the shell. It soon resembled a scalloped spinning top. A well-aimed blow from the cutlass removed two centimetres from the top. You now had an opening where you could put your lips to drink the sweet, refreshing milk. A little pick me up, afterwards?

'Cut it for me, please!'

Another blow from the blade divided the nut in two. Delicious, tender, white flesh you could enjoy with the scoop the vendor had cut from a piece of a shell.

In Trinidad, I would see the Indian vendors, hats pulled low over their eyes as they swayed on donkey carts, stationary, whip in hand. Laden with bunches of coconuts they would park next to the shrimp sellers and water melon vendors on the hard shoulder where the Princess Margaret Highway meets Valsayn. I would also see them in Port of Spain by Queen's Park Savannah enticing residents and tourists alike. Each time, I felt gratitude. Gratitude and relief for this sight which clung so miraculously to an ever-changing landscape. I did not see the same sort of coconut vendors in Tobago but I met others like them. People I swear had been rooted and then carved out of an early landscape.

Now stop it all. Stop! Stop! Stop it all!

Stop the traffic. Stop the vendors. Stop the people striding along the street, standing on the street corner. Stop them all. I wanted to take it with me. Safe. Intact. I wanted to protect it fom erosion. I wanted to keep it from the elements. This was where it ended. This was where it began. This was where the focal lens, the brain behind the thought blinked to retain the vision. This was where the visual presence of a concept would come to my rescue when the loopholes in my memory began to play tricks on me.

It would plough the arid reasoning. It would hold until my return. And that would be soon. Very soon indeed.

I had never heard of a flight leaving early. Late, yes. What was more, I had never heard of one sneaking off behind the passengers' backs. But this is precisely what happened to the early flight to Grenada that day. I arrived in the departure lounge of Piarco airport to find a handful of disgruntled people airing their views. The conversation was very animated and, from the gist of it, I gathered that some were enjoying a quiet drink in the bar when the morning flight took off. It simply upped and went. No announcement. No pre-warning. No nothing. So now we were all going to be travelling out on the same plane. We knew we would be travelling out on the same flight because the law of averages says you don't get left behind twice. Certainly not twice in the same day.

All but two of my companions were Trinidadian and we were all on our way to Grenada for the same reason. The island was celebrating the fourth anniversary of the New Jewel Movement's coming to power. I had heard a lot about Grenada from people with various backgrounds and assorted political affiliations. They had talked of the island with great enthusiasm. All had said it was very beautiful. The one island they would like to return to. So I was going to see for myself. The celebrations would be a bonus. I did not know anyone living out there. I was travelling armed with addresses of two guest-houses where I might possibly be able to stay.

There were three other female passengers, one of them

was white. She, also, was going because she wanted to find out for herself. For me, from my immediate base, it was a short hop. The journey had taken her half way across the world. She had come directly from Australia. Politics were her driving force. I was motivated by curiosity. She was supportive. By the time they called us to board, Margo and I were fairly well acquainted.

I walked down the steps, on to the tarmac and stopped dead in my tracks. All the passengers were being herded toward the same aircraft so there was obviously no mistake. Until that moment, I had never heard of an 'Islander', assuming that planes of that size were used on executive flights or as luxury helicopters. I could feel my heart starting to sink as the edges of claustrophobia began to close in. It wasn't even as if one could open the window. As I stepped in, the plane seemed to shrink. How was I going to cope with this? With the first seizure of panic, my instincts were to run. Get the hell out. My hands started to sweat. I strapped myself in with clammy fingers and grabbed the newspaper in the glove compartment. I made a vain effort to keep my mind off the problem. Margo came to sit next to me. She started chatting about something or other but after getting a series of brief replies fell silent. In the background, I could hear a heated argument about Panorama, the steel band competition. The issue was around who should or should not have won it. Most of the passengers were joining in.

'But boy, I tell you! They should never have beat that tune.'

'What you know 'bout it? You know something 'bout beating pan?'

'Look, I telling you – '

'Boy, hush your mouth!'

There was a gentleman in a black hat trying to get a

word in edgeways. He was seated in the same row as Margo and myself but on the other side of the aisle. Although I did not know it at the time, the tune they were arguing about was his. He was one of our top calypsonians and that tune had won him many accolades.

I chain-smoked for the whole forty-five minutes it took to get to Grenada's Pearls airport. The minutes ticked away, mercilessly. Stepping off that aircraft into the sweet, sweet air was like having a trap sprung.

The airport was small but you already knew it would be because everyone talked about the big airport being built and mentioned the old one in the same breath. I didn't expect to see soldiers on patrol and there were none. I am really not sure what I expected to see. However, I did not expect the immigration officer to be out of uniform. He was efficient, quick and pleasant. Outside I found taxi drivers touting for custom, the way they do at airports on any other island. These, however, were most definitely after the American dollar. No point in bartering. To a man, they wanted twenty U.S. to take you to the capital. I told every driver who approached, I would let him know. I was kicking my heels. I wasn't in any particularly hurry. In any case, after meeting such interesting people, it seemed a pity to simply jump into a taxi without saying goodbye. When you step out of customs, you are back on the out-side. There was an official also in plain clothes at the door making sure it stayed shut. I must have been the first in the queue. The others took a long time coming out. No tales of horror. Their baggage check simply took longer than mine. There was a camaraderie building up. Everyone seemed to be waiting on everyone else. Granted, of the eight passengers, three already knew each other. They were part of a research team from the university. Neverthe-less, almost the whole flight seemed to be drawn into a hub. The calypsonian was given VIP treatment and whisked away, telling us we must check him out at his concert that evening. Still no sign of Margo. I asked one of the others as he came out.

'She's held up at immigration.'

I wondered how serious the problem was. It seemed mean to go off and leave her. And then there were three. One of the other passengers was a Grenadian girl. During the flight she had kept herself very much to herself. She breezed past us now into the arms of her taxi driver boyfriend and they drove off at top speed. And then there were two. Mark Fitzgerald, who had been attempting to chat up Margo even before we boarded, had collared one of the drivers. He was now making sign language to let me know he was holding that car for us. The other Trinidadians had gone off in two separate cars after we had exchanged addresses.

Margo fell out of the door looking flushed and agitated. I knew it wasn't simply because she had tripped over her suitcase.

'Jesus Christ, I thought they weren't going to let me in.'

She explained the situation.

'Didn't you know?'

I suspected it would be the same on all the islands. Unless you were able to furnish the immigration officer with an address where you would be staying while in the country, you'd find yourself up against it. I knew before we left Trinidad that Margo had nowhere to stay.

'So what did you tell them?'

'I'll drop by immigration in town tomorrow and let them know where I'll be. Tried ringing a couple of places just now but couldn't get through. I'll try again when we get there.'

Fitz was whisking us into the waiting taxi. Like everyone

else on the flight, we were heading for the capital, St George's. Soon we had left the dust of Pearls airport for the dust of Granville, the nearest town. It would be like any other small town on a Caribbean island where the people were struggling to make a better life for themselves. Apart from the dust there was a curling sense of resignation. This curling sense of resignation followed like a trail of dust to mingle with my own thoughts and an unexplained sense of guilt. I was in a unique situation. I had come to the islands to see for myself. There was already something plucking at my emotions. Soon it would stretch them to a transparency so taut there would be times over those next few months when I felt they would snap. On every island I visited where I saw the people of the Caribbean struggling to earn a living, some part of me would remain. It would lie on that rocky dirt road to the Concorde waterfalls where I met Elaine, weary, using her cutlass as a walking stick. It would lie in Anse La Raye, where Mark would beg me to let him join me in England because, even at twelve years old, he felt he could not escape his fate. When the fish didn't bite, things were bad. And of late things had been bad. It would lie in Dominica's Roseau where an old woman buried her face in her hands and wept when she told of how a hurricane had destroyed her home. It would lie in the open cesspit of slums just a stone's throw from Guadeloupe's glamorous boulevard in Point-a-Pitre where despair was like an open wound on the faces of Haitian families. My emotions would knot and turn, twist and fragment in the whirlpool of experience. At times, I felt like a ghost who was haunting herself.

The taxi skidded to a halt just a couple of miles outside Granville. Fitz jumped out and ran up a dirt track leading to a small wooden house. He called out and, getting no reply, began banging on the door. He came back a few minutes later, to quiz a group of boys standing nearby, taking an interest.

'Them blasted people never at home.'

Some relatives who lived there, he told us, were handling a legal matter for him.

'Boy, let we go!'

'You should have let them know you was coming.'

Fitz's narrow reply was lost in the driver's impatience to be on his way. The winding road seemed to be hewn out of a madman's logic. The journey was so long it seemed endless. I tried to glean something unique and special out of those miles but eventually had to come to the conclusion that it was all relative. The people who sit on verandahs, 'lime' on pavements or stand chatting at stand-pipes, turn their heads to take an interest. Sometimes it was little more than benign. At other times, we held their curiosity until the car was out of sight. This was how it was with the children, in particular. For them, time was never the pressing urgency which had to be divided into parcels of vital minutes so that only a few could be spent in the motionless study of looking over your shoulder at something or other. For me, every child, every man, every woman was part of the phenomenon. I was as curious as they. I wanted to see how the island's circumstances affected them. Like a fool, I searched faces for visible signs. Scrutinized armpits for excessive sweat. I was looking for something among the udders of ripe bananas, among the dark green lushness which would begin to stir or move as if guided by some excessive force. I found none. I saw that the concrete houses, the wooden houses, the shacks were the ones I would find on any island. The struggle was still taking place. It had to be fought before it could be won. That didn't take much working out. You didn't need to be a genius to figure that one. I turned to look at Margo. Her thoughts were marooned on a similar island to my own. I felt they deserved to suffer there. We should both have known better.

'It's taking one hellva long time. You sure we're on the right road?'

I hadn't thought about it. But now that she mentioned it –

'How much longer before we get –?'

The words died on my lips. Margo's hand shot out across my chest as she pointed to what had drawn her attention. Fitz and the driver still chatting seemed almost oblivious. We kept it in sight until the road took a sharp bend. It had come out of the blue and held us riveted. Thirsty as we were for a sign, Margo and I had drunk in every letter. This one was hand-painted and official. It stood a good twenty feet by ten and announced 'Work Harder for Greater Productivity'. I settled back in my seat, content. There was no time now to dwell on it. We were coming into St George's. The car went up a steep hill which seemed to blur everything from view and when the road fell it seemed to hold the lights of St George's right under our noses. It was now coming on for early evening and the capital was hidden behind a pale grey veil. We knocked at the door and a large, amiable woman informed us that yes, there were two rooms to let. Margo and I decided we would share one so Fitz could have the other.

Our state of excitement was heightened by the fact that Mrs Vierney knew everything we wanted to find out. It didn't take long before Margo and I were seated in her living room drinking coffee and chatting.

Two women on their own in a Caribbean night, both obviously strangers and one of them white, could create some problems. With a Caribbean man in tow, it would offer some protection. The guest-house was situated on a hill which seemed to be cut in tiers. There were three roads, each immediately above the other. We could not see the one below the guest-house, any more than we could see the one beneath that one, which led to the Carenage. I fell in love with Grenada that night. I was left with an impression of houses being joined at a tangent and separated only by narrow passages, sometimes so slim you would have to squeeze sideways to get through. And the gutter was where the water gurgled not out of contentment and ease but from the power and force of use.

The three of us set out with light and happy hearts. There was something in the air like tiny filaments of wonder. It encircled us time and time again, binding Margo and myself round and round with incredible ease and then spinning us anti-clockwise. And the sounds weren't just from the people on the streets. It seemed to rise from the pavement to mix and mingle, stroking their words, giving them greater depth and meaning, smoothing abrasions, softening the sharp and angry tones. We went down towards the market. Down. It was a wide road which had the brakes on your leg muscles screeching. We walked past the market place to the sea front. I went down to the sea and there had a vision of the vastness of deserts until the black rocks broke the waves with the impact of a sledge-hammer on wafer-thin glass. It sent sprays leaping up out of the water. They were so high I had to jump away for fear. Fear of what? I told myself fear of being drenched. I shut the door firmly on my thoughts.

The others had gone ahead. I caught up with them in a shop where smoked hams hung like early Christmas decorations and food was the least interesting thing on sale. The inside of the shop was infinitely more sombre than the evening outside. It was a fascinating place where dark wooden stools seemed to grow out of the floorboards. The beer was lukewarm but we didn't complain. Even if Margo wasn't, Fitz and I were well aware we were paying a good deal less than we normally would for a Carib lager in Trinidad. To enter into the spirit of things, we had a second and then a third. I suspected that life on the island was going to be pretty good and I was convinced of it, totally won over and converted by the time we had walked the short distance to Queens Park.

We had to shove and fight and kick our way in. The place was packed. Once inside, the atmosphere relaxed. We settled down in a good seat for a long wait. It didn't take long to notice one essential difference between the audience of a calypso show in Trinidad and one in Grenada. The performance was going to start late. There was nothing novel in that. I have yet to visit a show in Trinidad which started on time. However, what I was used to was some display of exasperation when they were kept waiting too long. Mingled with this would be slow hand claps, boos and requests to have their money refunded. Nevertheless, despite all the indignation, should the waiting period offer records which were the current favourites, their enthusiasm would know no bounds. They'd be dancing in their seats, on their seats, and rendering the words to the music. It is a way of response one soon falls into. It becomes second nature. Unfortunately, it is the sort of bad habit one is often tempted to take out of the country. A bit like contraband. So while Fitz and I were reacting to the very late start in the only way we knew how, a sudden glance around the audience showed that, apart from a handful of people, everyone was behaving impeccably. Audiences in the Caribbean tend to consume a lot of peanuts and there were shells everywhere. That aside, the audience was sitting and waiting, patiently. Not even the hot calypso music being played by the disc jockey could tempt them.

Fitz's fierce whisper almost scorched my ears.

'Boy, what wrong with these people?!'

I had stopped whatever I was doing to sit quietly and ponder. I would now be obliged to rethink certain concepts. Unlike Fitz I was not so sure. I did not automatically regard my values as faultless. Finally, the show started. The first two calypsonians on the bill were warm-up performers. The audience received them politely. Two of Trinidad's top calypsonians were on the bill. As we got into the show, I realized what was going on. The audience was most certainly responding but not in the raucous fashion I was used to. It came as a shock to realize they were simply being more selective. After all the derogatory remarks I had heard Trinidadians make about Grenadians, here was a people we could learn from.

The show was now moving quickly. He came on stage looking splendid in a gold suit and matching shoes. It was evident right from the start that it was he the audience was waiting for. And they showed their appreciation accordingly. We were getting excellent value for money. Five Caribbean dollars for a show which would have cost twenty to twenty-five Trinidadian dollars. And it was a good show.

That first evening in Grenada was not a disappointment. But breakfast was. I had hoped for something traditional. Instead, ham and eggs were shoved under our noses. Even after I had finished it and four slices of toast with nutmeg jam, I was still hungry.

'What are you going to do with yourselves today? Maybe you should – '

'I think I'll just mooch around the Carenage and get a feel of the place.'

Margo could well have been speaking for both of us when she interrupted Mrs Vierney's question. Your first day on the island, independent of tourist guides, you mooch.

98

I had already come to the conclusion that market places were the pulse of the community. I would experience the same sense of coming together on every island I visited. It was a source of life and inspiration. It was where the people's sweat falls to be nourished under the weight of an island dollar or drops to ferment and sour in the heat of a disappointed afternoon. The market place in St George's was no exception. The noise and a variety of smells came to us before we were even there.

'I go see all you later.'

Fitz left us to pay his solicitor a visit. We walked into a beehive of activity and colour.

Studded round the market were stalls and small wooden eating shacks. From quite early in the morning, early that is by European standards, you could buy a plate of peas and rice, stewed beef with yams and plantains, roti with curried chicken. You could buy a glass of ice-cold mauby, homemade grapefruit, orange or any of the other local fruit drinks, in addition to any of the other run-of-the-mill soft drinks. Sugar cake, ginger bread, guava cheese, tamarind balls. And that was just to put you in the right frame of mind. If you needed pulses, rice, dried fish or soused pork you might need to go inside the market. If you didn't need them, why bother? Why bother to draw a curtain between yourself and the sun when everything else was spread out before you? The outside of the market was a selection of patchwork squares where vendors attempted to display their goods to best advantage, The patchwork squares were a pattern of work not yet completed. It was for you, a potential customer, to add the final touches. You did this, by merely weaving your way between the fruit and vegetables displayed on the ground and responding to the sounds made to entice you. The vendors were in various stages of relaxation. A few squatted. Some stood. Most were seated comfortably on low stools or chairs.

'Breadfruit, Madam? Three for a dollar!'

'Come, doo-doo darling! Come and taste. Sweetest oranges in Grenada.'

A segment of orange was shoved into my hand. Almost mechanically, I put it in my mouth and walked on.

'Hey! Hey! Where you going?! I give you – '

The same voice which barely seconds before had been so soft and inviting was now abusing me. In taking the piece of orange without buying from her, anyone within earshot would have thought I had as good as robbed her of all the money she was carrying.

'Okras, ten for a dollar. Okras! Young and tender!'

As I passed she made an enquiry.

'Making calaloo tonight?'

'Ripe plantain! Get you ripe plantain!'

I was treading an altar and being serenaded most of the way. They say empty vessels make the most noise. A number of sellers were sitting quietly under their parasols and straw hats. At their feet, heaps of firm red tomatoes and unblemished yellow-orange grapefruits spoke for themselves. They didn't need to be advertised. It was to one of these traders that I made my way for a hand of bananas. I suspected that as in Trinidad and a few of the other islands they were called figs. As the fruit known by that name in other parts of the world is not found in the Caribbean, no confusion arises.

'How much you fig?'

I tried hard not to sound conspicuous. She looked up from the basket work on her lap, took me in then went back to her work. It was a few seconds before she answered, her fingers working nimbly to twist and weave the cane.

'Bananas, three dollars a bunch.'

Something, perhaps everything, had given the game away. If she could tell me about 'bananas' then she knew I was a tourist and was charging me accordingly. I looked from the rosette of smooth and glossy miniature phallics to the vendor. There were a dozen or so bunches on the white calico cloth. This tiny variety was my favourite. Those being sold by other vendors were too ripe. Hers were just perfect but the mere idea of being ripped off had me turning my head to see if any of the other vendors were displaying prices for the same variety.

I tried to barter.

'Two fifty.'

I turned to look at her. We held each other's gaze. I was unaccustomed. It was my first attempt at bartering. In Trinidad, if a market person tells or displays a price, then it is fixed. Should you attempt to influence them you stand an excellent chance of getting a mouthful. Only towards the end of the selling day will they consider dropping the price rather than take the goods back with them. I was in two minds whether to give the woman the benefit of the doubt when the sight of Margo's altered image distracted me. I was about to walk towards her when a restraining hand held me back.

'Three dollars.'

Her price hadn't changed but the amount of bananas being offered for my money had. It was an offer I could not refuse. I took them and, handing her a five dollar bill, walked away without waiting for change. I could still feel her eyes on me as my thoughts somersaulted over mountains of soil banked against hard toil in order to reap meagre results. My thoughts also touched on compromises of living from hand to mouth and having a large family to feed. Finally, my thoughts went off at a tangent to settle inside a pin prick of depression.

Margo was wearing a pentagonal canework smile. She pointed to a newly acquired hat, worn low over her face.

'Cancer of the nose. We Aussies are prone to it. I've never been out in heat like this before.'

We wandered through the market buying more than we could eat. The atmosphere was fantastic. Positively magical.

Margo was to prove to be a source of wonder. She approached one of the market women and started asking about life on the island. Her timing was exquisite. Because Margo was such a natural, friendly person, she and the woman were soon engaged in a fairly animated conversation. I left her to it and went off to see what else was happening. The market place served two purposes. It was where you caught the minibus to take you wherever you wanted to go. There was very little public transport in Grenada. You had to squeeze yourself into one of the sardine-cans where, even when obliged to fold yourself in two so the next passenger could get in, the bus boy was yet shouting, 'Room for one more! Room for one more!' Or if you were more fortunate, you took a taxi. As a wealthy tourist, you could afford to take a taxi.

'Going Grananse, lady?'

I smiled indulgently.

'Grananse! Grananse!'

'Gwarv!'

'Sotows! Sotows!'

The competition was fierce. They were touting for custom. No minibus moves off until it is full and you would find several going to the same destination. If it was only half full, passengers must wait patiently until it was 'quite' full. It never took very long because people were constantly travelling to and from St George's. The capital bustled as much as any other commercial town. I paid a visit to a bank opposite the market to cash some travellers' cheques. Margo joined me in the queue. The cashier was a darn sight more pleasant and efficient than the ones I had to deal with in Trinidad. Less of the bullshit and more speed and dedication.

There was an effect of squares within squares. Little stalls outside the shops on the streets bordered the market. They sold anything from combs to kerchiefs, some sold teeshirts, others odds and ends of toiletries.

We walked down to the Carenage. Restaurants, souvenir shops, official and other buildings were located close to where cargo, yachts and pleasure boats were moored. Timewise, we were making good progress. A number of establishments closed from midday until two in the afternoon. Both the immigration office and the tourist board were nearby so this was where Margo and I parted company for a while. I bought some postcards and was on the Carenage writing them, killing time while I waited for Margo, when I heard a familiar voice.

'Girl, we just thinking about you and your friend.'

It was two of the Trinidadians from the flight.

'You enjoying yourself? How you getting on where you all staying?'

I told them we had no complaints so far.

'If you want to come and stay, we have room at our place. Come over tomorrow evening, let we crack a bottle of rum and thing.'

We remained chatting for a while before they left to return to Grand Anse. I watched the people come and go. There were a lot of Europeans, ambling along, cameras at the ready, taking in everything. I took them in while they watched this picturesque part of the city going about its business. Margo joined me.

'Have a mauby.'

I took her to the nearest café to recover from her visit to the immigration office. She didn't like the drink. Said she found it too bitter.

There was so much to see and so much to do. We felt it would be a good idea to plan the next few days even though the next few days possibly did not need planning. The official day of the celebrations was only a week away and there were things happening all around us. The productivity exhibition, several rallies and a full scale manoeuvre in the park close to where we were. Just a few of the things we already knew about. Margo was keen to listen to a speech scheduled to be broadcast that afternoon. The Prime Minister Maurice Bishop was out of the country. His deputy, Bernard Coard, would be making it in his absence. Back at the guest-house, I had a long, long shower, letting the jets of cool water cascade over me. Lulled into a delicious sense of security, I began to doze on my feet.

A light drizzle had started from early that morning. I stood on the verandah waiting for Margo and Fitz. The plum trees were doing a sun and rain dance as the breeze shook their branches. Muted iridescent tones were woven into streaks of rain. They came down like continual filaments spun by lightning fingers. And from below, way below where I stood, sounds rose to become decipherable. Snippets of conversation taking place on the Carenage drifted up the hill through all that greenery and rock to reach my ears. I understood what people meant when they talked about the hills being alive with sound.

The previous day on the Carenage, I had stood back to take a good look. Up in the hills, houses peeped out from behind thick, green foliage. I tried finding our guest-house. There were so many to choose from. Later the same day, Margo succeeded. We had missed each other at the rendezvous point and I had returned to the house. I hadn't been on the verandah long before I saw her coming up the hill. While on the Carenage she had been able to find the house and had seen me standing there, waiting.

'Okay?'

Her voice broke into my reverie. She stood in the doorway, adjusting the strap on her camera case.

'Christ, he's a pain.'

I didn't need to ask who she was talking about.

'That bloody man just won't leave me alone.'

Margo had a problem all right. In truth, we both had a problem. It was part and parcel of the same thing.

'Am I over-reacting?'

She had misread my expression.

'No, I agree with you. Fitz is becoming a pain in the arse.'

It is always a disappointment when people who show promise turn out to be very different from what you expect. Fitz was one of those black men who was dying to see what 'it' was like with a white woman. For convenience sake, he was good to have around. From Margo's point of view, his burning curiosity, in the short time we had known him, was beginning to make her life hell. I didn't come into it. He already knew what 'it' was like with a black woman. However, I was amazed at my lack of judgement. At Piarco airport, he had tried to create an impression and had succeeded. At the time, I sincerely felt that he may well have been someone of importance, in a position to take us around and give us a good time. Since then, we had caught him out in one or two lies. His family didn't own umpteen acres of land and he did not have lots of rich and influential friends on the island. He was a liar and a braggard. I could forgive him for that. The thing that had me cringeing and wanting to scream was his habit of saying 'Look! Look!' when he was about to say something he felt deserved your undivided attention. The even more annoying thing was, it worked. No matter how boring the topic, and by then we had heard several versions of his favourite conversation pieces, you found yourself turning to listen. We had discovered enough about Mr Mark Fitzgerald to feel it was about time he was on his way. At a discotheque the previous evening, what should have been an enjoyable time was spoilt by his continual pestering.

'I've had enough. It really is insulting. And he's so bloody crude.'

'We're going to have to give him the kiss of death. I know he goes back to Trinidad next week but we can't put up with his shit until then.'

Each turned to our thoughts.

'Look, I been thinking. Why you two don't come an stay in Grenville with my family. It go cost we nothing. They have breadfruit and coconut, orange, fig and thing growing by them. We go catch fish in the river. We could cook and thing and enjoy weself. It go cost we nothing.'

Margo continued fiddling with her camera. I was looking towards the Carenage. We hadn't heard him approach and even if we had, his presence was by no means a good enough reason to stop what we were doing.

'Look!'

A few seconds later.

'Look! Look!'

I turned to stare past him and he still didn't take the hint.

'Look! Look! All you don't have to worry about a thing. When we leave we give my cousin fifty dollars or so and –'

Margo and I looked at each other. One of us shook her head. The other looked towards the heavens. I can't remember who did which. He was trying to lure her into a false sense of security. It was obvious. Apart from anything else, the man needed someone to wash his underwear.

She told him slowly and deliberately.

'I don't want to go anywhere, with you.'

You would have to be some sort of moron not to take the hint.

'Look! Look! It go cost nothing. Only a few – '

'Look, Fitzie baby. Shut up about your blasted family. We're really not interested.'

He didn't believe Margo when she said it but he sure as hell believed me. He shrugged his shoulder and looked as if we had just kicked him in the groin.

'I just thinking 'bout all you.'

Margo exploded.

'Like bloody hell you are!'

Afterwards, we walked quietly towards the centre of town. Fitz left us to pay his solicitor a second visit. The whole purpose of his trip was to settle a legal matter involving some land. His father was from Grenada and had died leaving land which was now in dispute. Or so he assured us.

'I go have to make a turn to Grenville when I finish here but I go see all you later.'

We never saw him again.

It can't be the heat. Mad dogs and Englishmen aside, I am really not sure what made us decide to attempt the distance from the house to Grand Anse on foot. We really weren't sure how many miles we were undertaking. Perhaps, we were also being a little foolhardy. The fact remains that the walk to Grand Anse beach that afternoon turned out to be one of the most hazardous afternoons of my life. The road was not only narrow, it was narrow and winding. And it wasn't only narrow and winding, it was winding as if built by a drunken road-builder. It would disappear suddenly to reappear as a sharp bend. This we could cope with. The danger lay in the suspicion that life came cheap on the island. After the third car passed us without even attempting to slow down, our survival instincts found us not just stopping to let each one go past but standing well back. It was a very busy road with a number of minibuses doing a very lucrative trade. They were the worst culprits. Once or twice we saw what looked like near misses as one swerved to avoid the other. They knew the road. We didn't. However, I preferred not to think about the fact that, sooner or later, your luck runs out. With the number of tourists on the island renting cars and in particular Minimokes, the chance of an accident was always there. They didn't necessarily need to know the road to very quickly get into the swing of things. Of course, the minibuses slowed down when they saw us. Gesticulations ensued. The bus boy was touting for custom. On each occasion we declined. We recognised four different buses on the route. It took over an hour to get there, so naturally they passed us several times and every time they passed, they let us know about it. Yells, jeers and boos greeted us every time they drove past. With that and having to avoid the rest of the traffic, our nerves were pretty taut when we eventually arrived.

Meanwhile, we did our best to enjoy the scenery and most of the way it was pretty stunning. Every now and then we caught a glimpse of the sea. It lay between shacks, expensive bungalows and sheer cliffs. It lay on our right, blue and calm. Every time we saw it, we thought we had arrived. As we went, we enquired at every guest-house we passed for their rates. By then we had decided Mrs Vierney's was perhaps a little too expensive. Even though the basic charge of twenty-five East Caribbean dollars seemed reasonable in itself, what we had not taken into account were the extras. The hoped-for reduction in sharing a double room was not forthcoming.

Mad dogs and – which category were we? The sun fell

on the back of our necks and clung biting to our skin with teeth of molten lava. On we trudged. The mirage said we were on a fertile Caribbean island. In reality we were sifting desert sand between our toes. And we were! I'm not sure which of us glimpsed it first. Sandals in hand, we started running. Grand Anse beach bowed down to touch our toes, folding itself lovingly around our feet first, then our ankles. Our bodies were in full flight but we moved in slow motion angling against a stiff breeze which rushed in on a delinquent wave. How the devil we managed to stop ourselves from diving fully-clothed into the water, I don't know. Forethought is forearmed. Grand Anse was the best beach on the island. The longest. The bestest. Plush hotels and nightlife stretched along the beach. Grand Anse was synonymous with the finest and the best. But don't let the Americans get wind of it. Oops! They already have. An American medical school was situated here. After all, where else but a tropical island to sit under a coconut tree sipping pina coladas and ambling leisurely into the blue, snorkel in hand, when you're not cutting up bodies.

Forethought is forearmed. If you're going to Grand Anse, you take a swimsuit. Just as well. After that long, gruel-ling walk, the cool blue water swirling suggestively was, perhaps, more than we deserved. I changed in record time. Margo beat me to it. Her easy breast strokes as she swam out into the deep was the last I saw of her for a while.

I became a dab hand at floating on my back, floating on my back and avoiding collisions with too many bodies in the water. I was drifting out on a calm and keeping an eye on the action as I went. Life was for living, idling, relaxing. The tourists were for making a quick buck from. Mingling with the pink bodies slowly roasting on the sand were those of a darker hue. Exactly what they were doing was difficult to say but most were male. All seemed to have torsos hewn out of black granite. Whether lying on the sand next to a companion or trying to charm her into buying one or two items from his tray, all appeared to be selling something. The buyers were invariably female and white. Every now and then, I saw one of the female hawkers. Their wares were usually beach clothes.

'Nice dress for you, madam? Look at the colour. It will look so l-o-o-o-vely against your skin. I have just the shirt for you, sir. Why don't you –?'

Having heard it all before, I turned to float on my stomach for a while. I faced the horizon. But all I could find was the desert where they once put me to count the sands. One by one. One by one until I understood once and for all that every single grain was part of the drought. Every morsel, every particle of cracked earth, every breath which lifts sand like a gloved fist to your lips and forces it between your teeth then up your nostrils, was an agent of the desert. And their grand hotels on the beach stood on pillars made of sand and would very soon crumble back into it. It was guaranteed to slip through your fingers as easily as water and be just as elusive. It was all part of an illusion. Another version of delusion. Just one more mirage of life.

Much later, we began to count house numbers. And it was much worse than that. Neither of us was certain of the address. Carifta Cottages. That much we can remember. The question was which one. There were a lot of them. Some faced the beach, others had their backs to it. As luck would have it, two things happened almost simultaneously. One of the cottages had Police Station in large letters across the front. Great! Bet they know who's who and where. At the same instant who should we see strolling towards us but one of the people we were in search of.

'Is now you reach?!!'

I translated for Margo who was looking at me with a half-smile.

'What kept you?'

He was off somewhere. He would see us later.

'But the others there.'

It was a bit like the ten little Indians in reverse. There were a couple of strange faces. People we hadn't met before. It looked as if the whole side, in ones and twos, would be flying in for the celebrations. In no time at all, we had tuned in to the clinking of ice as we sipped rum and coke. Easy conversation was punctuated with quips and laughter.

'Why the two of you don't move in here? We have plenty of room.'

'Where you all staying sound really expensive.'

It was the second invitation we had had of that nature. Fitzie's motives had been dubious. Maybe theirs were also but Margo and I felt they wanted the novelty of more female company. There was only one woman in their group.

The cottage was fully furnished. Living room, kitchen complete with all necessities. The three bedrooms took as many beds as there were people sharing the cottage so a fixed rent was simply divided among those present. The more the merrier. Or the more the cheaper. We wondered later if that may have been another motive for the invitation. For the time being, we simply relaxed and enjoyed the company.

The minibuses stop running early. You could, of course, take a taxi but with the state of our finances, who wanted to turn tourist? Take a taxi and starve for a couple of days. If you are on a tight budget, it is as good as final. At about eight o'clock, we got out the playing cards. Like occupations of that ilk which start off being fun, in no time at all you are telling your partner that if you had a gun you would shoot him because he is a bloody fool. By ten o'clock we were at each other's throats and on our third bottle of rum. Hard-drinking, hard-bargaining gamblers. And the amount of noise we were making would have been reason in itself for the police to pay us a visit. They were only four cottages away. A car screeched to a halt. It wasn't them. A friend of a friend was going into town. Did anyone want a lift? Margo and I had to tear ourselves away. Since we would have to pay for our room at Mrs Vierney's anyway, we decided to get back that night even if we had to walk. Having been through it once in the heat of a Caribbean afternoon, a starlit night held no terrors. I had heard no rumours of the Grenadian night being unsafe for women.

'So until tomorrow then.'

And indeed the next sunset found us loaded to the teeth, staggering under the weight of bags and baggage. We had a room to ourselves. There were three beds in it but the other girl preferred to sleep with her boyfriend so they had the smallest bedroom to themselves. Three of the guys were in the big bedroom and the fifth was bunking in the living room.

That night, every night, there would be a disco, a show or something happening. Five East Caribbean dollars to get in and I would take twenty extra. On that, I could have a good time. Hot calypso blasting in your eardrums, you are jerked on to the dance floor like puppets, stopping only to turn with an outstretched hand as you stumble to the bar or reach to undo a zip as you queue for the ladies. Otherwise, you stand on the floor gyrating and sweating. Once again, you can spot the Trinidadians. We are the ones who don't know the meaning of the word inhibition.

The Grenadians and the tourists tend to take it easier. Don't get into such a lather about things. Don't tend to sing along with the vocals quite as loudly. Don't tend to move their bodies as if they are manipulating some wayward hula-hoop. Do not put as much effort into enjoying themselves.

The calypsonian appeared from nowhere to take Margo in tow. I didn't see him arrive. He wasn't performing there that evening. He was just enjoying himself. Partnering Margo on the dance floor, he began teaching her how to dance to calypso music. No more bobbing up and down in opposition to everyone else but a gradual coming together, an assimilation of cultures. We danced until we were told to go. He waited for us outside, surrounded by his entourage. Leaning against the expensive car on loan during the tour, he tried to tempt us back to his place. Either of us. Preferably both. I got the impression he didn't mind which one. We were, he told us, each in her own way a little different from the women he was used to dealing with. We promised to check him out over the next day or so. He was also staying in Grand Anse, holding out in a splendid little number with a swimming pool and close enough on a clear day to see when he was on the verandah. Margo and I visited a few times. It took only ten minutes on foot. But not the following morning. Out for a swim, she went out further than usual. She wanted to take a look at underwater life. She brought some back with her. While coming up for air, she trod on a sea urchin. The sole of her left foot looked as if it was suffering from blackheads. We were able to get one or two of them out but decided, despite the advice from well-wishers and seasoned sea urchin treaders to leave them to dissolve, to seek medical advice. She had said she wanted to see what the general hospital was like. I don't think this was quite what she had in mind.

The hospital was situated in the centre of town. The steep road leading to it was one of the main shopping areas. Business was brisk and lively. Cars coming and going; once again you had to stand back to let them through. There was usually a police officer on the dromedary's hump, directing traffic. As always, in full uniform. And as always, this included white cotton gloves. The initial impression was one of spotless white. However, I figured that if you had been standing around for a number of hours with all that dust, not to mention exhaust fumes, it wouldn't do to look too closely. As the day begins so early, by mid-morning it must feel as if you have been there for days. The police officer on duty was looking thoroughly fed-up. I offered a smile. She had my fullest sympathy. I was still smiling and she was still looking through me when Margo and I turned at her extended left arm, up to the hospital.

'Jesus Christ! We're going to be here for hours.'

The waiting room was packed and there was no one at the reception desk. After a while a nurse came bustling in.

'Act the tourist.'

I pushed her forward.

'What can I do for you?'

The nurse tried to look stern and efficient. She tried but appeared more surprised than anything else. I suspected they didn't get too many white tourists limping into casualty. We got fairly prompt attention. Prompt, that is, by comparison. I had heard the shortage of trained nurses on the island presented a real problem. Margo was passed on to a girl whose uniform looked too large for her. I turned away from what might be going on behind the scenes to what was taking place on the outside.

A number of patients in pyjamas and nightdresses were coming, going or relaxing on the wooden benches in the courtyard which led to the ward. A few of the patients were chatting to people I took to be visitors. It seemed a fairly novel way of going about things. Why make your visitors go all the way upstairs to the wards if you can come down to them?

I turned back to the screens where Margo was being attended to. Focusing on the space between the curtain and the wall, I glimpsed vague shapes as they came and went, moving in the shuttered light.

Funnily enough, Margo never said a great deal about what went on in there except that she really wasn't impressed. The nurse had applied some sterilizing fluid to the foot then bandaged it. In fact, the bandage was so badly done she had more problems walking than before. When we got outside, we had to re-do it.

Wherever you went you found vendors. The hospital grounds were no exception. A variety of sweet and savoury snacks and soft drinks were on display on both sides of the drive leading to the main entrance.

On the hump, the policewoman still looked as if she had the hump. Her white gloved hands spoke the same language of power and control. With the mask deflecting the midday sun, only her eyes and lines drawn tight across her forehead and the corners of her mouth reflected any emotion.

'Wave back, nuh? What wrong with you?'

It seemed a little bit indulgent and pretentious. I put my heart into it to make it look a bit more than a royal wave. Instead of just beaming a greeting my hands as well as my lips were working overtime. It wasn't possible to say just how many cars joined in that part of the activities to celebrate the fourth anniversary since the revolution but if the sparsity of parked cars on the roads was anything to go by, the support was pretty general. The car I was travelling in was part of the motorcade going around the island. The people lined both sides of the road, waving and cheering. Strange snake this. Whenever I looked over my shoulder, the level of the land permitting, vehicles serpented as far as the eye could see. And we travelled at a similar pace. 'Grow more Food. Build the Revolution.' I kept it in view until it was out of sight, just as I had done on my first day. Since then I had seen a countless number of slogans, all standing high above the ground. Several versions of the same message of encouragement to the people. They had never failed to draw my attention. I had never been able to go past any of them without feeling a surge of excitement.

'Forward ever! Backward never!' The words rang and echoed throughout the day. I was hoarse from the shouts. We had got out of the car a number of times to attend rallies. The tickling in my throat was also partly due to swallowing dust I had been shaking from my mouth and from my clothes. Members of the People's Revolutionary Militia were travelling in the back of the truck directly ahead of our car.

'Jacko! Jacko! How you doing boy? Is long time no see.'

The greeting had come from someone in the crowd and was directed at a young man in khaki uniform and cap sitting on the edge of the truck. He smiled a bleary response in the general direction of a group of people nearest to him. We had been crawling behind the truck for more than an hour. And during all that time, Jacko had been dancing non-stop. It was celebration time. He and the other young people with him, all in uniform, had been making their own music. The khaki shirt was now open to the waist and worn outside of his trousers. The peak of his cap had gone through a hundred and eighty degree revolution and now shaded the back of his neck. In terms of distance he had marched miles, his feet beating against the floor of the truck as his jack-boots crashed down on the open space. His knees came up again and again to almost meet his chin. But that was over with. Now, beads of perspiration trickled down his face on to his neck, to join forces with the sweat running from chest to navel. Every now and then, a khaki arm reached across his face to wipe the sweat. And the parched dryness in my throat made me swallow hard. Dry and arid road.

Again, I had to shake the dust from my clothes. This time, we had come full circle. We were back in the capital. No one was in any hurry to wend their way back to their respective homes. I was travelling in the car of a Grenadian gentleman I had met a couple of days previously. Margo was in the one directly behind ours with some new friends. The rest of the motorcade would be coming in for some time afterwards. I didn't care to hazard a guess as to what time the last of the cars would be arriving back in St George's. I turned to find the truck driving off. And yet Jacko held the bleary smile from all those miles back. And having smiled, smiled on. He smiled as if he held some secret vision, the sweetness of which none but he could comprehend.

'Now, all you understand the problem?'
    'Yes.'
    'Don't say when all you get in there, I didn't take time and effort to tell all you.'
    We answered in unison.
    'We won't.'
    'And all you still haven't changed all you mind.'
    'No.'
    'All you sure?'
    'Yes.'
    'All right. Well, tomorrow I go bring a cylinder of gas to the house.'

'Thanks. Thanks a lot.'

We walked out of the house in Government Hill, feeling very pleased with ourselves. But there were times during the rest of my stay on the island when I would have doubts about the decision made that evening.

The rest of the household were due to return to Trinidad. We would be left with a house far too large for two people, both size and rentwise. We had got to know Window through a group of Canadians who were staying in the house next to ours. Window was also caretaker, of sorts, of a house in Morne Rouge, rented only during certain months of the year. This was not one of those times so the house was empty. He would talk to the landlord. The cottage was only rented at certain times of the year for one reason and one reason only. The rest of the year, there was a water shortage problem. In fact, it was a very real problem. There was none. The opportunity of a two-bedroomed furnished cottage at a nominal rent seemed like the answer to our financial problems. We, perhaps, hadn't given it as much thought as we should have done. Things you take for granted are soon put to the test. Water for cooking. Water for cleaning. Water for flushing the toilet. Water for washing yourself and clothes. The umpteen times a day you put your hands under the tap or reach for a glass of water to drink.

The cottage in Morne Rouge was a short distance from where we were in Grand Anse. Moving simply involved a few trips on foot along a quiet road where minibuses did not travel. The cottage was situated at the top of a hill. The first of a number of dwellings which sloped down to the beach. A long row of concrete steps gave access. It overlooked the sea, giving a clear view from both bedrooms and living room windows. There were holiday apartments on the opposite side of the steps. Later, we would find out that although they suffered from the same water shortage as ourselves, provisions had been made for them.

Grenadian families occupied the houses on our side of the steps. A small space separated us from our immediate neighbours. Although we remained on only nodding acquaintance, after a while we felt as if we knew them quite well. The whole family, including the baby, made noise with a good deal of zest.

'And – and – and – and Michael I tired telling you!'

A little later:

'Michael if I have to talk to you once more, boy, I going to give you such a cut arse.'

Less than an hour later:

'I tired telling you!'

Whack.

'I tired telling you.'

Margo sitting at the living room table working on an article to send back to Australia winced every time the strap came down.

'Really puts a lot of effort into it, doesn't she?'

Michael's screams set the baby off. Between them, they swallowed every atom of tranquillity. The strange duet jostled for attention with everyday sounds which rose to the surface at that time of day. Intimate snippets of conversation would seep through their front door, into our window.

'Girl, if you know how the man did – '

'Is truth then?! Was a time when he was friending with a woman from Grand Roy. And when the two of them in bed, all the time he did want she to – '

'Child, I heard the man nearly kill she! The first thing he want do was –'

They were a large family. By the resemblance, we took the women to be sisters but it wasn't easy to say which children belonged to whom any more than which gentleman belonged to which lady.

Gas was expensive. Rather than using the gas cooker I assumed their landlord would have supplied, they cooked outdoors. The smoke from the coalpots would curl upwards, always towards our windows. The smell of whatever they were cooking would seep into our kitchen to dominate the smell of our own cooking. Every now and then, Margo and I remembered to joke about it.

'Christ, they're not cooking that again, are they? It's the third time this week.'

There were two wonderful occasions when, after a heavy rain, water began gurgling out of the taps. We filled everything we could find and for a couple of days enjoyed the luxury of fresh water for everything.

Water was now a very precious commodity. We became stingy. Buckets of sea water filled a barrel in the bathroom and was used for any purpose which did not demand fresh water. Buckets of fresh water were kept in the kitchen.

There were two stand-pipes we could use. One was on Grand Anse beach, the other in the grounds of a nearby house. The Cuban gentleman who lived there gave us permission to use it whenever we needed. So as not to waste much time, we acquired a routine. Every day, for one reason or another, we would need to go into St George's. We would walk down the hill from Morne Rouge, past the Radio Station, to Grand Anse. On our way, we would leave the empty buckets behind a hedge close to the stand-pipe. On our way home later in the day we would collect and fill them. The two or three showers a day I had once taken for granted were no longer a reality. Any opportunity to use someone else's shower was taken. So all in all, despite the sledgehammer of realization when the less romantic aspects of pioneering life hit us, we coped.

Being practical, we soon adapted to the umpteen trips it took down and up those steps. We were to discover for ourselves what had been known by others for centuries. Sand was an excellent scouring agent. Our pots and pans were taken down to the sea to be scrubbed clean.

My association with the sea was otherwise limited to twice a day. In the mornings in the name of hygiene and later in the day if I happened to be around when the heat of the mid-afternoon sun became too much for comfort. The sea presented a quiet front from any window of the cottage we chose to view it from. A quiet front when we crossed the sands to get to it, our footprints losing all signs of individuality among the many which had already been there that day. In the evening time, it presented a quiet front should we choose to patronise the discotheque on our stretch of beach. The moon shimmering in slivers of gold would often spotlight its presence. On nights when there were no shafts or daggers of broken light, it would murmur its presence or wash against our feet with a suddenness to catch us off balance. Always, much colder than we would have supposed.

'Garden of Eden all over again. So hazy and unreal. It's like being on another planet.'

Talking to myself. And was there really any wonder?

There were so many dream qualities to the day, I found myself inching forward, one foot in front of the other. When they talked about walking a perfumed path, I always supposed it involved a crowd of people armed with bottles of scent, spraying towards the ground as they went. I was walking a perfumed path. It was not the first time I had found myself in one of the nutmet-growing regions. Window had taken me on a visit to his village. I was so excited, I picked up the first, then the second. But this was

121

different. Then as now, some of the harvest lay on the ground. Cloves grew there also. Until then I had not realized they were part of a blossom. Indeed, I had never stopped to ask myself how they grew. And if I had, it was unlikely I would have given myself the correct answer. They were the buds of a specific cluster of white flowers. I was walking along a path where nutmegs seemed to grow wild. They lay strewn on the ground, many still inside their lacy red coats of mace. Overhead, the fruit hung like a split peach. The open halves still held their perfume. All around me were laden branches of nutmegs in various stages of development. Some had not as yet ripened sufficiently for the slit which would gradually get wider, revealing the red cloaked kernel, eventually allowing it to fall to the ground. I was walking along a path where nutmegs seemed to grow wild. But of course they did not. Although the area was not cordoned off, the trees were someone's property and the nutmegs were not going to waste. Sooner or later, someone would come to gather them.

Window's family had been extremely generous and given us a variety of fruit and vegetables to take back. In the same village, someone's garden had carried a rack with hundreds of cloves spread out to dry in the sun. During the course of the day I visited other gardens, other villages where racks covered with cloves lay drying in the sun. But, again, this was different. I had not seen how they grew. I had not seen the trees they came from. I had not reached the same pinnacle of awareness. Had not sensed an air of magic. I had not, at that stage, inhaled the perfume of wonder.

'This is where all you get off.'
  'Is here.'
  'All you get out here – cross the road and – '

'Is across there.'

'Don't miss all you stop!'

We thanked them, driver, bus boys, passengers alike. The walk began where the minibus had dropped us. It would take us up the the hill to the Concorde waterfalls. A long way up but we were in no hurry. We took our time, laughing and chatting as we went. We passed little nests of houses. I could not help but look in, wondering who lived there. Every now and then we came to one where someone was sitting on the steps or leaning on a verandah. On each occasion, we greeted them.

'Good morning.'

'All you going up to the waterfall, then?'

'Yes, we're going to see for ourselves.'

Sometimes, the conversation went further. Sometimes it ended with just a brief exchange and a goodbye wave from them and us.

The day went through some strange changes. Heat waves may have seeped through the concrete combustion which crumbled the stone slabs back into dust. We were travelling on a dirt road. Two figures suddenly appeared in the distance. At first, undefined. I could not tell if they were men, women or children. They came over the crest of the hill, moulded against the sharper angles of moving air so it wasn't possible to tell what speed they were travelling at. So deceptive. At first I took them to be a mirage. They came over the crest of the hill then seemed to mark time before coming forward in slow motion. Curtains of shimmering heat cut, dwindling the two bodies, still distorting shapes. The sun continued to strip and peel them, absorbing colour, blanching and draining them to off-white, white. They become fused into one form. A parallel predicament. The same identity. They redeemed themselves before descending the hill, reclaiming colour, shape and form as they came. Two women balancing full sacks on their heads, one was carrying a cutlass. How strange that while the sun was devouring them, it never once glinted off the steel blade. They came quickly down the steep incline. The sacks on their heads swayed only with the movement of their bodies. Their bare feet continued to stir the dust. One was middle-aged, the other, perhaps in her twenties. I had met her before. I walked forward to greet them, confident. The younger woman raised her hand. I started to lift mine also in a gesture of welcome.

'No!'

I thought perhaps I had not heard correctly.

'No!'

Her hand came up to hide her face.

'No!'

My hand fell to my side. Both she and the other woman were looking towards me, at me, through me as if I wasn't there. The object of their attention lay outside my immediate vision. Margo's voice eventually broke both the tension and spell.

'Okay. Okay. It's okay. It's all right.'

I turned to find her putting the lens cap back on her camera. My face still hovering on the brink of a smile, I moved one or two steps closer to the women. Their attention still riveted on Margo, they walked past as if I was invisible. The younger of the two was the more daunting. Her face had tightened into a mask of hostility. On her way down the steep incline, she turned from time to time to make absolutely certain. Her head swivelled as if on a slow pivot. The other woman continued her progress, down. She did not turn. Not once. Not once did either of them reach up to steady their burden. It was almost as if they were not carrying a load. It was almost as if the sacks had become an extension of themselves. They could never fall. I watched until they disappeared. It happened as suddenly as they had appeared. Sucked into the vacuum of the next hill.

Thick leather soles offered little protection against pebbles which now formed a layer between the soles of my feet and the sandals. Stopping to remove them I could not help but notice the pattern like a cross along my insteps. The only part of my feet protected from the dust which now reached to my ankles was the skin covered by straps.

'She was determined, wasn't she? She definitely didn't want me to take her photograph.'

I didn't answer. Head bowed, she walked slowly ahead of me, deep in thought. I was carrying the weight of a sudden depression where the abyss along every groove and rutmark had been hacked with the same piece of machinery. Where the whirr of feet trampling step by step through the passage of time was fossilized into the same grooves and rutmarks. The same abyss hacked by the one piece of machinery.

I stepped into the shadows which lay to my right. Barely feet away from where I walked, the river rushed in the direction we were coming from. It smashed around huge, black boulders studded along its path. Tiny pink and white blossoms were being carried along. Some came to rest inside the curves where the erosion of years had created temples. Safe havens where some could wash against the tide, protected from the turbulence until they faded, shrank to sink beneath the waters. Margo and I ascended the road to Concorde at our own pace. I continued in the shade, ignoring an open path where the sun blistered. From time to time, the river disappeared to come back into view. Voices ahead suddenly drew my attention to the crest of a hill. Margo stood talking to a woman who balanced a bucket. In one hand I saw the dull outline of a cutlass. In the other she carried a large box. I did not alter my pace. In time, I caught up with them.

'This is Elaine. She's got some land up here.'

The woman returned my smile. Almost instinctively, the two of us reached down to help her carry the weight. I listened while Elaine talked, leaving Margo to make conversation. I listened without lifting my eyes to meet her face. No longer protected by oblong shadows which stretched at a tangent to the brittle heat, razor-sharp strokes from the sun singed the hairs on the back of my neck. It continued clawing at my skin until Elaine had posed, stately, her cutlass at her side, for Margo's camera. She left us to take a path which led to her plot of land. I moved back into the cool, balming shade of the river's flow.

I believe we could hear it long before we saw it. Water screamed from a great height as it plunged to the depths below. The shout was deafening. I didn't need to listen. It came in, filling my senses. Yet somehow it did not seem able to reach the arid regions of my thoughts. Cascading down it bounced off vertical rocks before crashing into the river below. It broke the surface into endless splinters of ripples.

Could I even compare the height from which it fell with the distance from which the Caribs leapt? I am no judge of distance. I had gone with others to Sauteurs in the north of the island from where some of those early inhabitants had leapt to their deaths. Leapt rather than be taken prisoners by the French. I shielded my eyes to look towards the heavens. No, perhaps not that far. Perhaps, not nearly that far. I have absolutely no judgement of distance. All I know was that I could not walk along that path in Sauteurs to look down from the cliff's edge, as the others had done. I could not do it. Could not do it. Could not.

What a nuisance! We had already started scrambling

down the bank when we spotted them. A couple sat on a rock with their arms around each other. Her fair hair falling down the back of his muscular, black arm. Dreadlocks were pressed against the side of her face. The last people we expected to find up there. It seemed a bit mean to kill their last day together. She would be flying back to Canada the following morning. Margo and I scrambled back up the bank and continued on our way. We never did find out if that first waterfall was the one we were looking for. Somewhere, sometime later, we found a place where the river serpented far enough away from the road for us to assume privacy. Taking off our clothes, we stepped into the water.

Some rocks stood in an irregular circle, shielding a rush so the flow inside their pool remained fairly calm. But to get to it, we had to wade into water which though not very deep was turbulent. You found yourself stepping into eddies which whirled around your ankles and jets of water which shot like bolts against your feet. Margo's naked back simply held both arms at shoulder level to stop from falling. I held firmly to boulders, rocks, stones and, because the place was overhung by trees, branches also. Had it not been for Margo's presence and the overwhelming urge to feel cool, I would certainly not have put caution aside so firmly.

'Really strange pull from under the water, almost as if –'

Her last words were lost in the splash as she dived sideways through an opening in the circle. How strange she should have felt the undercurrents also. I thought, perhaps, of the two of us I would have been the only one to sense them.

I had seen this fire before. Elusive. It changes shape. Every evening I had watched as, curled into a perfect orb, it fell from the sky at a speed which had me wondering if an invisible hand hadn't reached up to pull it out of the heavens. It peeped out with a half-closed eye from behind the horizon. A circle of fire was being extinguished as it sank into the sea. Naturally. What else would happen to fire under the circumstances?

'Christ! This can't be real. It's got to be magic.'

Hardly an evening went by without either Margo or I phrasing the sentiment in some form or fashion.

A blaze of glory which screamed across the sky for the majority of the day would draw in its reserves and set. I would find myself looking at the phenomenon, spellbound. Sunset was apt only in so far as it described the process which was taking place. The word did not do it justice. I did not know a sun could set by simply falling from the sky to slip below the horizon. And where did it go when it was no longer contained? I had my suspicions.

We had met Milton at Grand Anse beach. He lived in a one-room house up in the hills overlooking Morne Rouge and earned his living by selling coral jewellery to the tourists. I would watch fascinated as he stripped the bark from the coral then bend and curve it through the flame of a candle to make one of his bracelets. I was never able to look at the flame without thinking of fire falling from the sky and Milton's hands reaching out to capture it as it fell. The precariousness of the slender black shape would come home to me time and again. If a fraction too much effort was put into bending the arc, it would snap. I held my breath as I sat and watched one day. I watched through the curtain of fire as it happened three times in a row. The snap seemed to come from deep inside his fingers and instead of a curved circle held between thumb and fore-finger, he would be left with two separate pieces. The jagged edges of their erstwhile union, blatantly obvious.

Milton would begin again. He would begin all over again.

Why were some days so much more precarious than others? A frightening cycle of near achievements. Beginnings with middles but no end. The crack sounded as if it had come from deep inside his fingers. So much tension in the very heart of that fire. The centre could not hold.

The centre did not hold.

'Where are the guards. Surely, there'd be some posted now.'

I was talking to myself again.

My last day on the island. My second visit to Point Salines. Milton had first taken me there during my early days on the island. The Grenadians were, naturally, very proud of their new airport. It would make the island more accessible and forge a stronger link with other Caribbean islands as well as the rest of the world. The once hilly terrain had had to be levelled, dredged and filled in to become the smooth ground which stretched clear down to the sea.

The runway waited.

Workers, Cuban and Grenadian alike, had been busy building the airport. No one had tried to stop us. We had stood and watched the trucks and bulldozers going about their work. A monumental task, yet incomplete.

That second time, I was on my own. But there we were. Clear down to the sea.

The runway waited.

Some hangars had already been built. I could see that for the time being they were being used to store building materials.

The runway waited.

The runway waited so close to the sea. Was it too near?

Would it begin to erode all achievements before they were even completed? What if the salt ponds which had to be dredged decided to reclaim their territory?

The runway waited.

So much of the runway had already been paved that it stretched like a road, out of sight. And so wide.

It might never happen again. Never again in my life would I be able to stand on any runway to see and hear the vibration and witness the magnitude of the vision as it threatened from the sky.

I could feel the heat beneath my feet. I could sense currents beginning to gnaw at the foundations. The shifting nature of pitch responding to an impetus from the midday sun receded behind potholes which rose above the level of a black volcanic flow.

President Reagan had made his speech about the new airport, just a few days earlier. He had said it was an air base being built to store ammunition and train the military. The island's foreign connections had been stressed. The one with Russia mentioned but the EEC's involvement in funding the project ignored.

Reagan's speech had sounded threatening. The People's Revolutionary Government had feared an invasion even then. Prime Minister Maurice Bishop told us to be vigilant. Be prepared. He had urged those of his people who had not already done so to join the militia. I had remained close to the radio, feeling a growing sense of indignation. I had come to love Grenada. Of all the islands I would be visiting, I felt it was where I would consider returning to the Caribbean to live. I asked myself, what would you do if the Americans were to invade right now? The sense of outrage dictated that if it came to a battle, I should stay and fight.

The next few days had seen a stepping up of military manoeuvres with the island being put on alert.

We held our breath and waited. We had waited. Only when we felt the danger had been well and truly averted did we exhale.

I had seen the river run clear and sweet. Clear, transparent images once looked back at me. I did not recognize the black, bubbling volcanic mass where circular pools like eyes rose above a deluge to bear witness. Bear witness. Bear witness to truth that the flow ebbed back to where the parched, open dirt road waited for your bare heels and the dust flew back into your face. Bear witness to the funnels of irregularities which sucked every atom of life from the vision. Bear witness to blind, staring eyes behind the closed, parched lips.

'Amber and the Amberines', the military exercise staged two years earlier and widely assumed to be a mock invasion of Grenada, was about to become a reality.

A gentle breath moved inside a fine speck of dust. I heard it like a long sigh before it was pulled into the sands to once again become sand.

Forward ever! Backward never!
Forward ever! Backward never!
Forward ever! Backward never!

It was interesting to witness the process in reverse. Joinie and I had stood knee to thigh watching them stream off the boat. There were now just as many making the trip.

Having determined to return to Tobago, the dilemma lay in deciding exactly when to travel. By the time I finally made up my mind it was another holiday weekend and all flights were fully booked. Not one to turn up at an airport on spec, I decided to take the boat.

By necessity, the act of boarding demanded some control. Once on board, however, chaos took over. They ran up and down the boat looking for seats, fighting each other for space. No matter how close you were to the head of the queue, it seemed as if you were never close enough. By the time you boarded the vessel, all seats had been taken. The process was an ingenious one. Dad, Uncle Rufus, Auntie Mae or Gran, should she be hale and hearty enough, would queue early to hold a block of seats for the rest of the family. The response from the passengers not at the absolute head of the queue or who didn't send an Auntie Mae or an Uncle Rufus ahead, varied only in the actual choice of words.

'Like all you take out shares in the boat or what?'

'Don't mind the rest of we. We is nobody. I can't quite place you face but I feel sure you must be royalty.'

'I pay the same money for my ticket and this old wajang spread she big arse across three four seat. What trouble is this?'

I was forced to be vocal also. My repartee did not compare.

'Is this seat taken? ... Is this free? ... Is it taken? ... '

I eventually found one. It was a straight-backed chair at a table for one in a far corner. All comfortable seats had been taken. I was wedged into obscurity. The bar was not far. During the next few hours I would make three trips to return each time with a full bottle of Carib lager. Otherwise, I sat and I observed. So much was going on. I would need to shut my eyes tightly and place fingers firmly in my ears to avoid it. I dare say there are a few white tourists in each boatload but this means of transport is, largely, the vehicle of the people.

The holiday spirit took over from the moment we boarded. Those who could not find a seat of some description took a pew on the floor. Later they might find themselves there anyway. I was one of the few passengers travelling alone. Lots of families. Lots of male groups. There did not seem to be any peer status. There were men in their twenties as well as forties in every group. A loud energetic game of cards was already on the way. From the start the atmosphere seemed geared towards a mini-carnival. In a mixed sex group, two guitarists were playing a calypso while the others harmonised. But all was not harmony.

'Turn down the music! Turn it down! Turn it down!'

A ghetto-blaster had been splitting our eardrums since the young man took his seat. A gentleman I took to be the guardian of our peace continued to remonstrate with him.

'If I have to tell you about that blasted noise once more you go – '

'How you could come quite over here where I playing my music good good and start making trouble? I ain't interfere with nobody. I minding my business. How all you people get to be so damn wicked?'

'I ain't telling you no more. I want that blasted music turn down. It too loud.'

'I do you something? Like you want people hear your mouth or what?'

'I giving you one minute then that thing going out the window.' The passenger turned to his female companion. Dressed all in white, tube top, shorts and sandals, she was wearing an expression which told the world she knew she was looking good. At the same time, her face showed the embarrassment of one who was at the centre of some unfavourable attention. He turned his head to talk to her in a voice loud enough for all to hear.

'The man come with he mouth swell up, swell up like I did tell he 'bout he mother.'

She laughed. Her laughter was a little too loud. Until then, only a few of us had been taking an interest. The guardian was making his way back to their table. As he got to within a foot of them the volume was turned down.

I was afraid to eat anything. It had been so long since I last travelled by boat, I could not remember if I was a good sailor or not. Hearing someone heaving over the side when we had only been at sea for fifteen minutes made me certain that I made a wise decision. Did Trinidadians go anywhere without their pot? There were two women with children, one a baby, sitting on the floor. Food was being dished up. It was well past lunch time. I had not eaten since morning but the sight of all that food did not make me hungry. I felt sick just watching them. And could a child that age really consume such a mountain?

'You not getting up to play 'til you finish that food, you hear me?'

There was no alarming movement, no lurching or swaying as I had feared. I had been warned that at some point I would be reminded I was at sea.

134

'Just wait 'til the boat hit the Borcas, girl. You go know.'

There was a lot of milling around, much coming and going. Some disappeared for a while, maybe exploring the boat, to come back a little later. Through it all, I stayed put. There was so much to see and enjoy. So much music. So much singing. So much laughter from children and adults alike. So much sound. The air was dancing also. The deck had become a visual, audible cocoon. A sense of being locked in had me shutting my eyes and swallowing hard. I suddenly found myself bolt upright in the chair. I became conscious of my mouth hanging open, my eyes fixed. Somewhere, a force was struggling to free itself. It was so close, so near. I could feel it. But the door remained shut. Eventually, its energy spent, it wafted to the floor. A wisp of its former substance, it seeped through crevices between the floor and its frame. Like a pinprick of light, only the bare bones reached me.

Five words of recognition. I repeated them to myself.

... Is that how it was? ... Is that how it was? ... Is that how it was?

Forced into a tight knot of anguish, they went down in the deluge. These passengers were in a celebratory mood. Celebrating what? What was there to celebrate? The fever raged on.

Children playing around me came to lean on the table. Yet I remained where I was. I did not budge. I did not stir. Camouflaged by filaments so dark and gloomy, the cobwebs attracted no shaft of light. It drew no attention. I may as well have been invisible. What was there to celebrate? In the final analysis, when the debris had crumbled into dust and the dust been swept under the carpet, what the *hell* was there to celebrate? The irony was bitter and exquisite. Every man, woman and child swore he or she was going somewhere. Every man, woman and child swore he or she had something to celebrate. So what the devil was I doing taking a boat going somewhere, going anywhere. I was going nowhere. What was there to celebrate?

When we hit the patch of choppy water they call the Borcas, my stomach lurched.

One of the women was busy mopping up vomit. The other was changing the baby's nappy. I had to turn my head and hold my nose, the combination was too much. They made hard work of it. Between them it was a slow, painful experience.

The coastline never shifted. For hours it appeared to be the same distance away, moving at the exact speed as ourselves so that every time I glanced out of the porthole, we seemed no closer. A sudden buzz of excitement told me we were coming into Scarborough. There was a mass exodus for the stairs. Strange, the sudden shift of attention. The change in scenery determined the direction of the cast. From the jollity, intensity and determination to wring every minute of pleasure out of an incarceration, they were once again jostling each other for space. People were now jammed between cars and vans, waiting to disembark. I felt a jolt as we came in. The release was sweet. Fresh air and people on the outside, their eyes focused on us. I had telephoned to say what time I would be coming. Gingo came towards me, jingling his car keys. He grinned as he took my case.

'How you keep missing thing so? Big big wedding here last week. We eating up and drinking up, partying for so. Everybody want to know where you is. You still in Trinidad.'

In truth, friends of Rita's and Kelvin's had got married a few days earlier. I knew about it but couldn't quite find the impetus. To be welcomed after the long painful journey, to stretch my legs and be on firm ground again and not know the danger of waves had me smiling like an imbecile. I had taken Rita and Kelvin some bottles of their favourite whisky. I doubt if they'd have minded if I'd arrived empty-handed, they were so welcoming. It was good to be back.

Thanksgiving Sunday. On the island it was a time to drop in and be made especially welcome with food and drink. If any stranger were to knock on a door, I sensed he would be made welcome.

'Let me take a turn.'

I looked down at the chunks of ice packed between the metal cylinder and the wooden tub. The ice was sprinkled with coarse salt to stop it from melting too quickly. I put my left hand firmly on the top of the churn and began turning the handle.

Soursop ice cream. My favourite. I was a child again. Tunapuna where I was born.

I had returned to the island a year earlier. I had stepped off the plane, apprehensive. The years between had been vast. My mother had met me at the airport. The road led through Tunapuna where I was born, lived and was brought up by my grandmother when my parents came to England to study. I had begged to see the house where I was born. Born and lived until my grandmother's death.

I had arrived too late. They had begun demolishing it, three days earlier. Only the shell remained. I had tried to retrace my footsteps back along the stepping stones to my formative years. The decision to make the return journey had been difficult enough without finding myself marooned as soon as I arrived. During those four weeks on the island, I felt uncertain of most things I saw. I could not stop looking over my shoulder at the desert nor could I stop sifting the memories which ran like dust through my fingers. I had hoped to find it all there on the island, waiting. I had not come prepared.

I vowed I would go back. At the earliest opportunity I would go back. And this time I would get it right. Cautious. I would watch carefully for the gradients and be alert to when the ground beneath my feet shifted. The next time, I hoped not to be caught unawares.

The wheel turned onwards. Clockwise. As a child I had stood on the porch of our house to take my turn at making ice cream. Then, as now, we would be celebrating something. Celebration time. Noise, laughter, visitors, lots to eat and drink. How many times did you have to turn the handle before the ice cream was ready? Nobody counted. Nobody cared. It was a labour of love. I would turn the handle through countless revolutions. Wheels within wheels, each moving at a different speed. And although an entity in itself, each formed part of the pattern, a piece of the history.

How many revolutions did it take?

We were under a house which stood on very high concrete pillars. The space doubled as both kitchen and laundry. In the far corner a figure was forcing clothes against a scrubbing board. The girl's downward movements were as regular and fluid as I hoped mine were. From time to time we glanced at each other, using the other's rhythm as a metronome. Even after she had changed the garments on the board, our movements synchronized as I continued to turn the handle.

Two women were doing the cooking. Three large iron pots, covered and steaming, had just been taken off coalpots. Serving spoons and plates were now being assembled. Food was about to be dished up. Stylas would be taking me to visit various friends and relatives. It would be extremely bad manners to refuse to eat or just sit there toying with my food.

When nature called, I found myself entering a hut a little

distance from the house. I would be visiting other houses with outside toilets while on the islands. A deep pit and around it a raised platform of some description. The four walls would be of wood, corrugated iron or concrete and there would be some sort of roof. I would follow the one simple rule for all of them – never look down. The lavatories were consistent in so far as they all smelled the same.

'She know we doing the round.'

Upstairs with Stylas, the women put our plates on the table and left us. I was relieved. Just a dumpling and two pieces of meat on mine. It was the first time I had eaten wild meat. It was manicou. I found the flavour strong, distinctive. Later it would be agouti. Later yet I would get a chance to taste turtle. Ice cream, fruit cake and more drinks followed. More people dropping in.

It was a while before we could move on. The village was humming, a buzz of activity. Houses full of people drinking, eating and just generally socializing. By evening, a few drunks would be blatantly in evidence on the streets.

And through it all the rain fell. It came in torrents with a sun making vain attempts to shine through. We had the car but in the main it stayed where it was because we were often visiting houses doors away from each other.

One might suppose that sooner or later you would knock on a door to find no one at home. This did not happen. Every house we visited had host and/or hostess, plus a number of people. I reasoned Stylas was obviously taking me to the more productive side of the village or visitors were largely coming from other areas.

Through it all the rain prevented the sun from shining down on a village aglow with hospitality, goodwill and open doors. No icy slashes of frosted glass obscured your view of the inside of their hospitality – for Thanksgiving Sunday, at least.

'Now, you sure you not too tired.'

'Boy, behave yourself! I a born Trinidadian. How I go be too tired for Buccoo tonight?'

'I go pick you up at nine then.'

'That nice.'

Stylas gave me one of his slow, easy grins. The one which said he and I were on the same wavelength.

He had once said he wanted to take me to the best. I was relieved his idea of the best did not turn out to be plush hotels where white tourists stayed, with cabarets and bands laid on specially for them. His idea of the best synchronized with my own. While it was impossible to get completely away from places frequented by tourists, we largely succeeded. It was one of those dimly lit clubs geared towards local and not tourists' tastes. There was just enough space for dancing. Just enough tables and chairs. A lot of excellent music and a good bar. Stylas had started taking me to the nightspot regularly. It had become one of our favourite haunts. Once, a young white woman had walked in with a black companion and once an elderly white woman in the company of a group of blacks. Apart from those two occasions I did not see a white face during my numerous visits.

The next two days, however, found me doing the conventional tourist bit. Gilbert Maynard, the man from the meteorological office, had called at Rita's and Kelvin's a couple of times after our first meeting. On both occasions, I was out. He must have given up because I did not hear from him again. He must obviously have got word that I was back on the island. When I returned from Buccoo that night, there was a message to say he would be coming early the next morning to take me sightseeing.

'Yes, I've heard it before. It's quite famous now.'

We were in Plymouth, west of Scarborough, standing in,

of all places, a cemetery. It was crowded with tourists taking pictures or hovering over the same gravestone. All were pondering the enigmatic inscription which included the words:

> 'She was a mother
> without knowing it
> A wife without letting
> her husband know it
> Except for her kind indulgences
> to him'

Maynard told me that for the past hundred and fifty years, visitors have been scratching their heads. Some had come to their own conclusion as to what the words meant. Let them continue to puzzle over it. I was more concerned with another monument. Not too far from the cemetery was a geometric construction, erected in memory of the Courlanders. I contemplated the reasons, pondering concrete angles, which could have brought this group of Latvian explorers to the Caribbean.

'What do you suppose they were *really* looking for?'

Maynard shrugged his shoulders. His eyes suddenly glazed over with inspiration. He began to spin me a yarn. I did not believe a word of it. I wished I knew more about their history. I wanted to know more about what took anyone so far away from their country of origin. I wasn't in the least interested in what the history books said. I was looking for something more profound. Perhaps, an easy answer. Definitely, an alternative one. I was well aware that what I was looking for probably did not exist.

Back in Scarborough, we visited Fort George. A main tourist attraction, it commanded a defence view of the harbour as it had during the days when Tobago changed hands thirty times. A dice of the eighteenth century, being played among Courlanders, English, French, Dutch and Spaniards. From the old battlement, we watched for two things. For a good five minutes we followed the boat from Trinidad as she eased into the harbour, twinkling every inch of the way. The harbour lights blinked and glittered as if glow-worms filled the space not only along the sea front but the coast line also, as far as the eye could see.

'Down there is Bacelot. Follow my finger. Watch for some green lights? You see them? That – '

The sights were pointed out to me, one by one. I glanced into his face and took with me a tinge of envy. So easy. So at ease in the place of his birth. His hand moved confidently from one area to the next. It was his and he knew it. During those six months, I didn't meet anyone who didn't know their own island. They knew the soil and the plants and the fish and that little beach tucked away from prying eyes where you could go for a swim in the nude with no one – tourists at any rate – to disturb you. Firm as rock, man, woman and child, they had stood in their own grounding.

Stylas, Gingo, Joinie and the others had taken me to places they felt would be of interest but certainly not as diligently and with as much dedication to the role of tourist guide as Gilbert Maynard. With them it had been beaches, parties, clubs and such. Things and places they would usually have done and visited. They would take me anywhere I wanted to go but, as a rule, sightseeing was not one of my particular interests. Whenever I was told of a place I should definitely make a point of visiting before I left the island, I would make a mental note, but at no time did I feel any overwhelming sense of urgency. Maynard took his role seriously and, strangely enough, on each occasion my thoughts would leapfrog beyond the present to cling firmly to a deeper sense of history. It made what would otherwise have been a tedious two days stimulating and occasionally disturbing. The following afternoon proved to be the ultimate experience.

When we got there, it was coming on to evening. There were pictures in the tourist brochure of an enormous iron wheel which stood in a wooded area. Moss, vine, vegetation and trees clung to it, grew on it, against it, along the spokes. It was all that was left of what was once a sugar mill. At the foot of the wheel was flat grassy land. The spot has since become a popular picnic site. The photograph showed a white couple seated with their backs away from the wheel. They seemed to be smiling at something in the distance. I had not asked to be taken there. Once again, Maynard had brought me to a place which had become a tourist attraction. And I, as far as he was concerned, was a tourist. There was no one there but us. I felt it the instant we arrived. The atmosphere was tight. An open zip had been yanked from the base to the top of my spine, closing the V. I could feel myself stiffening, almost standing to attention.

We may have unwittingly brought thin veils of night with us. Evening began to fall quickly. It was the magnet which also drew the birds and crickets. The monument may have stood like a neutered giant but it was certainly no relic. The place still held a great deal of tension. As evening descended it brought with it strange shadows and sounds. Was it just me or could Maynard sense them also? In an effort to fight off the fear I was beginning to feel, I turned to give him my wholehearted attention.

I liked Maynard's voice and I liked his face. He was big without being thickset. He often looked as if in need of a shave but the greying stubble never seemed any worse from one day to the next so I reasoned he was probably just not a very careful shaver. Despite myself, I had to turn my head towards that eye where veins strung taut at right angles to the pupil pulsed and throbbed inside a living force. Every time I felt it, I forced my attention back to Maynard. And every time it happened, I could feel my fear grow stronger. I was in danger of being drawn so close to the hub I would be sucked into the vortex to become a speck of dust on a lens which still looked on with impunity.

Maynard was probably old enough to be my father. The habit of screwing up his eyes and looking at through pin-pricks as if he was trying to suss me out remained constant. I eventually got used to it. There was also something mildly flirtatious about his manner. Nothing I could quite put my finger on but it went beyond mere teasing.

'Well, you must know better than me. A woman like you who been everywhere and done everything. I must seem like some little boy, compared with your experience.'

And so on. He never missed an opportunity. I moved closer to him for one reason and one reason only. I needed the reassurance of his presence to hold on to the present. I did not fear his taking advantage of the situation. My only fear was one of being overtaken by events. I feared the constant turmoil which can melt a solid surface so it becomes molten tar which ebbs to reveal potholes like eyes below the surface. Always, just barely below the surface. Eyes which stare back at you. I was always in danger of being sucked into those funnels. Unless I held fast to Maynard, this time I would become little more than a particle of ground despair before death. The hub was still stained with the dried syrup, blood which had been wrung ounce by ounce from African men, women and children. Now only the flack remained. Just dry bones. But the skeleton still stirred, creaked and moved.

Passengers drunk with fervour. The fever running high.

Drunk on the blood of their ancestors. And what in the name of all that could be understood and explained did they have to celebrate? Every man, woman and child swore they were going somewhere. What could they have to celebrate? When the boat hit the Borcas, I felt my stomach lurch. The women had wiped up the vomit. They hadn't done enough. It wasn't nearly enough. I could still feel danger come and go with every passing wave. Like tides which meet to cross then cross again, every meeting weakens the will and resolve of the other. This time I moved so close to Maynard that I was now standing directly behind him. And he talked on and on about something totally irrelevant to my predicament seemingly oblivious to the danger.

The second visit to Tobago had brought Rita and I closer.

'Well, how old you think I was?'

'Are you serious? You're only nineteen? I thought you were in your twenties. Twenty-five, twenty-six at least.'

Rita and I were sitting on the porch, relaxing. I'm not sure how the conversation got round to one of age. She began to laugh.

'I nineteen. Sweet nineteen. Is Kelvin who getting old. He thirty-two.'

Her expression changed. When she spoke again, her voice was low and confidential.

'I still think about my baby, sometimes.'

I didn't know where it was leading to. She was already walking towards some conclusion but I did not know where she was coming from. She paused, perhaps waiting for me to ask 'What baby?' or 'When?' I left her to find her way without my assistance.

'Not for Kelvin. Before I meet he. Was when I was fifteen, for a teacher at school.'

She went on to tell me the baby had died when it was almost a year. In Western society it would be put down to cot death.

'I still can't see how this child just stay so and dead.'

In Caribbean society it was sometimes blamed on something more sinister.

'I still feel they do he something. He was a nice little boy, you hear.'

I was not sure I wanted to know all this. She had opened a door, stepping full into the sunlight. I would have preferred her to remain in the shade. She should be somewhere which afforded a little comfort, at least. In the Caribbean, there is little stigma attached to illegitimacy. Rita would not have worried what I would think of her having had a child when so young.

'Had your children yet?'

The words came suddenly. A voice shouting in my brain. Where was I? Oh yes. In someone's house, on some island, at some other time. I had been forced into conversation with a woman I would not normally have passed the time of day with. The person who had asked the question was some years my junior, hardly more than a girl. A woman, I told myself, who could barely read and write. The question had been shot, from in amongst the bracken and foliage. I turned my head slowly to take the girl in from head to toe. Superiority fell to my ankles. And where was I, anyway? I don't seem to recall. Was there something they forgot to tell me? There is, undoubtedly, something else that I should know. Why? Was I under some obligation? I do not remember having ever been shown the stopgap between duty and inclination. They did not say it was a function, a mandatory function which I as a woman, a black woman, was obliged to perform.

'Since then I trying so long. I feel I can't have no more.' Rita's voice was still working in the background.

146

'How old are you? Nineteen, did you say? I don't see what your problem is. You've got your whole life ahead of you.'

She turned her head quickly, taken aback. She must have picked up something in the tone of my voice. I avoided her eyes, conscious of having directed my anger at her. It was nothing more than a general response. And why me, anyway? Why choose me to confide in? We changed roles. I was standing in an open doorway, bathed in the full glare of sunlight. A stranger in your doorway. Not as unfamiliar as she might be. Welcome her in.

'I still miss that little boy, you hear.'

I was, nevertheless, a stranger. Why the confidence? Maybe she simply wanted someone to talk to. Instead of a close friend, sometimes who better than someone you hardly know. Better yet someone you know will not be staying long. Someone who would not have time to get to know the people you know, well enough to betray your confidence. So you take a chance and you trust a stranger. Trust she will not change her mind about staying. Trust that she is only passing through your life as she promised. Trust she will not stay any longer than she said.

'I trying so hard to give Kelvin a child. Is months now I going to see this woman who say she can help me. All kind of exercise, massage, bush and oil this woman giving me to drink. And, girl, it real expensive. I ain't tell he about it, yet. But he always quarrelling now about how quick I does go through money these days. Girl, I 'fraid to tell what I doing.'

I didn't want to know all this. Didn't want to be privy to all the intimate details of her life. Didn't want to any more than I did two days earlier.

'I 'fraid that if I can't give he a child he go make one with someone else. And you can't trust them girl round here.

Gladys and Mavis call theyself friend but I does see what they doing. I does see she, Gladys, smiling up in Kelvin face. She have a man of she own but she still want mine. Paco, she and the child still living in the two-room board house 'cause all he money does go on gambling. He never have no money. How he could buy she things?'

Tell her the things you cannot chance to tell anyone else, she will not betray your confidence.

'Is soon I go have to start thinking about holding down a little job to pay this woman. Kelvin tell me last night, he feel I have a sweet man and is there all he money going. I think he serious too.'

She made a noise. I believe it was meant to sound like laughter.

'I somehow feel I can't have no more.'

Yet again, I had been looking for something which does not exist. Every situation had its flaws, its dark side. There is no such place as paradise. I went to meet Rita and help her along the way. I had almost forgotten to take human frailties into consideration.

'For heaven's sake, you're nineteen. You're only nineteen. Give yourself a break. You've got time on your side.'

'Had your children yet?'

Where was I? The random recall was inclined to confuse. Memory did not always sift as carefully as it ought. There was something I wanted. Something I had to do. What was it? Ah, yes.

I wanted a present for my mother. Something she could varnish, admire, then put on her shelf and dust from time to time. I found the last resting place of the conch. The pink shells lay in a heap. All sizes of irregularities. To have discovered this haven where fishermen discarded the shells of their catch seemed really something at the time. I selected one I thought would suit her fine and tucked it under my arm. But I made the mistake of looking over my shoulder. The dusty footprints led up from the valley to where I was standing.

A souvenir for my mother's shelf.

What shelf?

The shell was soon cupped in my hands. I did not realise I was lifting it to my mouth until I felt it against my lips. Hard and familiar. And the name of the game was random selection.

A souvenir for my mother's shelf.

What shelf?

I forced all my breath through the aperture. It took every ounce of strength out of my body. The second time, I could hear the sound loud and clear.

The third time I blew the conch, they came down from the mountains, machete in hand. The cry which stung their lips was one of freedom. Rebellion was in the wind, seeking out the eye of the hurricane.

A present for my mother's shelf.

What shelf?

'I so 'fraid I going to lose Kelvin.'

Rita's voice brought me back to her for a little longer. Did I dare to tell her? No, I could not. The stranger already knows more than she should. The suitcase in my head was being sorted and had been for the past forty-eight hours.

I had been alone in the house when Gladys dropped by, two days earlier.

'Where Rita?'

'Out for a while. She'll be back later.'

Gladys had made herself comfortable in one of the armchairs. Looking around the room, she started muttering, as if talking to herself.

'If she up to she old tricks, again, could be hours. Habit like she own does die hard.'

149

She paused to give me a sidelong look as if waiting for me to prompt her. I had my back to her at the time. I caught the glance purely because for some obscure reason I happened at that precise moment to glance in the mirror. I didn't want to know. I didn't want to know any of it. It was still early. I had been enjoying a languid morning and was about to make myself some breakfast when she arrived.

From the kitchen I could hear her. Louder now.

'If she think people don't know 'bout she, she lie. Tobago ain't big enough.'

I tried clattering, making as much noise as I could to drown the sound. But she was determined. The more noise I made, the louder her voice.

'So much baby she must be throw away before Kelvin see she. Is no wonder she can't make no more. I tell you.'

It wasn't just her words which now set me trembling and tight with rage, it was the laughter which accompanied them. Once heard, never forgotten. Fangs sharp enough to search out and bite into that sack of anger.

I stormed into the living room.

'Wasting the man money with she – '

By the time I got to her, I was controlled enough not to shout or hit her. That anger was now rolled into two tight balls in either fist. I knew the rest was in my face and she could see it quite clearly when I bent over her. I had never been able to come to terms with Gladys's face. It was wide and flat like a landscape without clearly defined features. Something I never felt able to take in in one look, but would need to explore section by section to get a clear and related picture. Gladys did not interest me sufficiently to put myself to the bother. Even as I stood over her, little more than a mouth, nose and two eyes with barely any reflection.

'You are *supposed* to be a friend of hers. You are *supposed* to be a friend.'

I was conscious of my voice being slow and quiet and of the landscape in front of me going through dark changes.

'And since you *are* supposed to be a friend. I would be grateful if you would act like one when I'm around. Okay? Do you and I *perfectly* understand each other?!'

I wasn't expecting a reply and did not get one. I went back to the kitchen and, directly afterwards, heard the front door slam.

Trust a stranger. She will not betray your confidence.

Gladys knew I would not go back to Rita with what she had said. Trust a stranger. I suspected her reasons were twofold. Satisfy her own envy and force a wedge between Rita and myself by letting me in on information she felt I should know.

I did not want to know at the time and I wanted to know even less when Rita began confiding in me.

I had made no firm decision as to how long I would be spending on the island that second time round. I told myself I would see how it goes. As and when. As and when. As and when it goes and as and when it went.

Trust a stranger.

Since the incident with Gladys, I had been listlessly turning things over, holding each article up for inspection, indecisive as to where each should go. But the suitcase was now packed, closed, ready, waiting for the sunrise. Everything had its place. Little changes. The dust rising up from the empty dirt road parches your throat, fills your lungs. It obscures the vision with the bizarreness of its clarity.

Trust a stranger.

'Had your children yet?'

I took the shell from my lips and turned towards a new clarity of vision. My reply to her question came too late. Or perhaps, it came just in time.

'No. I blew their brains out before they were even

conceived.' The note was so swift and so sharp, it demolished all comprehension.

A present for my mother's shelf.

What shelf?

I threw it over my shoulder, back among the heap of other discarded shells. Pink and lifeless. Their substance gone, they lay forgotten. Obsolete.

'What shelf?'

'E–e–e–e–eeeee–nerts!'

The upper and lower jaws crunched together before the sound came again.

'E–e–e–e–eeeee–nerts!'

The professionals. A band in whom I took special delight. I first encountered them at the bus station in Port of Spain but didn't really begin to appreciate their true potential until I arrived on this island.

There were four I particularly noticed. All personalities in their own right. The one with the dreadlocks had gold crowns and always wore a pair of sunglasses with mirror lenses. Leaning towards him, you would find yourself looking down at your own reflection. The distorted contours of my face would stare back as if taken by surprise. I never once got a glimpse of his eyes.

Bridgetown, Barbados. A bus station with market place situated nearby always makes sense. The entrance to the market hall was only yards away. There were also stalls in the open air. Reach out and pay for the mango while hurrying to catch your bus.

Just a stone's throw from the bus terminus in Bridge Street, the busy commercial arm of the capital rotated. Pulsated. Much to keep you occupied should you feel strong enough to resist one of the professionals. In the harbour nearby, cargo boats and small craft nestled one against the other. A picturesque setting. But there was a feeling, a sense of erosion, no different from the one you experience in any port flanked by old buildings where trade of a hard-bargaining nature once flourished. My sixth sense asked if bartering of a more odious nature may not have taken place here. And when the idea began to take shape, every one of those black, scarred, decaying bricks became a powerful indictment. When your imagination blinks hard enough, it can take you down and you may not be able to sift the possibles from the probables. Far less damage to your equilibrium to simply turn and face the professional. Look at him. His hand was lifted towards the second wall of glass which separated you from him. The hand was raised not in obeisance or greeting, in the understood sense of the word, but in offering. He was holding something out to me. It was a small packet. The contents of the packet were wrapped in a brown paper bag. The brown paper bag sat neatly in the palm of his hand. His lips parted again to reveal – the sun. A cache of golden sunbeams lit his mouth. The sun glinted, trapped among his teeth. Reflected against the steely, glinting ivory, stars twinkled, ebbed, revived. Ebb and revive. Ebb and revive. I had heard of dazzling smiles but this was ridiculous. Heart-shaped gold crowns framed the gleaming ivory. A mouth as precious as his should, I felt, definitely be insured. And if any doubt remained as to who he is and which fraternity he represents, the bottom and lower jaw once again separate as he utters a sound which has the tongue trembling against the roof of his mouth for a good three seconds.

'N–e–u–r–t–s!'

More succintly.

'Nuts!'

And to qualify it. He was, after all, his own production and marketing man.

'Get your lovely fresh roasted nuts!'

The other three were just as distinctive. In addition to the specific touches which added that little extra to each character's personality, all wore a good deal of jewellery. They certainly looked more affluent than any others I had seen. I was forced to the conclusion that selling peanuts could be a very lucrative profession.

Many tourists use the buses in Barbados. Hardly surprising. It is a good, reliable service. Clean as well as cheap. I wondered if the professionals had become part of the tourist attraction. The proximity of the tourist trade, in effect, providing the soil in which their personalities could flourish.

I never thought I would ever find myself in a situation where I would be able to watch that hive lulled to the point where it slept. It hadn't occurred to me that the mains switch at the bus terminus could ever be thrown.

It was June and the Cannes Brûlées festival to celebrate the cane harvest was now well on the way. Baxter's Road mall is a street carnival, part of the celebrations.

On my third night in Baxter's Road, I missed the last bus. I had a straightforward choice between staying all night or leaving early enough to catch that vital link back to Christ Church. I was unsure. In the frenzy I forgot about the dilemma for just a little too long. Suddenly felt that I had had enough for one night.

'Let we go try, nuh?'

Sol, my companion for the evening, took my arm encouragingly. A native Bajan, he said he *thought* we might still be in luck. It wasn't easy. We were now moving against the flow and it felt as if we were the only people going in that direction. Everyone else was either using another exit or coming in fresh for the dance. You had to elbow your way past throbbing, gyrating couples. Blue jeans being the order of the day, swaying backsides were twitching ecstatically to calypso or reggae. The music blared from strategically placed speakers. Pushing our way back to where Baxter's Road met Tudor Street was an experience which involved a change of pace. Walking to lolloping to jigging then frenzied dancing before going back to walking. There was some sense of betrayal attached to moving past music without responding.

The final bus had gone. The entire terminus was fast asleep. We sat awhile contemplating the phenomenon. On the far side of the terminus the final sparks of a defiant flame still glowed. Blood still flowed from this commerical arm. Life hummed in traffic which seemed to be concentrated on one street and one street alone. People came and went. I was not too sure what it was all about. So how was it I could not even get a taxi? We made our way back to Baxter's Road. So strange. Two worlds where there was no overlap. You were either in the lull of the midnight hour or hurtling into a fever of noisy celebration. The wavering flame from the flambeaux provided the light for their stalls. The flames from the flambeaux and the fire from the coalports threw an eerie light on the people passing directly in front of them.

Baxter's Road was known as the street which did not sleep, even when there was no carnival taking place. Sizzling fried fish, roast corn and a variety of other delicacies could be bought from vendors who lined the pavement, burning the midnight oil as they fanned their coalpots. In keeping with the tradition of the Road, the celebrations began in the evening and continued until morning.

Hundreds of revellers, mainly black Bajans, packed the street. Music was only part of the entertainment. There were competitions you could enter. Most were taking place on the makeshift stage, erected halfway along Baxter's

Road. I was not too sure how they managed it. The road was no wider than any other and the stage was taking up a fair amount of space. We had to squeeze around it or push our way through the throng.

'You think I is part of the pavement? Get off my blasted shoes!' Standing on tiptoe on someone's feet, I still could not see what was taking place on stage. The platform was too low for my vision and the spectators were six deep.

I had been on the island about six days now, staying with a Trinidadian family who lived here. Friends of my mother's. Extremely hard-working people out on business most of the time. I was left to my own devices. It gave me the opportunity to make discoveries and come to my own conclusions. These had been largely uneasy times.

From where I was staying in privileged Christ Church, the bus to Bridgetown took me through an area where there were some chattel houses. Chattel houses, the unnerving reminder of slavery. They were the cabins which could be transported from site to site as slaves were moved from one plantation to another. The only permanency was the foundation on which the house was mounted. That chattel houses still existed in Barbados and were being lived in by the poor left me looking at much that I saw after that through the wrong end of a telescope. Shuttered like blinds which open and close, it let in just enough light from time to time for me to absorb certain details. I logged them much the way one would photographs, to come away with a number of images, each of which represented an incident or scene. Disjointed and incomplete, each impression was joined to the other by nothing more stable than a question mark. So much remained unanswered, so much inconclusive. I threaded them on to the same piece of string and went back to them from time to time, reshuffling, rearranging much the way one would pieces of a jigsaw. I wanted to make a picture, something whole and concrete. Nothing would come, just a series of incidents linked to the same island.

My passport claimed I stayed on the island for seventeen days. In reality, it was less than a week. Breathless. Breathless, uneasy times where whole days sunk without trace. I cannot recall the larger part of my time on the island. Only a handful of pictures being shuffled, rearranged and dealt like a very careful game of solitaire.

The only image which remained intact was the one which showed a mouthful of gold, the gyrating backsides of Baxter's Road and Bathsheba. But then layers of glass, double glazing and the sizzling heat of friction protected me from the cold.

Two English friends came at the same time I was there. I already knew of the problems white women holidaying alone on some islands could encounter. I had also heard of serious incidents which had taken place. One Bajan woman explained.

'Well, you can't blame the boys and them. Some of these women come here asking for it. They come to pick up black men and that's about the size of it.'

The woman had taken the conversation a step further.

'Was a time 'pon the buses when we'd get up and give seats to tourists. Not so now, child.'

But Caroline and Vanessa had steady boyfriends in their home town. They hadn't saved hard so they could travel thousands of miles to spend two weeks being laid by black men. Their own circle was multi-racial enough for them to do that without leaving the district, least of all the country.

Grantley Adams airport was manned by personnel less austere than those at Piarco. However, what it lacked in hostility, it made up for in frosty sophistication. At Piarco you got a taste of what you sensed might be coming when the sweat started pouring off you while still in line, waiting to get to immigration. The air-conditioning at Barbados airport left me feeling super-cool.

Nevertheless, the sophistication in itself invoked a sort of distancing and aloofness I did not experience at the other airport. It was an intricate complex. So much radiated from it. You encountered a network of souvenir shops, cafés, and an excellent bar before even entering the main building. When I went to meet Caroline and Vanessa, I feared I would have the opportunity of exploring every bit of it. As usual, the people you are waiting on are always the last to emerge. I was beginning to wonder if they had missed the flight when I saw them coming through the exit. Less than a week later, their smiles had turned to disillusion.

Some three miles from Bridgetown is a beach called Rockley. Some of the better hotels on the islands are situated there. It was the closest beach to their guest-house. One day, they met two nice young men who offered to take them on a tour of the island. The details of how they arrived back in Rockley, penniless and distraught, went on the police files.

I felt uneasy on the island. Uneasy. Uneasy more so than on any other island I would visit.

'Christ, they were vile. Such filthy mouths. We couldn't bring ourselves to repeat some of the things they said when they couldn't get what they wanted.'

I had not forgotten to pass on the advice. It was one of the first things I warned them about.

A cricket match was in progress on one of the islands when we went to the police station to lodge a complaint. The officer taking details made hard work of it. A slow tedious process. Action and enthusiasm coincided with the less interesting moments of the transmission.

'You sure that what was said?'

There was, also, red tape at its finest. Everything seemed to be going down in triplicate or quadruplicate.

'You absolutely certain about that?'

Did they doubt our word? Do sane people lie about things like that?

'We will follow it up.'

'There they are! That's them!'

How was it that two young men as distinctive looking as the ones being pointed out still hadn't been picked up. We were on Rockley beach where fine white sands form an easy cushion for your body and coconut palms rustle above your head. If you can find one strategically placed, you can bask in its shelter. The blue turquoise sea comes up to wash the sands. It could be paradise. Constant sun from the moment you step off the plane. Exotic fruit. Markets offered several varieties of mangoes, bananas and a wealth of other Caribbean fruit and vegetables. All this and Caribbean cuisine. It should be paradise. The choice of entertainment could keep you busy and amused throughout your stay. The Jolly Roger Cruise takes you aboard a boat crammed with other fun-loving people. Food, drink and music galore as you sail around the island. Nightclubs offer a myriad of acts. The country has lush, undulating, tropical vegetation.

' – and if you don't shut your blasted, fucking mouth, I'll give you – '

He was a police officer. He knew I was carrying drugs. He would take me down to the police station and what he wouldn't do to me when I was there, wasn't worth talking about. The venom was directed at me. Why? Later that same day, I had dared to intervene when another beach bum had accosted Vanessa. The onslaught left me weak and shaken. It was like a knife ripping me from stomach to neck. The hand went into the cavity to claim the womb.

A beach bum, audacious and confident enough to impersonate a police officer. What if he *was* one? I tried to dismiss the thought the instant it entered my head. After that we all three avoided Rockley. I, also, lodged a complaint. It could have been these plus a number of other incidents which caused the beach to be raided a few days later. They worked in pairs and it wasn't only women who were at risk, couples had complained of the man being insulted while the woman was molested. It was also a place where drug dealing was carried out. But it wasn't enough. It couldn't be enough. And by then, in any case, it was far too late. No sunshine. No frivolity. Nothing could dispel that dark cloud which remained, followed and would not go away. Worse, no apology or attempt at recompense on my part could erase the incident. Every time I looked at Caroline and Vanessa I felt guilty. They in turn became guarded and suspicious. And who could blame them for that?

I fell in love with Bathsheba where the Atlantic played havoc with the coastline. But this eastern side of the island was rugged, untamed country anyway. There would be no place here for the gentler rolling of the Caribbean sea. Barbados is known as Little England and this is Heathcliff country. The terrain looked hewn out of the same landscape which forged the moors. Carved by the same granite builder. They must have brought him with them when they arrived in the seventeenth century, eager to recreate the home environment.

The mould was a curious one. For more than four hundred years the island has been the most popular among the Caribbean for the English, and relates too closely to the albeit erstwhile mother country to be ignored.

The warning had gone out just a couple of days previously, reminding the people of certain precautions they should take now they were into the hurricane season. From the hotel verandah having a lunchtime drink, I could see fishermen struggling with boats in the water. Coconut palms were bent almost double. Their branches blown backwards like human hair in the wind. The sea, often angry, was raging. Waves beat against the rocks. And these were just strong winds. I sipped a Caribbean punch looking on at what might soon be a storm. A glass wall separated me from it – for the time being.

There was something on the island which spoke without using a voice. It was written in the landscape. The language was one which dramatized events through the terrain. I had seen the calm and the passionate separated by a mere stretch of land. It said everything I felt. It voiced emotions I was reluctant to admit. There was passion and there was drama. There was no Soufrière as in St Lucia, Grenada, St Vincent, Guadeloupe. No volcano to erupt at will or simmer, fuming, constantly on the boil or asleep with one eye open, breathing smoke beneath the surface. But there was a violence which lashed, and would surely be diminishing one side of her coastline more quickly than the gentler Caribbean on her west.

Barbados was unique. Unique in its history. Unique in the cultural divide which separated blacks from whites. Unique in its geographical position. Shaped like a leg of mutton, the island lies at a tangent to the other islands. It is located at a tangent to the rest as if to assert its uniqueness. It was the first island to be colonised by the English. Unlike the others, Barbados never changed hands.

Sol tapped the map with his finger.

'You see? No land between here and Africa. Look 'pon the map. See for yourself.'

162

Yes, she was outside of the semi-circle, excluded from the ring. There was a straight line between her and West Africa. They lay on the same latitude. No buffer existed between that continent and the island on the turbulent side claimed by the sea. Meanwhile, the placid Caribbean lapped at her west coast. I wondered if there could be some possible point on the island, some pinprick of land, some spot, some place inside her, where the two forces met, having serpented, insinuated their way inland through river and stream. In the very heart of her, perhaps? What then? Bearing in mind that the Caribbean is not always placid nor the Atlantic turbulent.

'Blue dress!'
I had been told the population density was higher than on any of the other islands. I got a sense of it when I visited one of the streets in the capital. The street was so narrow and the houses stood so close together you could see into the front rooms of the people on the opposite side of the street. You could see, without any effort, what they were doing. There was no room for privacy, no place for coyness here. My business was your business is their business. How did they exist within a boil of claustrophobia without going mad? Hemmed in by neighbours to the front, neighbours to the side, neighbours to the back, where did you find space? Where could you look for that patch of ground where you could just draw a circle around yourself and say, this is mine?

A people on the waves, of the waves. On a boat, on dry land, packed to overflow.
'Blue dress!'
I tensed.
'Blue dress!'
I faltered for a few seconds before walking on.

'Blue dress! You can't hear me calling you?!'

The woman's voice was challenging.

I was in slow motion on an asphalt line which separated one row of teeming wooden shelters from another. In my zeal, I must have looked in on her too closely. Aware of a possible confrontation, I tried to walk away as quickly as I could but the asphalt was getting softer with every second and I still needed to gain half the length of the street. I was trying to get away but every step was taking me down. As the pitch began to melt, I found myself moving in slow motion along an endless road where every step was an effort. I had to fight to make any forward movement. My feet and ankles were sucked into holes which felt like clamps around them. As my thoughts raced back to the incident on the beach and how much it had taken out of me, I fought hard to free myself. My breath came in short, sharp bursts. Slowly but surely I was making progress. As I saw the main road ahead, panic began to ease.

'What wrong blue dress? You 'fraid I go buss your arse?!!'

The same voice, now coming from some short distance behind me. She must have followed me part of the way. Other voices joined her in peals of laughter. Once heard, never forgotten. Raucous and uninhibited, it stripped me to the bone. Trembling like a leaf I gained safe territory on that next road. I did not dare to even chance a backward look. It was like coming out of someone else's runway on to your own. You don't slacken your pace until the muscles become too tired to move; only then do you chance a tentative glance over your shoulder. Only then.

'You can tell by their features.'

Sol's voice was not loud enough for anyone to hear and take offence. He did not have a car so we were taking a bus ride. I had asked about the rednecks, descendants of the poor whites. Their standard of living no higher than the poor blacks.

'And how they speak.'

I strained my ears to listen but I was sitting too far away for what they were saying to the driver to reach me.

Even when they intermarried with negroes, he told me, the children's features remained characteristic. We saw many of them. Strange. Like a brand. The colour of your skin singles you out. Your facial features tell your history. The habits of hundreds of years become the deficiencies of centuries. When they came to the island those hundreds of years ago, they were eking out an existence from the sea and some farming. It was a short journey from there into the 1980s. A community within a community. As if a wheel had got stuck in a groove and finding it was getting nowhere, continued to turn, nonetheless.

I went back to the cards, reshuffling them. I looked long and deep at each one. Closed my eyes before turning them face down. Concentrated hard to try and draw every ounce of marrow from the bone. It remained dry and hollow. I could feel the shape which curved and dotted when I ran my fingers over the ridge. Could feel this question mark. I traced the outline. Mountains and hills. The mystery still remained. The barrier, the remoteness between me and the island stayed firmly in place. I could scratch no deeper than the surface. So much had been left out. So many details still locked away in a drawer for which I could not find the key. So elusive. So fragmented. The peanut vendor's mirror-sunglasses loomed up, reflected in them was a serious-looking woman, lips pursed, the width of her forehead narrowed by the furrows which rippled along the dark waters of images which had been flung back. My business is your business is their business. The lost reflection of a head on a silver salver was recovered in that dark mirror every time the god figure turned his attention towards you. So elusive. So fragmented. So distorted. The memory wrapped its plunder in cotton wool, keeping it safe. Buried. I could neither find nor unravel this cocoon. In desperation I ripped one of the cards. Unfortunately, the first one I picked up was that of the island herself. Felt it. A tremor before the card was even completely torn in two. A full stop. Two last memories rushed in.

Returning to Christ Church late one evening I could hear calypso music coming from our street. A party was being held just a few doors away from where I was staying. As I went past I was tempted to take a peep through the fence. I stepped back in disbelief.

'You know there wasn't a single non-white person there. And would you believe all that lovely music was going to waste. They were just standing around chatting. No one was even swaying to the music.'

My friends only laughed.

'You're forgetting you're in Barbados. You're not in Trinidad now, you know. Is so they does carry on.'

I remember thinking at the time, it is as if time has stood still. The other end of the spectrum from the rednecks. Nothing has changed for them, either. They are still the élite. Wheels within wheels turning, in different directions.

I was walking a path which led from the house in Christ Church to the nearest beach. It took ten minutes. Yes. I went there many times. That was part of it. Often, I would sit on the same fallen coconut tree, its trunk now partly buried in the sand. It was where I first felt the tug of forces pulling in opposite directions. I had parcelled away the time spent on that beach just thinking and watching. Close to my feet would be shrubs which could flourish in the sand while other plant life fought for survival among broken crab shells and other small creatures of the sea which littered the beach. The sea would wash its victory of eroded memorabilia on to the sand. And even though the waters were too stormy to be safe for swimming, there were always a lot of people not only on the beach but in the sea. One day, when my thoughts were perhaps too deep for me to notice what was happening around me, I got caught between lines of grey crossing the sky. Everyone else seemed to have noticed them before me. Two small boys who only minutes before were leaping towards waves as they came thundering in, were now scampering into their clothes. Everyone had disappeared. The beach now miraculously deserted. It was extraordinary to watch a sky being reflected in the sea, as it grew darker and darker. The sea had become an extension of the sky. I could not tell where one ended and the other began. I could no longer find a horizon. Not even a thin grey line to separate the two. There was no division. Those choppy waters were daunting enough when they were blue. Now they roared, lashed at the shore and clung to the air, also. The air grew black. It was as if minute particles of spray had impregnated the atmosphere. I jumped to my feet and began running along the path back to the house. The storm broke. There was no place for me to shelter. Every house I passed on the way looked shuttered. No sign of life. And it is not always easy to knock on someone's door to say, 'Excuse me. You don't know me. I am a stranger but could I come in for a little while to shelter from the storm?'

Caught between the lines of grey crossing the sky I had temporarily lost my horizons. Only one was found again. I regained it in the ripped halves of that card. Even after I had carefully glued and firmly smoothed the two pieces together, the serrated edges of their join remained visible.

Even with my eyes closed, I could always find it. No matter how lightly I passed my finger I could still feel the backbone along the surface where the dividing line existed. Sometimes, I swear I could feel it tremble.

'You mean you going to St Lucia and you don't know anybody there?! Girl, you mean you don't even know where you staying?!'

I told them not to worry. I had been to the library the day before to make a list of a few guest-houses. When I arrived on the island, I would ring and make my reservation. No, I really didn't think they would all be full. So I went to join other passengers in the departure lounge and began to worry.

What would I do if for some reason things started going wrong? Who was I going to turn to? Who did I know on the island? It could be a very lonely business. Would everything turn out okay?

Paranoia sank in the presence of what confronted me. We were being ushered towards a plane *definitely* smaller than the one which took me to Grenada. To make matters worse, there were thirteen of us waiting to board. The obvious connotations registered. One empty passenger seat. I was able to shave one or two layers from my worries by adding the pilot and his assistant to the final tally. Strapped in, trussed with knees almost under our chins, it was a comfort at least that they didn't have us entirely at their mercy. They hadn't gagged us so we were able to discuss it among ourselves and not, necessarily, in hushed voices. I think we all felt as if some bad joke had been played on us. And if the pilots didn't like what we had to say about the mode of transport, tough luck. Hoots of derision and comments were flying like blue darts towards the cockpit. The American woman seated in front of me had a particularly loud voice.

'Oh my gard, this is arful! These people have gat to be joking! I should have taken the goddam boat! We ain't gonna make it!'

The pilots continued their preparations for take-off, unconcerned. Nothing to do with us. We're only going along for the ride. Shuttered and straight-jacketed, it was hell. Totally airless until the plane had gained altitude. My claustrophobia was like a very quiet knock on a door for which there is no key. The straightforward choice lay between telling them to let me out because I had changed my mind or sitting there and getting on with it. So I took a chance. I sat there and got on with it.

'Look down there.'

The Bajan gentleman sitting next to me had his hand on my head. It was a vice strong enough to move me like a puppet in the direction he wanted. He was showing me the Barbados coastline ebbing in the distance. Bathed in sunshine, the clean, clear sands edged with a frothy white collar could have been made with one continuous stroke of an artist's brush with the blue sea added for effect. It was definitely picture postcard stuff.

With thirteen passengers bonded together by a common grievance, it wasn't long before we knew a little about each other. On the next leg of my journey, St Lucia to Dominica, I would find it otherwise. On an aircraft of a similar size, the passengers remained as remote and distant as if the barrier between them was more than just a narrow corridor. On that flight, the order of the day would be confinement without flexibility. On this one, I soon forgot my discomfort and the time quickly passed. I fell silent to sit back, close my eyes and try to relax. Suddenly, a jab in the ribs.

'Look over there.'

My Bajan companion was drawing my attention to something.

'Oh, yes.'

I winced, rubbing my side.

'I can see. We're just coming in.'

We were coming in to Hewanhorra airport. There was space enough to swing as many cats as one wished. A runway like the giant's causeway opened up ahead where the big jets come in to land. We lost five passengers here, including the American lady. She hadn't been told the plane went on to Vigie and had arranged for a taxi to take her there. There was a lot of scuffling going on behind me. Suitcases were being unloaded from the pile of stacked luggage. Funnily, I hadn't noticed them there before. And stranger yet when my eyes scanned the remaining luggage.

'Where's the rest of the suitcases?'

There were eight passengers left on the aircraft. I could only see two suitcases and neither of them was mine. What trouble was this?

The baggage controller continued about his business until he was good and ready to come back and answer my question.

'There's space for luggage at the front of the plane. Sometimes.' He stressed the last word then paused before continuing in a totally disinterested voice.

'Sometimes we does put the extra luggage there. Sometimes it does arrive ahead of the plane and sometimes, it does arrive on the next flight.'

And how many don't arrive at all? I asked myself.

His final words as he wheeled the luggage trolley away were delivered just as nonchalantly.

'You could check in the front, if you want.'

I wasted a couple of precious minutes staring after him

in disbelief. I leapt off to make a quick sprint towards the cockpit. The baggage hatch was open and there they were. A stack of them, including my own, nestling happily together. I now had to go back and report to the other passengers. The belly of the plane was so close to the ground, all it took was a good stretch before I was back on board. They were waiting anxiously for my verdict.

'And sometimes, they does get it right.'

I was surprised at the length of time it took to get from Hewanhorra to Vigie. Coming down over lush green valley and hills, we negotiated the airstrip located just outside the capital. Something was beginning to come home to me. Outside of the second you set foot on an island for the first time, it is a name. Nothing more. You may have spoken to a number of people who lived there or had visited. You may have read a dozen books about it. It was still just a name. But from the moment you rip open that veil which shields it, you have arrived. You are there. Your actual knowledge when you are ready to leave may still not be brilliant but the barrier is broken. The island is no longer just a place on a map. I never lost the sense of wonder at actually arriving on an island. And there I was in St Lucia making that leisurely stroll across to immigration, but something was wrong. Something was very wrong. A strangeness I had not met before. Something warding me off, not to an alarming degree, but distancing me, nevertheless. It wasn't until I was in the queue, waiting my turn, that I realized what it was. My erstwhile companion drew my attention to it with something not far short of a karate chop.

'Hear that?'

I listened and recognized it for what it was. French patois. For some reason which I never did find out, there were a lot of people both on the tarmac and in the immigration hall. Far more so than I would have thought necessary. They were speaking in excited, hurried tones and, much to my annoyance, I never did find out what was going on. I had heard French patois spoken before, both in Trinidad and Grenada, but the occasions were rare. To hear it being spoken all around me was like a giant step out of the darkness. I already knew it was the language the people spoke among themselves. I listened, hoping to understand a little. I couldn't make head nor tail of anything being said. I stepped forward to take my turn at the immigration desk as the Bajan gentleman's heels disappeared through the door marked exit. Less than five minutes later I was following in his footsteps. He had disappeared into thin air.

The tourist board had a kiosk just inside the arrivals section. And that was how I came to meet Cecily Devereux. Strangely enough, there was something about the name of her guest-house which appealed. Even before I left Barbados I may have known that when I arrived, I would be staying there. While looking through the list of guest-houses in the directory, the one which fired my imagination was 'Belle Africaine'. Anyway, I would see when I got there. I had somehow forgotten all about it until the clerk showed me a list of accommodations. There it was again and by all accounts not too far from town, the beach and at a price I could afford.

She owned and ran the guest-house. It was her policy to collect guests from the airport. This was complicated by one issue. There was a taxi driver hovering at the immigration desk who was, supposedly, giving me advice also. All he had done, in fact, was answer yes, yes, yes to my questions about guest-houses. It seemed as if I had no sooner replaced the receiver than she was there. When he realized he wasn't going to get the fare, he was absolutely furious. An argument started. In patois and English. He claimed to have recommended her so to have cheated him out of the taxi fare really wasn't on. After all, he wasn't part of the tourist board set-up. And he most certainly wasn't hanging around the airport for his health. She gave in. As she explained later, it really didn't do to get on the wrong side of the airport taxi drivers. However, the driver was now so offended, he refused to take me. It was left to another driver. Cecily Devereux had already driven off telling them they were welcome to the fare. I was very pleased they managed to sort it out between them because I was beginning to wonder if I was going to be left stranded.

I stepped out of the taxi feeling a little sour. What I should have done was left them to it and walked. The place was just round the corner. After I had paid him the fare he wanted, I wished I had walked. Travelling light, with just the one case, I could have made it in less than ten minutes.

The lady was waiting on the doorstep wearing more or less the same expression as when we had met. It was a sort of smile-cum-grimace. You meet someone for the first time and something about the person tells you it would not be wise to get on the wrong side of them. Cecily Devereux was one of these people. I did not realize the rate was quoted in US and not East Caribbean dollars until I'd put the phone down. We tried ringing back to clarify things. By then it was too late. The lady was already on her way. The clerk suggested I spend a night there and work things out after that. So it certainly hadn't sweetened her temper when she found out she didn't necessarily have a week's booking seconds after being accosted by a ranting taxi driver. She was very anxious that I should stay for the full week, offering me the sort of concessions I found difficult to refuse.

'You won't get a better deal than that anywhere in St

Lucia.' The room was dreary and shabby. A hole in one of the floorboards was letting in sunlight. It was big enough for me to put my hand through. There was something so strange and ominous about that hole I always gave it a wide berth. I wanted somewhere I could settle for the next seven nights. I couldn't work up any enthusiasm about checking out some other place to find out if she was right or she was wrong. With my tight budget the chances were that all the places I could afford would not be any better and it was doubtful I would get a pot of tea thrown in every morning as well as the reduced rate. At the time, I was pleased with myself for having struck what I thought was a bargain. It turned out that business was bad. Business was so bad I was the only guest but I didn't find out until later. And the lady wanted her money in advance.

'I'd like the money before you move in. When I make special deals, I prefer not to take chances.'

This was new to me. I had never stayed anywhere where you paid in advance. It didn't occur to me to argue with her and in any case, it meant I wouldn't have the worry when I was ready to leave.

What she meant was, now she had me she was going to make sure she hung on to me. One basis for the concession was that I no longer ate breakfast. All I needed was a pot of tea. For the next three mornings a big, ripe, juicy mango was placed beside the things on the tray which the boy who assisted her brought in. After that, no mango. Just tea.

The day I received the last mango, a couple arrived. An Oriental lady with her European companion. It was not the blend of continents which intrigued me so much as the goings-on during the night. I woke to the sound of screams accompanied by a hasty retreat from the place they were coming from. The footsteps did not stop until they reached our landlady's rooms.

A quavering voice reached me, out of the darkness.

'There is, there is a small hanimal in my room.'

Cecily Devereux's voice pierced the night.

'Animal? What small animal?'

A man's voice.

'There is a creature in our room.'

It was slow but more assertive than the woman's. The alien quality of the English language manifested itself in his search for the appropriate words. And I never did fathom the language he and his companion spoke in. Three sets of footsteps made their way along the corridor back to the room. Cecily Devereux's was the first voice I heard.

'Good God! It's a mouse! Haven't you seen a mouse before?!!'

The woman protested.

'I want to move to another. I do not want to stay in this room.'

I must have been more tired than I thought. Somehow, against the background noise of bags being moved, I drifted off to sleep. Bags and Cecily Devereux's firm, determined footsteps as grumbling, duty-bound, she assisted in the transfer from one room to another.

I don't know how they managed to escape her the previous evening for in the morning I could hear her working from what I now suspected was a well-worn script.

'I'm going to make a special deal with you and when I make special deals, I like my money in advance.'

As things turned out, the only person to gain from the transaction was Cecily Devereux herself. The performance about the small 'hanimal' was re-enacted that night also, from the stage of a different room. This time, it degenerated into personal abuse.

'And where the hell are you from, anyway, that you don't know a mouse when you see one? You trying to say they don't have them in your country?'

The lady's companion jumped to her defence.

'There is no need for that.'

'Jumped' is, perhaps, too strong a word. His careful, hesitant English no match for Cecily Devereux's in the time factor which squeezes the passion out of words, leaving them devoid of any sting.

The guest-house seemed large. Whether it was or not is not really relevant any more than whether or not they ran out of rooms to move to. The fact remains that the next morning I met them in the hallway with their bags packed. On my way out, the third heated argument was raging. This time, it was the one concerning how much refund they felt entitled to. The landlady insisted they wouldn't be able to get a damn thing until she had gone to the bank. The short space of time between being given the money and banking it was a positive pointer towards her alacrity.

I did not see the couple again until the end of my stay when we were all on the same flight, bound for Dominica.

Cecily Devereux attempted to bend my ear.

'With all that food they had in their room, what the devil did they expect? Some people are so blasted cheap they'd rather live on bread and cheese than buy decent food. They brought the blasted things with them, in their rucksacks.'

Flashing her the sort of smile more often used by the deaf when they can't quite make out what is being said, I closed the door quietly behind me.

The feeling of alienation was still with me. I felt isolated. Isolated by words I could not understand. English was the official language but the people spoke French patois among themselves. French words which had not been remoulded made the aperture through which I could sometimes see light, but on the whole conversations around me gave the feeling of walking in the dark. This included life in the guest-house. My landlady spoke to Monica, her cook, in patois. She quarrelled with her in that tongue also. One afternoon there was a fever-pitch argument between Monica and the refuse collector. Even if the words were lost on me, the sentiment certainly was not. Nor was the trail of garbage.

The alienation therefore was nothing to do with environment and everything to do with language, which fused history and people to an anchor of place and fate.

A common factor of grief was the vexing question of transport. A number of islands had, at some point, courted the railway, but it proved to be uneconomical so the road became the only means of travelling across the islands. I wanted to go to Vieux Fort in the south, just to see what it was like.

That Sunday, it didn't take long to realize there would be no minibus to take me there. Sunday service I believe they call it. However, I wanted to get there and wasn't going to give up easily. I had already asked a gentleman sitting behind the wheel of the only minibus in the square. He had said no. I went back to him. He was still chatting to someone who was lolling in the back seat.

'Can you take me part of the way then?'

He smiled at his companion. This time he actually looked at me before replying.

'I may be able to take you all the way.'

I wasn't certain what he meant but decided to take his words at face value. He was about to pick up some people and did not know if there was going to be space for me, also. It all got very involved and complicated but the fact remained the minibus was going in my direction. We took off towards Marigot to pick up the group. The driver's companion was offering a personal service. He climbed the hill on our right to fetch four of them then knocked at the large house just below where the bus had stopped. Picnic baskets and bath towels were soon climbing in.

'It's going to be good, eh, mum?'

A strange sensation rushed through me as an accent which clearly defined the speaker's country of abode made me realize how far we both were from the adopted country. Every now and then I was reminded I was in exile. That morning was definitely one of those times.

It turned out the driver had rented a minibus to take a friend's relatives, visiting from London, on a tour of the island. At first, I was simply an outsider muscling in on a planned outing because I desperately wanted to get from point A to B. I was one of four extra passengers and for a while we picked up passengers and let them off whenever the driver felt able to cram more people into the vehicle. It all helped towards the petrol.

The road was steep and the scenery beautiful. Undulating tropical calm revealed itself with magnificent nonchalance. Every twist and turn of the road offered a view of rolling panoramic slivers coated in paradise. Breadfruit, bananas, mangoes and other trees bordered the roadside in hazy sunshine. We came to where, looking down on my right, a row of brightly coloured fishing boats nestled in the bay, tilting in the waves which washed against their stern. The bay looked remote and idyllic. It didn't seem to belong to anyone or anything. It just cosseted itself. I asked the girl sitting behind me:

'What's that place?'

Her voice held a strange tedium. She looked at her companion before replying.

'Anse La Raye.'

I held the view until overhanging branches and a steep rise took it from me. It seemed so perfect.

I don't know how long Les Pitons had been visible but it wasn't until someone pointed it out that I became aware of the two mountain peaks ahead of us. They stood dominant behind an unwavering white veil. The air changed from a warm, pleasant ripening heat to an acrid oppression. A stench like rotten eggs wafted into the vehicle. I had never experienced anything quite like it.

'What the hell is it?'

'We coming to the volcano, girl. Is Soufrière self you smelling.'

We seemed to be travelling up a dirt road towards open ground. There were a few cars, mainly white tourists. Camera in hand, some were climbing towards what I now saw to be smoking Soufrière basking in her own sulphur perfume.

'Want to take a closer look?'

Martin, the driver, was offering to accompany me. I certainly didn't want to go as far as Soufrière's belch and look down into her gaping mouth. I said I would walk part of the way. Some odd thoughts were running through my head as I scrambled up the side. All were linked to ideas of libation for the spirits. The fury of the Gods. The need to appease an open anger. I could understand the thoughts which could link a volcanic eruption with the occult.

'I don't want to go any further.'

Martin looked at me curiously, smiled then went on alone. Back on safe ground I could see figures disappearing towards the furnace.

'Want to buy some, lady?'

Whenever there is a sight which might attract tourists, there was sure to be someone selling souvenirs. More often than not, an attractive, muscular young man. I shook my head. He was about to assure me it was exactly what I needed when Helena came towards me, smiling.

There are outsiders and there are outsiders. Apart from the passengers picked up en route, there were two other people who did not belong, did not form part of the circle, Helena and myself. She talked to no one except the man she was with. Albert. He was Martin's co-driver. Slim with good bone structure, she would have been attractive had it not been for some strange mask which tightened her features. I could see from her face and the way she carried herself she was not a well woman.

It was easy to get to Soufrière. You park your car and walk the short distance to pay homage. Helena and I had gravitated towards each other in the short time between parking and returning from my walk to Soufrière.

'Come, take a bath with me.'

Only then did I remember my swimsuit and towel were still on the chair at the guesthouse.

'Don't worry. It'll be okay. You won't need them.'

I followed her away from Soufrière to a place where there were overhanging rocks. She helped me down to a secluded spot shaded by heavy foliage where one of Soufrière's sulphur springs formed a small waterfall. While Helena was undressing, I put my foot under the cascade. I don't know why I should have been surprised to find the water so hot. And it all seemed a bit privileged. Two naked women bathing under the hot springs of a lazy volcano. I didn't like it, at first. Hot, sulphur water on my naked body wasn't quite what I would choose in the heat of a Caribbean mid-day.

Helena's voice bubbled through the water.

'It is good for you.'

At the time, I did not know about its curative properties, any more than I was aware Helena had joined the excursion specifically to make the trip to the sulphur springs. She was ill. She did not know what her sickness was. There seemed to be no diagnosis of it. It was one of her few free days as cook in a large hotel.

'And you must drink some, too.'

I drew the line at that. Soufrière may touch my body but none of her volatile waters would reach my insides. And we weren't the only people. Sounds which reached me confirmed there were others just as keen as Helena. The towel she had brought got rid of the worst of it but it wasn't until a little later I was able to wash away the evidence.

'Why you want to go to Vieux Fort? There's not much to see and I don't think you'll get back to Castries tonight.'

It wasn't only Martin. Some of the others were trying to tempt me to stay and go on the trip round the island with them.

'Why you don't stay? We have enough food for you.'

To prove the point, a leg of fried chicken was passed slowly under my nose. So strange the way things work out. I was trying to find a way, some way of getting from one part of the island to another. Nothing more. But now I was being drawn towards a circle of strangers. And then there was one. Helena remained on the periphery. I suspected, somehow, preferring it that way. When we stopped to picnic she ate nothing. She said she wasn't hungry. I noticed she hadn't any food with her and she refused any which was offered.

Someone passed me a plate of peas and rice with beef stew and a glass of mauby.

'Martin was saying how much he likes you.'

His sister was one of the party. The same girl I had asked about Anse La Raye. He was looking at me and smiling. I suspected I knew what the score was. A Caribbean woman with a different accent and style made me that little bit different from the women he was used to. The prodigal had returned and the generosity of the fatted calf was sometimes overwhelming. Never, at any time, did I assume it was rightly mine. I never took it for granted.

The English accent belonged to the young girl. She was with her mother and aunt. Both women were St Lucian born but living in London for many years. The girl was born in London. We were all holiday-making in an exotic setting. The irony of it came like a strong and restless wave flowing through my head, leaving debris in its wake.

Some time was spent on a beach near Vieux Fort and I had to admit there really wasn't enough to keep me there. I took them up on the offer to see the rest of the island. It was a wonderful day of enjoying other people's company. Sadly, I could feel Helena slipping away, almost as if my being accepted into the fold signalled her rejection of me. By the time we dropped the family off and got back to Castries, she and I were like strangers. I don't think she even said goodbye. I was left with the memory of a retreating figure and the sad, haunted face with a straw hat which obscured her features and the floral dress as she took her time walking up the street. She walked alone. I never saw her again.

Evenings in the Caribbean are a time to take to your bed if you are sick or very elderly. Life begins early in the day and continues until late. By the time Martin dropped me off at the guest-house, it was not so close to the bewitching hour not to consider going for a drink.

Martin became my steady companion. Through him I got to know many of the bars on the island. Little drinking places off the beaten track, no more than shacks with a lively reality, were the ones I liked best. We walked into one which was lit by just three candles. The flame on the table where two elderly faces sat playing dominoes wavered slightly but remained as unconcerned as they did. Having discovered Carib beer, I had stayed with it. The temperature of the lager depended on whether or not refrigeration had reached that part of the island. Or whether the ice truck was delivering. At any rate, how readily ice could be obtained. The barman's face remained impassive before the glowing flame. His smile greeted us long before he made any physical movement.

'Hey, Martin. Long time no see. How you doing, boy?'

Everything was done in slow motion, ordained partly by his physical bulk. The rest could be put down to the general temperament of life on the islands. The unreal quality of the stage where one or two people dropped in during our stay was made even more pronounced by the fact that neither player seemed to notice us. The slamming of dominoes on the table and the occasional 'Bring another beer there, Ralpho!' was all we heard.

Fisherman's Feast is a day set aside on some of the islands for celebrating the 'catch'. The person at the tourist board told me there would be festivities in all the fishing villages.

'And Anse La Raye?'

'Yes, there also.'

The idyllic dream state had conjured up a shaded bay where brightly coloured boats washed against the sea. A special day spent in a special place.

Martin made a confession.

'Veronica and I come from Anse La Raye.'

I remembered her reaction when I asked about the village on that first day. It seemed almost as if she now disassociated herself from the place. She had seemed weary.

'I'll come and meet you when I finish work.'

I hadn't realized we had passed through it as well as viewed it from a distance. I did not know the decaying boards of poverty which lined the road where we had stopped to get soft drinks not that long before I had seen the view from the hill was the centre of Anse La Raye. Had I done so I would have reconsidered spending the day there. The veneer of Utopia had fooled me totally.

Not only was Anse La Raye far different from what I had supposed but the day also fell short of what I had hoped for. I had already missed some of the festivities when I got there, even though I had set off fairly early that morning. And the ones I hadn't missed weren't going to be taking place, anyway. I wasn't sure whether inflation had caught up with them or less significance was being attached to Fisherman's Feast than in earlier years.

Life in the village was being lived either in the streets or on the beach. The houses looked to me like slats of weather-beaten board. Some doors were wide open. I looked in on what was sometimes just two rooms. A living room led into a bedroom with a separate kitchen at the back. A few women sat on doorsteps plaiting each other's hair, minding their babies, talking or just looking on. Music was coming from various sources. In a room which could have been a bar, I saw couples moving to music which seemed to fill their bodies with inspiration. On the beach, a woman sat making lobster baskets. The finished sides of the baskets rested against a tree while she worked on, bending, contorting the pliable cane to weave the pattern of her will.

'Things are hard. It's not like it used to be. The men don't get the catch like they used to. I don't know why that is. I don't know.'

She talked to me while she worked on without stopping.

Men were congregating on the beach. A hut made of branches protected some of the more ardent gamblers and drinkers from a determined sun. I watched some of the bleary-eyed revelry and some of the bleary-eyed revellers watched me. Largely with little more than mild curiosity. The boat builder worked in confinement. He planed his wood under the protection of two parallel sides of board and a roof made of branches.

'When does the boat race start?'

'You missed it, Miss Lady. You should have come earlier.'

And he planed on, shaving slivers from the virgin side.

I was there for the day but within a short space of time I began to feel trapped. I could have made do with one third of the time I was now obliged to spend there. The rest of the day would be spent going round in circles repeating and redoing what had been accomplished or done before. It presented a very frustrating change to the pattern I felt was beginning to emerge. Instead of a spiral of progress, my life was being divided into a section of grids with each square the same size as the one adjacent to it.

I sat on the jetty looking up at hills where the road clung to a sheer drop and where from time to time some vehicle rode past. Overwhelming loneliness inspired by other things including the constant patois sent me once again in search of Miss Iona, Martin's mother. I had tried seeking her out when I first arrived.

'Is up there Miss Iona living.'

I followed the hand as it pointed to what seemed like the highest point on the hill. I noticed how the road curved. I also noticed the distance between where I was and where I needed to get to. The woman stopped me from setting off on a wild goose chase.

'But she not there right now. She with her friend, the Frenchman. He live in the house just along here.'

I would later come to understand the division between the inhabitants of St Lucia, Martinique, Dominica and Guadeloupe more clearly. I already knew of the long and bitter battle fought between the British and French for possession of these islands. One of the islands had changed hands thirteen times. St Lucia and Dominica remained with the British. Martinique and Guadeloupe were departments of France making the inhabitants French. This did not register until I arrived in St Lucia and later Dominica. It always seemed strange to hear the Martiniquians and Guadeloupians referred to as *French*.

Miss Iona's Frenchman opened the door. At a glance I could see the attraction. Something more than just the wide-brimmed panama hat singled him out as being different from the other men I had seen in the village. He looked the way I imagined the early French settlers dressed, instead of a simple fisherman as I was assured he was. The Frenchman spoke no English.

'Elle n'est pas là. Elle est partie.'

I had to make my way up the hill to Miss Iona's. On the way, three people overtook me with ease. When I eventually got there a very attractive girl in her late teens opened the door. Martin told me he and his mother did not get along and he seldom visited Anse La Raye. His one concern was for his sister, Esmelde. The only child still living at home.

'Yes, I am Esmelde. Come in, please.'

She led me into the living room of their humble home. A woman in her late forties, still very attractive, came in from the outside kitchen. She wore her headscarf tied at the back like so many other island women. There was something fiery about her. I could imagine in her youth she must have been very high-spirited.

She began giving me a profile of Martin the second she found out who I was.

'Martin is not a good son. He does not help me. If you know the bills I have to pay. If you know the –'

She was sizing me up as she spoke. Her eyes travelled slowly from my shoes to my hair and then back again. It may have been the natural curiosity mothers have about the women their sons are involved with. With the talk of 'bills', I began wondering if she thought I may be a soft touch. Generosity and magnanimity aside, there are always a few who think all tourists are rich. Martin had not talked of the conflict between his mother and himself but I suspected the blame may have been on both sides.

Esmelde brought a glass of ice-cold water without waiting for me to ask. The only spark of real interest I received from her mother was when I mentioned the Frenchman. Her eyes lit up.

'Ah, the Frenchman. He is *such* a nice man.'

She went back to the kitchen, humming. Esmelde and I went to sit on the porch. It gave a clear view down to the bay. The sound of children's voices, laughter and music rose from the valley.

We didn't speak. We sat on the porch each engrossed in her own thoughts. Martin had told me Esmelde was just eighteen. She was very pretty with large eyes, a pout and flawless skin. I wondered how long they would last. How long before the ravages of circumstances begin to take their toll. The strength of the island women was something taken for granted. They worked hard to make ends meet. The responsibility of supporting the children was sometimes theirs and theirs alone.

When Esmelde eventually spoke, her voice was very quiet.

'Let's go for a walk.'

We closed the gate behind us.

'Maman, we won't be long!'

We started walking back in the direction I had come. After a hundred yards, we turned on to a gravel path which led to a tiny beach. The path was steep, loose gravel had me picking my way carefully. A lone set of footprints led diagonally across the sand to disappear among the rocks on our right. The road was cut out of the hill. I could see a figure bobbing along the path behind the rocks. We sat on a log, our bare feet in the sand, the only people on this solitary stretch of sea which rolled against big boulders.

'Are you really from England? Can you help me?'

I could sense her restlessness long before she broached the subject.

'There's nothing for me here. I want to get out.'

This was different from what I often heard. It is usually America. Second choice, Canada. Great Britain invariably came a poor third. Some islanders felt life out of the Caribbean was sure to have more to offer. Even nowadays with all the evidence which has been accumulated they still feel the erstwhile mother country is a place worth emigrating to.

I told Esmelde I did not think England was for her but we would discuss it later. She had to go out that afternoon, we agreed to meet in the village later.

The restaurant I had passed earlier, recommended by Martin as a good place for lunch, was still closed. Situated where the road leading down to Anse La Raye met the one from Castries to Soufrière, it was near enough to the main road to be spotted by any tourist or adventurer. I waited for it to open, watching the cars, lorries, minibuses going towards or away from Castries. Every now and then one would come down into Anse la Raye. The restaurant remained closed.

The Indian proprietor of the café where I eventually settled for a light lunch was a much-travelled man. He was friendly, relaxed. Nothing about him suggested resignation.

'I been to all the islands. All of them.'

And I believed him. Why shouldn't I?

'Why did you come back here?'

He shrugged his shoulders.

'Who knows? You have to settle somewhere, at some time. I was born here.'

If you take a little soil from the island of your birth with you, you never lose your way. Is that what they say? Even if that wasn't quite it, I wish I could have been on the island to see the homecoming they gave him.

I walked through the village trying to gather my thoughts. The second and third time I hoped to see something I had missed on the first occasion. I watched the houses, the people in the street, walked to the new school then, as far as where a farmer kept his pigs. When I got that far, I knew I had reached my boundary.

As the afternoon wore on, activities changed accordingly. The smell of cooking reached me from various sources. A woman squatted outside her back door, fanning a coalpot. The energy of her determined labour caused the wood to flame and crackle. I was becoming a familiar sight. I watched them and they watched me. They had seen me come and go twice before and you don't need to understand what is being said to know when someone is talking about you. For the most past, it was idle curiosity. I returned the smiles and courteous greetings. And what had I seen so far? People locked in a state of inertia or so it seemed. So much was ebbing away or being taken.

The children took a particular interest in me. A couple of boys, no more than twelve or thirteen, stood close by as I lit yet another cigarette while waiting for Martin.

'Is it true you from England, Miss Lady?'

'I was born in Trinidad but I live there, yes.'

I heard myself reeling off the facts, as if I had been programmed ... born ... Trinidad ... present ... abode ... England. It sounded as if I was attempting to justify something or, more accurately, place myself in a definite category of belonging. The boys came to sit closer. They wanted to know all about life in England. I had to tell them what snow looked like. After all, they reminded me, they had only seen pictures. What did it look like falling from the sky?

They were wearing home clothes. School uniforms had been exchanged for shorts and tee-shirts which had seen better days. Dust and sand were already on their legs and bare feet.

'Will you be my pen friend?'

Mark, the more determined of the two, felt he and I should keep up a correspondence. He took over the conversation. His friend slipped quietly into the background, just listening.

'And then one day, will you send for me?'

I turned my gaze towards the sea, watching the bay as it curved, jutting into the ocean.

'Send for me one day, please.'

The green foliage of the peninsula tapered into the distance.

'Please let me come and join you.'

I followed the coastline as far as my eyes could see. It disappeared into the sea.

'And what would your mother say?'

'She will be pleased.'

And how did they do it? How could they spend their entire lives facing the sea? Every morning when you wake, it would be there. That giant expanse of water stretching into infinity was always there, slashing at your door. Mocking you when the hurricanes hit and when the fishing boats come in with little more than what it takes to line your stomach. How did they cope? First Soufrière with her ever-gaping jaws and now this hungry, bottomless void. I swear I would go mad.

There was a time when I was trapped in a melting asphalt jungle which brought houses already too close together, closer yet until they shared the same intake of breath, exhaled the same noiseless scream of outrage.

– but that was another country.

There was the sudden screech as an impatient driver brought his vehicle to a halt. I was beginning to recognize Martin's style.

'Esmelde's been looking for you.'

He had just come back from the house. In truth, I had simply said I would meet her back in the village. I had not arranged a specific venue on the assumption that Anse La Raye was small enough for us to find each other. When I settled into a shady spot, I had not stopped to consider I would certainly be out of the range of vision of anyone on the road.

'I'll write first.'

I pocketed Mark's address.

'Don't forget.'

I promised him I would not.

There was something here I had not touched, had not even come close to finding. There was a door which, blind-folded as I was, I could not hope to find unaided. My only chance would have been to stumble on it by accident. I had not even scraped the surface of this place. There is another Anse La Raye. It lay beyond the façade where they stood guard on their doorsteps and watched me as I explored the periphery of a reality. They didn't really have me fooled for one minute. I saw what I saw and I know what I saw from the outside as the hill rose and I looked down at the bay, that Sunday afternoon.

I wanted to ask Martin. Wanted to say to him, 'Come on, now show me the rest.' But I had never seen him so guarded. The places he took me to before we left were the ones I would have been too self-conscious to walk into by myself. He knew all the people. Introduced me to a few. All the while, he remained cautious. Tense.

He did not want to go back to the house again so I did not get to see Esmelde before I left. As we rode out, I had to turn just once. It would not have been possible for me to leave without the one backward glance. I took it. Mark was still standing where I had left him, looking. Just looking. I blinked and he had gone. Surely, by now, tucked up in bed for the night.

But I took that last memory of him with me, kept it safe between a square of glass and the framework of promises. So how was it I did not get a reply to that first letter I sent him nor the next?

It doesn't matter. I will have to return one day, in any case. I will have to go back, catch them unawares and find that door. When I do, I will enter it.

Vigie Beach was some short distance from the guest-house. Cecily Devereux went for a swim there, early every morning. I visited it twice during my stay. There are people's beaches and there are tourists' beaches. Nothing to do with a deliberate attempt on the part of the tourist board to separate the visitors from the masses. Everything to do with the obvious truth that hotels in the Caribbean are, invariably, close to beaches some distance from where the people live. Wherever possible, I used the ones frequented by the islanders. More alive, less preoccupied with lifeless bodies in scanty attire, their beaches were vibrant with activities geared towards enjoyment of life rather than getting an even suntan. I regarded Vigie as a people's beach and went there simply to be by myself. There is a definite dividing line between what you want and what you get. Floating on my back, I closed my eyes to feel myself drifting away. It was Saturday. Children's laughter, howls of amusement kept drawing me back to the present. Every time I opened my eyes and looked towards the beach, I could see the amber dreadlocks of the young man now sitting close to where I had placed my things. When I looked again, he was in the water. I wanted to be by myself. It was nothing to do with suspicion of other people's motives, I simply did not want any intrusion into my private thoughts. He was good-looking with mid-length locks. There was something very gentle about him. He swam around me in ever decreasing circles. Nothing pushy or overtly obvious about his tactics. Quietly persistent, he soon wanted to know all about me, then he made me an offer.

'My house is up on the hill. Why don't you come back for dinner?' Something told me I would be as safe as I wanted with him. At the worst, I might encounter a wife and children.

'You like fish? I can cook it good.'

He spent the best part of an hour trying to persuade me. The beach was getting crowded. As it got busier people began drifting down to the far end. A disused cemetery separated the lower stretch from the airport but you could largely forget it was there. Less populated than the side closer to the road, it was here you would imagine yourself able to get more peace and quiet.

'You don't like fish? I could cook chicken instead.'

Children with beach balls and such had mums and dads in tow. A young amphibian came splashing past me, closely followed by another set of flippers and snorkels. The sky was an extraordinary shade of blue, clear and deep. There were just four isolated clouds, pure white, they looked like balls of flattened cotton wool.

'I have some okras. A nice pelau with chicken and shrimps?'

The sun's golden aura produced a cocoon of what should have been perfect bliss.

'You prefer the chicken curried? I can make roti, you know.'

The concept of being suspended on an undulating, temperature-controlled current of air would normally have produced a feeling of well-being.

'Well, beef then. A nice beef stew with peas and rice. I have fresh pigeon peas growing in the garden. Nice and fresh.'

The noises around me became louder and more persistent. Shrieks and splashes bounced off the front of my swimming costume. Quite suddenly that wide band of noise began to narrow.

'Accra and float?'

It was shrinking as if being sucked into a vacuum, ebbing gradually until only the original level of noise remained. I closed my eyes to be taken down with it. When I opened them again, he was standing over me, looking thoughtful. Smiling wryly, he told me the conclusion he had come to.

'Well, girl. It look like you really not hungry.'

The market place in Castries was as colourful and exciting as any other in the Caribbean. Bright parasols flanked the pavement where vendors sat plying their wares. I always passed through the market on days when I happened to be in town. There was a good variety of cooked meals for sale and lunch was often bought from one of the market stalls. There were traders on the pavement in front of the market as well as along the street running adjacent to it. That angle of Castries boasted a generous variety of sale goods. There were a number of small shops on the opposite side to the main entrance. Their wares were not confined to the inside, but spilled on to display counters on the pavement. Whenever I needed cotton wool, comb or knicker elastic, this was where I would come. The general effect of these two cavalcades of display separated only by a stretch of asphalt was extraordinary. Like other markets, this one seemed to be a central meeting place. The restricted pavement space was made even more restricted by people who stood chatting in twos, threes and larger groups. I gave up attempting to manoeuvre through tiny spaces and joined those who also found they made quicker progress by walking in the road, taking their chances with the vehicles.

The fish, poultry and meat market was at the back of the main hall. These trades were monopolized by men just as the selling of handicrafts, souvenirs, fruit and vegetables were done largely by women. The main hall was a light, airy building ringing with noise and laughter. If you were seriously looking for souvenirs then the first impression you might have was that you had certainly come to the right place. It was this which made Castries market so special and different from others I visited in the Caribbean. I fell in love with a beautiful cane rocking chair. If I could, I would certainly have taken it back with me. And there were other pieces of furniture equally well crafted. The most unusual feature of the market was its clay. Baked terracotta ducks with hollowed-out backs, large enough to support a myriad of small items, are utility in one of its simplest forms. Other more elaborate pieces had been designed primarily for decoration.

I looked at a coalpot. It was a beautiful clay item. A present for my mother's shelf.

What – ?

– but that was another country.

I understand a good deal better than I did then.

Utility as opposed to display. Use generates friction. Friction stimulates growth.

A real coalpot but too heavy for me to carry. I would buy one anyway and arrange for it to be sent on to her. It would be a gift much treasured for speciality dishes which did not taste the same when attempted in a conventional oven. Competition was fierce. With more than a dozen traders selling almost identical goods, there had to be something about one of them which would make you want to buy from her, as opposed to any of the others.

'What you want, darling? Come let we talk business. You want both pairs? If you want both pairs, you can have them for a dollar less.' The voice was no more seductive than any of the others. I made the fatal mistake of glancing up at her. I was hooked. On the afternoon before I left St Lucia, I staggered out of Castries market clutching an armful of ducks and drakes, two miniature coalpots, plus the real one for my mother. They were all bought from the same trader, for one reason and one reason only. She had my grandmother's smile.

Geest, the banana entrepreneurs, take passengers on the cargo boats which go from Barbados to St Lucia then on to Dominica. The trip is a regular run. Bananas are the major export of the two smaller islands. The days when one could travel on banana boats for little more than it would now cost to buy a roll of film was not within the living memory of anyone I met on the islands. I was told I could make the trip from Barbados, overnighting in St Lucia before going on to Dominica. It seemed like a viable proposition until I calculated it cost virtually the same to go by plane as it did by boat. On inquiring further, I also found out it would not be a sloop with the captain hanging on bravely to bunches of bananas and one crew member rowing while the other kept the flag flying, even in gale force winds, by strumming his guitar and singing the banana boat song. The boat I would have travelled on was pointed out to me. It was like a small ocean liner. I would probably have found the passenger quarters accordingly equipped.

It seemed like the re-run of an old movie to find the same boat in Castries harbour one morning. I had forgotten all about her but she was to dog me for a while. I would be watching her as she came into Dominica and we would meet up again in St Lucia on the return leg of my journey.

One of the first things I did when I arrived in St Lucia was to ring Clive, to let him know when I would be arriving in Dominica.

Martin came in good time to take me to the airport. Cecily Devereux stood on the porch bidding me a grimace-cum-smile farewell. I was the only guest apart from those two nights. Now the place was empty. She would miss me, no doubt. And I would miss Martin.

I would be missing him even sooner than envisaged, the flight was leaving on time. Another Leeward Islands Air Transport islander. Dominica's main airport at Melville Hall was badly damaged during the hurricane so flights were diverted to Canefield, the airstrip just outside the island's capital, Roseau.

'We will meet again?'

'I promise you, I will be back.'

I went to join the other passengers in the departure lounge.

The nightmare vision of a sea swelling up so high around me that the boat was swallowed up became a sort of reality as I opened my eyes to the sight of huge waves on a midnight sea. The crossing was more than rough, it was awful. A boat totally at variance with the sea rocked and jolted its way from Dominica to Guadeloupe. By early July you were well into the hurricane season. Gale force winds which bend coconut palms and almost blow you off your feet have you crossing your fingers in the hope that it isn't the start of something else. After Hurricane David, with the damage still very much in evidence, you hoped to heaven there wasn't going to be a next time. As the boat heaved and groaned, I thought of a woman in labour.

Any romantic notions of banana boats or cargo boats had soon flown out the window when I went to the harbour. They took off like a jet. I was determined to make the journey across to Guadeloupe and mentioned it to Clive while staying with him and his family in Portsmouth. As luck would have it, there was a boat which made the trip once a week from their harbour. It left at midnight on the Sunday and returned the following Wednesday. I had just ten more days left in Dominica. It was Friday and we discussed it. It would surely make some sense to take the boat that very Sunday. So Sunday afternoon found me at the harbour, passport and the necessary amount of East Caribbean dollars in hand to pay for the trip. I would have to meet the captain and agent, as did all passengers, before travelling that night. My eyes were riveted on a strong carrier, twice the size of anything else in the harbour. She lay anchored, high and sturdy in the water. Oh, good, I said to myself, that'll get us there in no –

Clive followed my gaze.

'No, not that one, this one.'

I looked to where he was pointing.

Some friends in England had a cabin cruiser. I am no expert on boats but I swear she was no bigger than that. Theirs was a vessel any sailor would be proud of but with just a few of us on board we were continually bumping into each other. So where the devil were they going to put the fifteen or so passengers rumoured to be making the trip?

Seaworthy was the last adjective I would have used to describe her. The boat looked as if it was being kept together with glue, string and possibly the odd nail. The paint, what there was of it, was blistered and cracking and I'd swear the boat hadn't seen a scrubbing brush in some considerable length of time. There was no doubt in my mind that it wouldn't last the journey. It was fragile, unsafe and the woodwork looked as if it was rotting.

My horror-stricken face must have said it all. Clive immediately broke into a stream of praises about the boat's virtues. It had been in service for years – all the more reason to my mind for sending it out to pasture. The captain was a very able man with a great deal of experience. I found out later he and Clive were cousins. As he talked, I watched what was going on around me.

A number of vehicles were parked on the wharf. They were unloading crate after crate of grapefruits, limes, mangoes, dasheens, boxes of anthurium lilies, cane baskets. You name it. There was so much of it, it was fast filling every available space on the wharf. And there was still more coming. But what was quickly pickling my brain was that it all seemed destined for the one boat. Unable to stop myself, I moved as close as I dared. The cargo hold seemed bottomless. There were two men down below. They seemed a long way down. Two other crew members were throwing boxes down to them. And as they looked up, all I could be sure of was the whites of their eyes. And just supposing they were able to load everything? Just supposing that when the hold was full they were able to stack the rest on deck, the boat would be so low in the water, anything could happen. At the best of times I am no sailor. This would be madness.

'I am *not* going on that!'

Eleven-thirty found us picking our way in the darkness. He, with a torch in hand and me, holding a canvas bag. The road from his family's house to the harbour is unlit. There was a wind so strong it almost took your breath away. The forecast for that evening had not been particularly favourable. Rain with the possibility of thunder. I am still not sure what caused me to change my mind but in the five minutes it took to get down to the boat I went over it once again in my head. All in all, it was one hundred times more convenient to make the journey from where I was, rather than going all the way back to Roseau. The rest was something to do with throwing caution to the wind, spirit of adventure, a once in a lifetime experience. Anyway, I had paid my money and they were holding my passport, so there wasn't any going back. I'm not too sure where my survival instinct figured but one thing was certain, not very highly.

The instructions were that we should wait at the small jetty for the rowing boat which would take the passengers to where she was anchored, now some distance from where she had been earlier. There seemed to be just the two of us waiting to board. It was still and silent. The harbour lights threw strangled, yawning reflections in the water as, very slowly and cautiously, a man in a rowing boat approached. Above the black, choppy water I could see the merging form of oars, torso and boat alongside the rhythmic beating of the sea as he came closer. And as he came closer, I realized it was most certainly just as well there were only two of us because that was all he could take.

I am no sailor. At the best of times I am wary of the sea. Even when she comes lapping fondly at my toes, placid against my back, I remain suspicious. So what in the name of all that is clear-cut and logical was I doing, allowing myself to be lowered into a rowing boat which seemed to pitch with every stir of the ever-increasing wind and did not look any more seaworthy than the vessel which spawned her? Looking straight into the black, bottomless sea, I stepped as daintily as I could into the boat. Common sense prevailed. You sit where you can achieve some sense of balance. It was the woman getting in behind me who almost tipped us all into the water.

'Woman, don't hold my collar! You go throw we in the water!'

The boat swayed as if it was a hammock. Sitting on a plank of wood and holding on with fists of steel, I sent up a little prayer. Not even a crowbar could prise my hands loose.

'Jesus Christ, woman! What is wrong with you?!'

She was, if appearances were to be relied on, about to sit on his shoulders. Clive was leaning over the edge of the jetty warning me in hushed tones to be careful where I kept my money. He was still giving me last-minute instructions as the boatman began rowing away from the jetty. They came over loud and clear. I must make sure and enjoy myself. I gave him a long, silent wave to let him know his words had been heard and understood. I was still waving as he became smaller and smaller in the distance.

The three of us moved silently through the night. No one spoke. All that could be heard above the almost silent sea was the swishing of oars as we moved towards the bigger boat. I took each movement of the oars as they came. I was totally uncomfortable and very apprehensive. Something I noticed, but which in my determination to be strong, resilient and not give way to panic had not really registered until that moment, was that the boat was leaking. I felt it as I stepped in but there was now more water around my ankles than before. And worse yet, we were very low in the water. I was experiencing a very complex mixture of emotions which I couldn't be bothered to analyse, safe to say that anger was in there somewhere. I didn't give a damn what my fate was, provided he didn't hand me a tin can and tell me to start bailing because he would sure as hell know what it was like to feel an oar across his head.

Every stroke of the oar took us nearer our destination. At first the distance had seemed insurmountable. The distance from the jetty to the boat looked like miles. It was a comfort to know that there was help waiting to haul me and my belongings aboard.

The deck was stacked to capacity. Presumably, anything they couldn't fit below was left on top to brave the elements along with the rest of us. There was some bailing going on below me. The gentleman in the rowing boat was preparing to make another journey. It would appear we were two passengers short, There were nine bunks. Three sets of three. In the semi-darkness, I could see all were occupied. And if they hadn't been they certainly were when my travelling companion slipped neatly past me on to the bunk I was about to investigate. It was unlikely I would have been able to sleep, anyway. However, I would have preferred to have a choice in the matter. I didn't know what to do with myself. I went back on deck to find I was not the only person with nowhere to sleep.

'Ah, Miss Johnson.'

Well, I certainly couldn't imagine what he and I could possibly have to say to each other.

'Miss A-a-a-a-h – '

The captain was looking at my passport and attempting my Christian name. I had more or less switched off. He continued his attempts at breaking the ice. I strongly suspected Clive had asked him to 'look after' me. Suddenly, it was as if he had a vision.

'When you are ready to sleep, you can share my bed.'

'What?!'

'You can get in next to the girl who's using my bunk.'

I returned to the cabin to take a closer look. Two of the bunks were being shared. Each had two female passengers sleeping head to toe. The idea really did not appeal to me in the slightest. I went back to the foredeck to sit on one of the crates and was still sitting there when the rowing boat returned with our last two passengers. By then it was close to midnight. The crew went through the motions of whatever it was they went through before the boat sailed. I dare say I was in their way, but I really didn't care. The boat turned through a clear arc to sail out of harbour. There was a lot of coming and going in the engine room. One crew member kept going up and down the stairs under the bridge. The orange light of a lantern glowed and faded at almost regular intervals. I sat back and closed my eyes. All I could hear was the steady and not very soothing hum of the engine.

I may have drifted off because I suddenly started. The boat was rolling. A strong wind was tossing her. My head was involuntarily turned to the right. Dominica's coastline lay black and ominous, held like a rock between the sea and a midnight sky. I could find no stars. I could find no light, only shades of dark blue and grey throwing the darkness into relief. Occasionally, I could see tiny electric worms serpenting across the sea. I sat down for two hours, tossing with every whim of the turbulence. And yet strangely at ease. Powerfully at peace, I was allowed to simply sit and be by myself. There was something very unreal about the situation. A dream-state was accentuated by the hard, unyielding coastline still very much with us, still holding us to her. Such a weird sense of resignation. It was as if time was standing still. Surely, we should have left Dominica behind, hours ago.

With the rising wind came rain. Torrential rain forced me to abandon the deck for the bridge. The two other passengers on deck were now also attempting to squeeze into the tiny space. Lunacy. There was nowhere else to go. Two of the bunks were empty. One was carrying the captain's briefcase containing passports and other documents. The other bunk belonged to Vincent, a crew member. He was busy doing something or other down below and had made it quite clear no one was to use his bunk and he had no intention of sharing it. To all appearances, the crew had priority over the passengers where sleeping accommodations were concerned. I was inclined to believe it was nothing more than their own rules and regulations which they made up as they went along. 'We have to work hard on this boat therefore we are entitled to a good night's rest.' I reasoned that even if all the bunks were in use – two people in each, there still wouldn't be enough sleeping accommodation. We were keeping the captain company. Four of us on the bridge. Only one was navigating. And the storm was now truly in earnest. The sea rose, taking the boat with it. The sea ebbed and the boat went down as if the floor has been pulled from under her. The boat was on a helter-skelter. My stomach was the least of it. We were having a rough ride without all the fun of the fair. Sitting behind a wheel, we involuntarily swayed from left to right, right to left. We went from side to side moving almost in unison. Moving at the whim of the sea, of the storm, of a boat which we no longer seemed to control.

'A storm. And it's hurricane season, isn't it?'

The captain looked at me and grinned.

'That's right.'

His voice was incredibly cheerful.

All the excitement was wearing me out. I was soon dog-tired. All efforts to keep my eyes open proved to be of no avail. Not even the concept of peril on the sea could shake off the weariness which clung to my eyelids. Did I dare chance it? Was I really that desperate? Physical exhaustion overcame all aversion. I elbowed the woman across to her half of the bunk and dropped into the available space. My waterproof jacket was the pillow between her feet and my head. And if she wanted to spend the rest of the night picking my toes out of her ears, that was entirely up to her.

How could it be I was the only person disturbed by it? There was complete silence from the bunks. As peaceful as babies they remained oblivious to the heaving boat while I continued to toss with every movement. And how could anyone in their right mind sleep? How could anyone with an ounce of sensitivity or awareness of life allow themselves to submerge and sink like a stone when their very lives could be in danger? I reasoned they must lead very blame-less lives. I shut my eyes to hold tightly to some strange emotion and concept of religion beginning to tickle my brain. The feeling sunk to my stomach like a trickle of warm, slow liquid. I went down there with it and may have stayed for a while. I was the boat. I am the boat. But this was not the hand which had so often reached up to take me below the surface. These waves closed in like a grappling iron. Their razor-sharp tentacles began to suck my life-force, draining my energies the second they touched me. And then voices were there also. They were urgent. I started. Opening my eyes I found nightmare and reality had merged. The sea was indeed coming in. Had any of it been a dream? Had I not simply watched, as waves grew larger and larger until we were no match for the sea? One wave towered high over the boat.

And then the captain was yelling at the crew. Two of them tumbled out of their bunks, trampling three bodies bedded down on the floor. In the faint light, I recognized two of them as passengers who were on the bridge earlier. The third was a crew member. The captain was still yelling at the crew. Someone on the aft deck was juggling with chains and ropes. He was drenched. We heard it and saw it. A wave towered high above us. Seconds later, the sea came in. The two passengers, now fully awake, leapt to their feet, shouting and swearing. It was over as quickly as it had happened. Whatever safeguard which needed to be done was done. All we were left with was the aftermath. And through it all the sleepers slept. I remembered the sight of legs being peeled out of soaking jeans. Bags being moved. We had all been instructed to remove our shoes before getting into the bunks. My sandals were soaked.

It all happened during the tight hours of darkness which squeezed me minute by minute during a long and useless night. The storm still held us but by now I had grown resigned.

I was able to drift off to sleep for a while. As I was slipping through the net, a figure stormed past, still swearing and cursing. And the last impression I had as the net closed was of a wet, naked bottom brushing against my hand. I was awakened once again by the sound of dragging chains and loud voices. This time it was because we had reached our destination. The crew were leaping ashore, ropes in hand. I looked about me. The bunks were just starting to stir.

Point-a-Pitre. My first impression was of a grey colonial texture. This was accentuated by rain which was bucketing down. From where I lay, I could see beyond the aft deck to a line of sheds. People were sheltering in front of some of them. All were looking out to sea and therefore obscured from my view as the rain ran in rivulets from the grooves of the corrugated iron roof. The rainy season had precipitated us. It was the first torrential shower I had witnessed in almost a month.

The sight of running water only heightened my discomfort. I was dying. I could not tell the last time I felt so uncomfortable. My bladder was bursting. It went without saying that there was no toilet on board. Not only was there no toilet but neither were there any facilities for one's basic needs. I certainly did not regard a bucket, plastic or otherwise, as being quite the done thing. At least, that was what I was offered a few hours earlier. He had yelled his instructions across the boat.

'Nathan, get a bucket for the lady!'

I told him to forget it.

I tried not to think about how desperate I was but my discomfort was never that far away. Earlier that morning, a potty had been passed between two women then emptied overboard while most of the men were busy docking. It was all done so quickly and discreetly I almost missed what was happening. A little later when I realized I could well have asked for a borrow, it was too late. The other passengers were waking up and the crew now back in the

208

cabin. I lay there like a lump, afraid to stir in case I had an accident. We were waiting for the customs officials. The captain did not want anyone leaving the boat until then. At last, I could stand it no longer, as he walked past, I let him know how things stood.

'I'm dying. I've got to go ashore for a pee.'

He gave me a roguish grin.

'Well, I did offer you a bucket, last night.'

I ignored him and repeated my request. There was no denying the urgency in my voice. Customs officials were not due for another hour or so. He, probably, felt he could trust me. I was in any case, still in his care. I wondered if I could last until I got there. I felt cauterized from the waist down. I could appreciate it was only a temporary state of affairs but I had almost forgotten what it was like to feel human. I had almost forgotten what life was like before I found myself in that predicament. The toilets really weren't that far away. I tried to maintain some dignity as I made my way, so as not to betray my plight. When I got there, I found it was the type where you have to squat. My preoccupation had almost blinded me to the fact I was now in one of the French departments.

I thought my young friend had grown restless on board and was looking for a way out because the captain had only allowed her off the boat so she could accompany me. But no, there she was waiting patiently. And no, she didn't want to go herself. She simply wanted to show me the way there and was now waiting to show me the way back. I was now able to think rationally. No longer disadvantaged, my senses were now acute and in perfect working order. I became aware of almost everything I had been blind and deaf to earlier.

From the minute I set foot on the boat, I had felt like a stranger. Again, very much the outsider. The conditions which they regarded as being acceptable were to my mind intolerable, but I jogged along as best I could. I had felt like the odd one out because it was all new to me. Again, the only person on board who didn't speak French patois. The impression I had of Dominica even before I went there was of an island where everyone knew everyone else or, to be more precise, everyone else's business. In days to come, I would understand why the impression remained with me. The passengers were laughing and joking with the crew. I could pick up one or two phrases from time to time and get the gist of what was being said, but it was largely lost on me. The conversation switched from patois to English.

One of the bags which had been soaked belonged to a passenger making the trip across for a holiday. She held one crew member and one crew member only responsible. The one who took the bag off the bunk, where she had left it, and put it on the floor. She was furious. Apart from anything else, she had no clothes to change into when she got off the 'blasted' boat. An extremely animated argument was taking place with some passengers joining in. They took sides. Mainly hers. Why the hell he had to go and put the woman's bag on the 'damn' floor?! The argument was like a ball which shifted from court to court, from patois to English. Vincent was defending himself. I mean how was he supposed to know what was going to happen. Sentences started in English were finished in patois. The captain himself joined in, accusing the man of being responsible for the majority of things which went wrong on the boat. Vincent was almost in tears. I found him the most abrasive, the biggest in height and build and also the ugliest of the crew members. So, to discover it was possible to reduce a man of his measure to jelly came as an interesting surprise. He retreated to the aft deck to sulk and the woman retreated to the bridge to continue complaining to the captain.

The atmosphere settled down. An oldish woman turned from her conversation to say something to me in patois. I smiled and looked away. She repeated what she said, waiting for an answer. There was silence as everyone else waited. Their eyes were on me. Eventually, I had to laugh as I made a confession.

'I don't understand patois.'

One of the men said something and everyone laughed.

I was feeling very sheepish because she now had to speak to me in English.

'What is your name?'

I told her. She now wanted to know where I was from.

'Ah, I come from Trinidad, too. Arima. You know, Arima? But I live here many years. Last time I been back, eighteen years, now. Went for my son's wedding. He marry an Indian girl.'

Her skin was like creased, tan leather.

'I live in Guadeloupe twenty-five years now.'

I wanted to ask how come but did not. To some extent it seemed irrelevant and to some degree the answer was obvious. In the old days, the people of the Caribbean came and went among each other's islands. If you liked the place, you stayed. For a while, at any rate. If you didn't, then you moved on. You moved on to some other island and you did not necessarily ever return to your own. In those days, there were no restrictions. You came and went. Your own small island was the incentive and inspiration. Curiosity, restlessness and a sense of adventure were your oars and when you left you took them with you. The island where you were born was always with you in spirit. I thought of this as I looked at her. She must have been in her sixties. I sensed she may have had a hard life. Her grey-green eyes were alive and full of expression as she spoke. I felt sad as I watched and listened.

And when it came down to it, where and what were roots, for heaven's sake? A people on the waves, of waves. Often at sea. Whose fault was that? In essence all you were doing was attempting to pacify the restless, hungry spirit in its quest for an answer it might never find.

My thoughts went back to the proprietor of the café in St Lucia. How many hundreds of miles? How many thousands? I should have asked him. Should have asked. Should have done. Should have.

Yes. Had I known at the time there was a question which needed to be asked, I would have asked it.

I was fascinated by this woman. Madame Rico as everyone called her. I wanted to know more about her and the other women. There were six of them making the trip every week. Every Sunday night they took the boat across to sell their fruit and vegetables in the market, returning by the same boat when it sailed on the Wednesday night. There were goods on board belonging to sellers who hadn't made the trip. They would be flying out to Guadeloupe that morning to meet the boat. The other women were friendly, suspicious or apathetic. The normal combination of personalities you get when travelling with a group of strangers. The market women and the crew were like a family. As regular travellers making the journey every week, it really didn't surprise me.

And the rain came down. Passengers were still waiting to leave. We wouldn't be able to do a thing until the customs officials arrived. On the aft deck some were performing their ablutions. There were a couple of barrels of fresh water. A lot of scrubbing and brushing was going on. Toothbrush and toothpaste very much in evidence. All within the realms of decency. When I was able to find a space, I joined them.

There was a lot of fooling and monkeying around

between the regular passengers and crew while I played a waiting game. Someone I had met a few evenings earlier had promised to ring some friends in Guadeloupe and ask them to meet me. He knew I had no contacts, not even somewhere to stay. But as the evening wore on, he had become more and more inebriated and I felt the chances of his remembering were slight. However, I received a message on Sunday afternoon to say there would definitely be someone at Point-a-Pitre to meet me. I waited, watching hard for a person who fitted the description I had been given. Ah, here was someone who could fit the bill. A man wearing a trenchcoat and carrying an umbrella was coming towards the boat. He was now speaking to the captain.

'Madame Rico, s'il vous plaît.'

Someone had sent Madame Rico a flask of steaming coffee. I remember thinking at the time, the lady must be well loved.

The message had said eight o'clock. The person would be there to meet me at eight in the morning. I waited as the rain fell. Relentless. Grey-faced façades of concrete effigies. Unbudging, unyielding, uncompromising. And how good was my French these days? I hadn't needed to put it to the test. Here, it was the official language. I needed a crutch. Somone to help me over the next few days. As I watched the rain, my thoughts were doing slow somersaults. I was being gradually drawn into a different circle. As time went by and still no sign of the people meant to be meeting me, the captain asked Madelaine, one of the market women, to find a cheap guest-house where I could stay. It was now almost nine o'clock. Customs had been and gone but, with the rain still pelting down, only a few passengers had left the boat. Madelaine said she had to leave the boat on urgent business anyway. She would inquire for me.

I watched her pick her way through the rain, a diminutive figure behind a large, black umbrella. Threads of water either bounced off or cascaded down it. This was far from what I had envisaged. Crestfallen, I couldn't be sure if the stony, faceless buildings obscuring my vision would have been as awesome had it been the sun and not rain in control. It might have been some sort of compromise. Colonialism, its face and architecture, remained constant, rain or shine. What had I envisaged? Did I have any preconceived ideas about what I would find when I arrived in Guadeloupe? Apart from someone there to meet and take me around, little else. Certainly not Guadeloupian girls in madras robes and foulards, waiting at the quay, ready to dance the beguine as soon as my boat came into view. So few have crossed your path. See how the rest go by as if you don't even exist? I was one prodigal few knew about and the majority didn't care. Did you think all the islanders would have been out in force just for you, one moth-eaten traveller plucked from exile back into exile?

The fruits of someone's ablutions made a dash for freedom, didn't make it. Floating blobs of processed toothpaste and greyish, soapy water dashed in after as a chaser, dissolved beneath a hammering from the rain and the sea's natural action. I felt as if I could, as if I should, begin all over again. I was still wearing the jeans and blouse I had worn when I boarded the previous night. Despite all my efforts, I still felt sticky and uncomfortable. I squirmed inside my underwear. This wasn't me. I longed for a shower and a complete change of clothes. No, this wasn't me, at all. So who the hell do you think you are? A little bit of discomfort and you start twitching. The man who said he had arranged for someone to meet me in Point-a-Pitre was something in the government. I had hoped for comfort. I had hoped to be looked after, Taken here, taken there.

Yes, that was what I had hoped for. And what had I got? Where had I got?

I had got as far along the archipelago as I was likely to get. I had reached the zenith, the pinnacle of my travels. I had not visited all the islands I wanted to get to but it didn't matter. It really did not matter.

My journey had come to a natural conclusion. I felt that even if I could afford to, it would not be possible for me to go any further. A closer look at the map and I understood better. Aesthetically, most people preferred to describe Guadeloupe as being shaped like the open wings of a butterfly. Split both north and south at a forty-five degree angle, there was little doubt in my mind she was the mother of those islands from Dominica down to Grenada. They had all been shot from her open, sulphuric thighs. They lay in a gentle curve below that apex. And how strange, the centre still held. Well, almost. Basse Terre was separated from Grand Terre by nothing more innocuous than the Rivière Salée. The boat was nestling close to that channel between the two halves of the island. A natural barrier. I could go no further.

But what of Barbados? Even now, what of Barbados? Still too unique to belong, she lay orphaned, motherless, outside the arc but on a similar latitude to St Vincent.

In those silvery waters I would find a mirror image, the reverse of all things my eyes and mind could reach and grasp. What if the revelation were to be taken further?

What if Guadeloupe was the manifestation, the physical result of that pull I felt on the other island, so obviously an outsider. What if she did, after all, belong to the group. Every prodigal has a home. What if –

'Miss Johnson.'

The captain's voice pulled me back. Mesmerized, I could feel myself absorbing every glimmer of light which bounced off the water. My thoughts were taking me far enough.

'You seem a long way away.'

I shrugged my shoulders and flashed him a smile. It was Monday, the boat would be back in Dominica on Thursday morning. I would remain there another ten days before retracing my footsteps to Trinidad. And the next time I found myself in the departure lounge at Piarco, it would be to catch the flight back to Heathrow. Happily, until then, miles upon miles of rain separated me from where I was and where I would need to get to.

Time was money. The sellers who came by plane arrived at the wharf to collect their goods. On a grey, unforgiving Monday morning the rain started to ebb, taking with it more passengers from the boat. The waning process continued. As the passengers said their goodbyes, I was able to see more clearly who were market people and who were not. None of the male passengers were traders. The only male trader in the clutch had come by plane. And his was big business. He and his wife were helping Nathan and Keith, another crew member, to unload crates of fruit and vegetables. Time was money. Two of the women who came by boat worked for him. The market where they sold was near. It was an outdoor one but they would, nevertheless, be able to find some shelter. The ubiquitous parasol was waterproof enough for any weather. Time was money. Soon, it was just the captain, his crew and myself. I began to feel guilty for I suspected had it not been for me, Madelaine would have been back long since, to set up her pile of provisions alongside the other women.

'And where are you and the others going to stay?'

'Right here.'

He tapped the stern, lovingly. I should have guessed. In fact, I probably already knew but asked out of idle interest.

I could not seriously imagine him being separated from his precious boat. And the crew probably didn't have any say in the matter.

'It's all right. You can stay with us.'

Madelaine was at my elbow. I had not heard her return. The same woman I had shared the captain's bunk with, I swear at some point during the night I had kicked her in the head. The vexation of having a sleeping body rolling back against your own every time you pushed it away had got the better of me. She was small, almost dainty, fine-boned and slim. But she looked strong. She wasn't like the others. There was something which singled her out, a sort of reticence. That morning while the other women chatted from their bunks, she hardly joined in. Head resting on her arm she had smiled at all the witticisms and sympathized with the rest. I suspected she may also have felt awkward about having to share a bed with someone who was more than just a stranger. A complete stranger. This was the first time we had spoken. She was shy and awkward at first.

I could not help but smile to think of Clive instructing the captain to look after me. Perhaps he would have had some explaining to do if he had let me wander off in the rain not knowing where I was going. But again, I would like to think he would have attempted a solution without any prompting from Clive.

And Madame Rico? My thoughts darted to her. She was much older than the other women. On such a cold, wet day I hoped she would be all right.

I would be staying in a house in Abymes. It was where Madelaine always stayed and, of late, Thea, one of the other women. The rain had stopped, I stepped off the boat, past the customs building into Paris. Well, it may as well have been. Martinique was known as ''ti Paris'. I knew Guadeloupe was regarded as showing less French influence

217

than the sister island but if the replicas I kept seeing were regarded as showing less influence, I felt I would probably not like Martinique. The shopping arcades, parfumiers and particularly the pâtisseries were all keen reminders. Yet, just a stone's throw from a boulevard lined with palm trees and a park with its beautifully manicured garden, were the worst slums I had seen on any of the islands.

Madelaine had customers other than the ones she sold to in the market. To these customers she sold wholesale. The dasheen, yams and eddoes would be by the sack and not the kilo. One of them had asked Madelaine to get some weights for her scales. The provisions had been delivered earlier. It was just the weights we now had to take her. The woman's shop was in immigrant quarters in surroundings which degenerated from poverty to abysmal poverty. The settlement was well hidden. No tourist would find it except by accident. If they did they would have the common sense to turn and walk away as would any white tourist who tripped on a core of hungry eyes and raging hearts. The yawning sore began somewhere along the edges of the pavement and ate its way inside. The kitchens were open, bare lean-tos. They did not spill on to the streets so much as recede inwards. Pots, pans, coalpots, lean-to dwellings and bundles of life existed close to the edge. Belongings looked as if they lived out in the narrow street so close yet so far from tourists' eyes. You followed the poverty no matter how far into the centre your eyes strayed. Unlike Barbados, there were no indignant lips to curl around words which left you in no doubt of how they felt about your looking in on them. The outrage seemed to be turned inwards. Eyes looked up, looked at you, through you, out the other side at some distant lasting vision. And your eyes could not contain the sight of them nor hold their gaze either – for markedly different reasons. The sight of you did not satisfy, it still left them ravenous. The sight of them filled me to the extent where I had to look away. And when I did, my eyes fell on portals without doorways then backed away to where the children played. Somehow the children always played. I had never before been so close to a fire that I could feel it parch my tongue. My tongue remained moored to the roof of my mouth. There was, in any case, little to say.

Later, I asked Madelaine about the settlement.

'Haiti. Most of them come from Haiti.'

'Why here?'

'Maybe, the language.'

Because both islands speak French? Is that what it was?

'It's the same language wherever you are.'

'What?'

'Nothing, Madelaine. It really doesn't matter.'

We were talking of some seven to eight hundred miles. They were a long way from home. A long way to bring your rags and empty bellies. Had they been told it was the promised land?

It did not go away. Nothing made it better. The more I saw of the boulevards with their palm trees, the more my thoughts went back to that narrow street. The more my thoughts remained on the edge of an open cesspit of poverty.

After taking me to the house in Abymes, that first day in Guadeloupe, Madelaine had gone to the market to join the others. She worked until mid-afternoon. The house was not that far from the city centre nor the market, for that matter. After a shower and change of clothes I walked into town, despite a rising temperature. I went straight to where the women were. At first, I watched from a distance. They were, naturally, in competition not only with the Guadeloupian market people but each other. Madelaine and Thea shared the same pitch. They were the only vendors who called out to the customers, trying to entice them. They vied for the same customers.

'Viens, viens! Ici moi vends le mieux.'

'Ici! C'est meilleur marché!'

I did not understand all the words but the technique seemed to work. I went over to chat to them, especially Madame Rico who sat with a box of mangoes at her feet. I faded once more into the background in order to come to a more accurate conclusion. What was it to her, a profession or a way of life? I suspected the latter. She was getting too old for the constant travelling. The women made the overnight journey to sell their goods in the market for three days before returning home to repeat the process the following week. That journey backwards and forwards every week would mean they did not see a great deal of their families.

Somewhere along the line I had caught a bug. All the symptoms of 'flu relegated me to an early bed that night. Madelaine and Thea, both very religious, went to a prayer meeting. Out of interest, I would have liked to have gone with them. Madelaine had gone long before I woke. She had left a message to say she would be back by mid-day. The house was at the back of a grocery and café. The proprietor lived there as did Yvonne, a young woman from Dominica. I decided to wait for Madelaine in the café. Yvonne came in from the shop where she worked. I listened while she chatted. She talked about having spent some time in Antigua before coming to Guadeloupe.

'I had my children before I left Dominica. They still there with my mother.'

Had yours yet? I waited for it. She changed the subject, leaving me with amnesia and momentary loss of direction.

'They don't like us here.'

Still not sure where I was. What did she mean, 'us'?

220

'They think they better than Dominicans and St Lucians. Say we don't have style. Don't know how to speak real French. They only want us for the worst kind of job.'

The proprietor came into the café and she retreated back to the shop where a customer was waiting. Monsieur Thiebault was a man in his sixties. The previous evening, his eyes had flickered over me with fractional interest. It was the sort of reception you give a stranger purely out of courtesy. He addressed me now with the same politeness.

'Bonjour Madmoiselle. Comment allez-vous?'

'Je vais bien, Monsieur Thiebault. J'espère que vous allez bien, aussi?'

I was being deliberately pedantic.

He stopped wiping the table and turned to look at me, his expression one of naked amazement.

'Mais, vous parlez Français, Mademoiselle. Et vous le parlez bien.'

'Mais non monsieur. Une fois je le parlais bien mais j'ai oublié trop de mots. Maintenant je parle un petit peu. C'est tout.' The twelve months in Paris as an 'au pair' were many years behind me but I had retained a reasonable accent. It was this which had impressed Monsieur Thiebault. When some of his friends came into the café, a little later, he had to show me off. I had to speak to them in French also. With Yvonne, he spoke Creole. The shop was empty again. He called her and said something in standard French. She did not understand. I could feel her confusion. He turned to us, his voice mocking and sneering.

'Elle ne comprend pas ce qu'on dit.'

So whose fault was it if she didn't understand French? Blame the erstwhile or perhaps not so erstwhile masters. She was not to blame. Like other Dominicans I had met, she spoke good English. Among themselves the people spoke French Creole but English was the official language.

My experience among St Lucians was similar. It was English spoken with a French Caribbean lilt, with Creole among themselves. The Creole spoken by the Dominicans was not quite the same as that spoken by the St Lucians. By the same token, both Martiniquians and Guadeloupians spoke French as their official language plus a Creole. The French patois spoken by them was different from the one spoken by the St Lucians. Because the idiom is a basic combination of old French and some of the African dialects, peoples of the four islands were able to understand and converse one with the other. However, the patois was so far removed from modern-day French that unless the people of Dominica and St Lucia learnt the language they could not hope to understand. Whether the Creole was French, English or Spanish patois, it was the language of the people, a means of identification which remained specifically theirs.

I churned it over very very carefully before addressing him.

'Quel dommage, Monsieur Thiebault, que vous ne connaît pas l'histoire des Antilles. N'oubliez quoiqu'elle ne parle pas Français, elle parle Anglais parfaitement et vous ne connaît mieux qu'un ou deux mots. L'histoire des Antilles n'est pas sa faute. Croyez-vous que c'est sa faute qu'elle ne sait pas parler Français?'

He and his friends had been amusing themselves at her expense. She had had to stand there like a moron looking from one to the other, wearing a vacant smile and expression because she could not understand what they were saying about her. I had tried at first not to interfere. I was, after all, a stranger, an outsider, but I became so disgusted I could not sit and listen to it any more. I stepped in. I did not pretend to express myself perfectly but I know I got my message across. While his friends had the decency to look reasonably abashed, Thiebault's face tightened. My words had been addressed directly to him. How dare I, a woman, show him up in front of his friends? He, the owner of the café where I was sitting and the owner of the house where I was sleeping, even if I was paying rent for those two nights. That was the sort of pompous idiot he was. I had sensed it from the start. For a minute, I seriously thought he was going to hit me. Worst of all, I was a woman. But I was ready for him. His pride could not have been any greater than my anger and disgust. I regarded the game he was playng as an obscene betrayal. Even if I could be bothered to shred my thoughts finely enough to detail the ground debris of my emotion, I doubt if he would have understood. He continued to hold my gaze, his face rigid. Suddenly, it softened. He gave me a reluctant smile.

'Oui, Mademoiselle. C'est vrai. Vous avez raison.'

I had listened carefully to Thiebault and his friends. Their pronunciation was different from mine. It was all part of the conditioning. Thiebault as full of admiration because I spoke French with an accent closer to the masters than his own. History repeats itself. This sense of entrapment bore the hallmark, the brand of slavery. I turned to Yvonne.

'If Madelaine comes, tell her I won't be long. I'll be about fifteen minutes.'

I wanted to get away from them. The taste was still in my mouth. I walked out of the gate and turned left. The asphalt was wearing thin at the edges of the road and formed an irregular pattern until it faded into dust and pockets of tiny stones.

There was a bakery close to the house. A delicious smell of mid-day baking was rising from it. I looked in the window. It was the rhum baba which caught my attention. That took some doing. It was an interesting window. I resisted as long as I could before throwing caution to the wind. I went in and bought two rhum babas and two delicious fruit slices. I felt incredibly depressed. The food might help. I was walking and eating, trying to console myself.

It was a narrow road. If a lorry met a similar vehicle, they would not be able to pass each other. As it got nearer to the main road, it gradually widened, and as it got nearer the main road there were less houses and more shops. Diagonally opposite the bakery was a bicycle shop. I crossed the road and went past wheels upon wheels of revolutions with circles within circles. The islands shared a common experience which went beyond the open canker of one people enslaving another. A shifting population of Arawak, Carib, European, African and others. Turn within a tornado of centuries and the stones which were stones became the sands of the beach. The wheel which continued revolving was grinding more than just the juice of sugar cane which had been left to go through a cycle of fermentation. The volatile spirit reeked even on the cleanest breath. A stench of decay and habit was strong, even in the whirlwind of time.

I don't know how long she had been walking towards me before I spotted her. Her washing blowing in the breeze. The heat waves which cut at her body distorted her shape as she came over the crest of the hill. The sack balancing on her head fused to become an extension of herself. She seemed to mark time before coming forward, smiling. Handling the ground provisions left her hands, arms, legs, and shoes, not to mention working clothes, despite the apron, covered with soil. Her head was tilted to one side as she squinted against the sun in her eyes. Hands buried deep in her apron pockets, it was a stance I would always associate with Madelaine. Whenever she came to mind, that was how I would always remember her.

'Shopping this afternoon?'

She nodded. I did not mention the incident and, when we got back to the house, Thiebault was out. That night would be my last one there which was perhaps just as well.

She showered and changed then we walked back into town. On the way we met a group of young men. Madelaine went up to one of them, smiling. He seemed just as pleased to see her. They stood chatting for a while. I did not ask, she volunteered the information.

'My twins' father.'

'Your what?'

'The father of my first two.'

'Really?'

'Yes. Really.'

'How many do you have then?'

'Three.'

I found out later that Thea had four.

Madelaine's twins were eleven. The youngest, nine. All boys. Her mother lived with them, looking after the children when Madelaine was in Guadeloupe. I was beginning to understand a little better where she was coming from.

As we walked into town, I began to get a better idea where they were all coming from. They were tough and ambitious. All the women had dreams which went beyond petty trading in Point-a-Pitre market. The francs from their sales would be used to buy goods, largely toiletries, to take back to Dominica. Even after customs duty had been paid, Madelaine said she found it made good sense. She, herself, had opened a small shop. The goods would be for her shelf. I didn't ask about the other women but, reading between the lines, suspected they were buying for other shopkeepers.

She assured me the purchases were a good deal cheaper than in Dominica. The alternative would be exchanging francs for their own currency but to sell for East Caribbean dollars would not be favourable. They would lose out.

I never doubted that in some instances the women grew their own fruit and vegetables. I also suspected they were paying much less to make the trip than I was. But when all was said and done, the cost of living in Guadeloupe must have been considerably higher than in Dominica for them to go through all the trouble. The goods they bought while on the French island would certainly be the incentive.

They were shrewd and they were wily. It was a tough world and if you wanted to survive you have to pull out all the stops. Madelaine's long-term ambition was to open a bigger shop but she would be interested to know what else might be on offer.

'What's it like in England?'

I told her more or less what I had said to Mark and Esmelde. We agreed it wasn't for her.

Despite everything, I still hoped against hope the people would turn up. Every time I went to the boat, and there were a few occasions, I inquired. It was on one of these visits that Keith invited me out. If nothing else on that second and last evening, I would get a chance to sample some of the night life. He came to collect me, waiting in the café until I was ready. Until I was good and ready. We took a taxi to a nightclub he always visited when on the island.

I was extremely disappointed. He did not know me, so could not know my values were the opposite of what he supposed them to be. I had a growing impression of Guadeloupe as the tropical playground of the metropolis. What price freedom? There was no pretence at anything else here. It left me with a hollow uncertainty. I wanted to meet and talk with the people. So far, it was just Monsieur Thiebault and his friends. That said nothing at all. How valid were the impressions I had gained without actually being given a chance to verify them?

'Why didn't you take me to a club for Guadeloupians?'

'This is.'

'I mean black Guadeloupians.'

'I didn't think it mattered. Thought you'd like it here.'

It was an hotel, all palms and swimming pools. Friends on the islands would have been ashamed of me. This was everything I had been avoiding, right down to the barman in a bow-tie. The constricting values allowed little room in which to curl a cynical lip. There was a sprinkling of black faces, about the same amount you would expect to find. It was curious to watch the beguine being danced to a rhythm which was almost authentic but more exaggerated. I got involved in a heavy rum cocktail which would not leave me alone. Earlier in the day I had been eating to console myself, now I was drinking for exactly the same reason. We took to the dance floor and stayed until all dancers were asked to make way for the floor show. The main act turned out to be not the ubiquitous limbo dancer but a contortionist.

As the compère was about to walk on stage, a young woman walked in. Obviously delighted to see him, she flung her arms around his neck. He completely ignored her. She tried to catch his eye as he walked back to the bar. He went past her table without even glancing. Gradually, it dawned on her and when it did, she went crimson. Her white escort was trying hard to pretend none of it was going on. The compère said something to the people he was drinking with, they turned to look at her then chuckled.

On the dance floor, I found myself glancing at her from time to time. She was in pain, extremely embarrassed by the incident. And, to some extent, she was now the floor show. Everyone had seen.

For heaven's sake, woman, get up and go. Walk away from it! I kept willing her to leave. Her presence was making me more and more uncomfortable. The relief to turn and find she had finally left. It had taken the best part of an hour. What had I seen? A white woman had thrown her arms around the neck of a black man in a dinner jacket and bow-tie. And he had made her look a fool. It was nothing to do with skin and nothing to do with anything else. It was everything to do with skin and everything to do with the rest. An incident which didn't even remotely involve me had left me tight with anger. Until that moment every pore of my body had breathed awareness of class and colour. Under normal circumstances I would assuredly have dismissed her as a silly, naïve bitch with more money than sense. But these were not normal circumstances. Caution. Tread warily. One foot in front of the other before the impulse, pulsed.

I saw her as a sort of victim. A victim of circumstances. Just an incident. One in millions like a grain of sand in a desert of the universe. His reasons were his own. Nothing to do with her and nothing to do with me. It had happened and that was sufficient.

Under the magnifying glass, the skin lifted and fell. Very gently. A growing indignation had left every follicle sensitive to the fire which singed, even at a distance.

The incident was nothing to do with me but I had felt it. One woman to another, I had felt for her.

Christ, she looked tired!

I winced at the sight of the hooded, reddened eyes and tension lines on Madelaine's face. But it was a happy smile. She had sold everything. It was over for another week.

Before rendezvousing at the bus station to go to San François in the south, she went back to the house to shower and change, then went into town to do more shopping. In that mid-afternoon heat, she would have gone from shop to shop looking for bargains. On the previous afternoon, I had started to wilt long before she had finished. The gruelling pace she set herself was too much for me. She never let up. Her pace never eased. I had been to the market on all three days, just to watch. Everything about Madelaine was brisk. She sold more quickly and twice as much as Thea. Hers was a quiet impatience.

She was pushing towards that vision but overdoing it. She was pushing the dream of progress too hard and too fast. She was tough and energetic but that was not necessarily enough.

My last day in Guadeloupe. I had offered to meet her earlier in the day and take some things back to the boat. While I did this, she went back to do yet more shopping.

She fell asleep almost as soon as we set off. I did not have the heart to wake her. She slept all the way, until we arrived at our destination. While she slept the bus stopped for passengers to board or descend. They reminded me of Trinidadians because they dressed with the same flair. I waited for it, hoped against hope. No, it would not happen. There would be no fire and brimstone on this or any other service I was likely to travel on. The audaciousness was not there. The passengers who boarded together chatted quietly to each other. That was all that broke the silence as the conductor took them from where they were to where they wanted to get to. I began to feel homesick. The audaciousness was not there. I looked at the faces around me. They seemed to betray a sort of despondency. A façade? Like the city itself? Behind a placid exterior lay the true expression. I wondered how many of them supported the Resistance. How many would go out and take a stand? How many would go out and fight to liberate their country from the French. Dignity and freedom. I knew enough about the island's recent history to understand how audacity could sometimes be a fire raging behind closed doors.

The afternoon turned out to be abysmal. I was racked with guilt. She should have gone back to the house to rest. She was too tired to be any fun. Difficult to say exactly what I saw. Little remained with me. The mood of the afternoon took care of that. We wandered through San François looking at this, doing that, until she began to get irritable. At which point I insisted we took the next bus back to Point-a-Pitre. Whether she would have rested had we spent the afternoon in the city is debatable.

She remained an enigma. But that may have been partly my fault. Despite all I had seen, all I had heard and all I knew, I still did not see Madelaine as a market woman. She was playing a role and playing it to the hilt but she was not like them, those women who spent their time between two islands. Half the week in Guadeloupe, the other half in Dominica. Like the island itself, they straddled the waves. Children from thighs of ambitious labour remained within a gentle curve. Not far. But Madelaine was not like them. Like them and yet unlike them. An outsider. Easy. Easy. Lock onto the concept turn once then gently pull away. Easy. Easy.

It was a means to an end. She had style and a sort of reserve they did not possess. Even with her face and body grubby, calling to the customers to come and buy, she retained that dignity.

How did the scales balance? They tipped in and out of favour. Largely, out of favour. I had not seen nearly as much of Guadeloupe as I had hoped. Had not been able to get to Basse Terre, the other half of the island. Again, perhaps entirely my own fault. If you want something

230

badly enough you can get it. I should have gone for it, not let the language nor anything else get in my way. I should not have waited, hoping something – someone – would turn up.

How did the scales balance? Madelaine held some weights all the way from Dominica. Within hours of arriving in Guadeloupe, she handed them over to a woman who owned a shop in the immigrant quarters of the city.

They tipped out of Madame Rico's favour. I was afraid for her that Wednesday evening. When we got to the boat she was already there, huddled on one of the bunks. What could there be in it for her at her age? Hunched over her box of mangoes, she had looked older every time I saw her. What could be in it for her?

An ageing woman, she should be resting, putting her feet up and enjoying the fruits of her labour. One of the other women opened a bottle of bay rum and began stroking the liquid across Madame Rico's forehead. She lay back on the bunk to rest. I went to her.

'I not feeling too good. When it rain like that, it does get into my bones, girl. I does feel it in my bones.'

Business had not been good. I knew she had not sold as well as she had hoped to. She closed her eyes and turned her face to the wall.

Scales balance. Alternately, they tip in or out of favour. There was a night when not just Madelaine but everyone on the boat held weights between palms of hands turned upwards in prayer. Words of supplication were on their lips. I had asked about the outward journey. How on earth did they manage to sleep on a boat riding such stormy seas? One of them shrugged her shoulders.

'You get used to it. But I tell you, there was a time when I thought we'd breathed our last.'

Madelaine had been making the trip for about two

years. Some had been doing it for longer. The experience they shared was the night the boat stopped and refused to budge. I could not help but shiver at the thought of such a tiny speck against the vastness of a Caribbean sea. The men took it in turns to dive into the black night to find out why the engine was not running. I could imagine how every minute must have seemed like an hour. Stillness and tension on the inside. The sea on the outside, waves purring against the boat begging to come in. Long before they realized that something had got caught in the propeller and been able to free it, I would have felt the sky fall in. I would have freaked, screaming long and hard into the night. No, perhaps I would not. I would have been still and at peace. Resigned. *Death by drowning*. All through the long hours of that night, I had fought hard to keep the words at bay.

I willed myself to place my thoughts as carefully on the scales as if they were a feather. Grabbing the nearest bunk, I shut my eyes firm against the oncoming night. I slept fitfully on a sea infinitely calmer than the outward journey and woke in the morning to my own restlessness and impatience. I wanted to be gone, to get off that boat once and for all. The week had folded. A neat crease along the centre. Both halves a perfect match. We berthed at Portsmouth harbour to wait for customs officials in the pouring rain. Another grey morning but there were no conditions on this one. No grave colonial structure but trees and houses. Neither gaining precedence over the other and lots of space between the two.

'Where are you going? Come back here!'

In my haste to get away, I had swept past some men sitting in the back of a black van. They were customs officials, parked between the jetty and the main road. As a passenger with nothing to declare, certainly not an armful of toiletries, I was told I could leave the boat.

They were in no hurry. Nice and dry under big, official umbrellas. I couldn't believe the first drop of rain which fell from one of the spokes to meander along the entry and exit stamps from Guadeloupe, St Lucia, Barbados and the more recent ones from Dominica. Another drop of rain fell on the page blurring the letters. The stamp being used by this official looked as if it had been dipped in water. How the devil did he manage to get rain on the ink pad? And my troubles didn't end there. He went through my bag with great care. Rain soaked me and my belongings. My former companions were all on the bridge. A long, watery wave to them still at sea, and from them to me. Then I turned to walk towards the rest of my stay on the island.

Dominica is said to have three hundred and sixty five rivers. Presumably, one for every day of the year.

I would be hard-pressed to compare her with any of the other islands I visited. She has a natural, unspoilt and dramatic beauty. There was nothing gentle or placid about her contours. Lush hills rose to sharp peaks then fell away to deep valleys. Because of the mountains, the island gets more than its fair share of rain. Rain forests.

Her landscape is so stunning she successfully courts disaster. The most northerly of the Windward Islands, Dominica bore the brunt of the hurricanes of '79 and '80. The people had no sooner started to rebuild from the first when the second came. Knowing this, I could understand the meaning of what I saw. Houses which looked what they were, homes which had been patched. Under the circumstances, who could blame those who felt there was little point in attempting more. As soon as you had finished, a third might strike. In Dominica, I saw entire coconut groves which looked as if the heads of the palms had been lopped. Far more damage than I saw in St Lucia. In the late evening they looked awesome, stretching like huge phantoms against the sky. Someone explained how the colossal winds bent the trees until they snapped.

We landed at Canefield Airport located a few miles from Roseau, the capital. It was only large enough for planes of the size used by LIAT. I decided to spend a day and a night in Roseau before travelling up to Portsmouth in the north of the island to stay with Clive and his family for a while. I met Russell over lunch at the hotel where I was staying. He, also, had just arrived.

Dominica was once the thriving lime-growing capital of the Caribbean. That was during the days when Rose's had their vast lime producing complex in Morne Valley. Russell had come from one of the other islands to work in Dominica. It was his job to advise the local farmers on how to grow the crop to best advantage so they would be more self-sufficient. I saw the cables which ran from the hills where the limes were once harvested to the complex for processing and I saw the whitewashed concrete shells of a once thriving industry. The end of an era. Until the island was able to revitalize this side of her once thriving export industry, she would remain a largely monocrop, banana, country.

One of the first things Russell and I did was tour the island. As a stranger, he, also, wanted to see for himself. We drove through the extraordinary rain forest for what seemed like a verdant eternity of ferns and trees. The forest, now a national park, boasts some six thousand acres. The island balances its own deficiencies. While it is not the obvious place to aim for if you are planning a beach holiday, the interior provides its own surprises. Many of the rivers aren't just wide, they are very wide. Every now and then we came to a spot where layers of sand had been pushed against the bank so you would quite unexpectedly find a tiny beach just large enough for two, hanging shy in the shade of tall trees. Sometimes, we would see women washing clothes in the river. As a child in Trinidad I did not live close to a river, yet somehow I always felt as if I had come home. The sight would stroke a longing in me to go down and join them. It always looked so ideal, so natural. The boulders in the water provided a place where you could spread the clothes to bleach. Reality lay in the packet of washing powder on the bank. On one particular occasion we could hear loud voices coming from below the trees. Driving past we saw wet clothes spread on boulders while heaps of dry clothing lay on the bank. A group of laughing women were swimming in the river. We turned the next corner to find ourselves in a banana-growing region. Fruit lay rotting on the ground.

'Come on! You can't be serious.'

I had just been told bananas below a certain standard could not be sold for export. I could see row after row of banana trees, blue transparent bags protecting the ripening fruit from birds and pests.

The unmistakeable stench of the fruit as it lay rotting by the roadside followed like a trail of carnage. The sight stayed with us for almost a mile. The smell remained for a good deal longer. That is what lay on my left. On my right the hill was dotted with a number of wooden shacks. 'Our house is on a hill, you know. It overlooks the sea.' Well, there is truth. And truth. There are hills, hills and yet more hills. There are hills where the people can squat without fear of property developers breaking down their doors. Hills which only the poor want to climb. Non-residential, marginal drainage, marginal electricity, marginal living standards. Water from stand-pipes half a mile away. Pull the green grass of freedom from under them. Replace it with concrete, then transport it to an urban setting. Slam them so close they huddle together for comfort, so close they inhale the same stench, exhale the same razor-sharp breath of despair. Now you can use a collective noun to describe them. Shanty towns. A pinprick of light at the centre of the hunger begins to eat inwards. Ravenous, it grows larger, devouring all hope until it is even sucking on the marrow. Only the socket remains, the bare bones, lifeless, staring at you, through you, out the other side at some distant lasting vision. And you can't go home worse off than when you came. There will be no fatted calf, only disappointment.

There are hills and there are hills. There are hills which only the poor want to climb. There are hills which only the poor *have* to climb.

I looked from my left to my right and then back again. Even though the policy had been explained to me, I still did not understand. It did not make sense.

We were travelling on the east coast to Marigot and would spend the night there. The coastline, far below, stayed with us most of the time. Castle Bruce came into view long before we got to it. As remote as the hills. And we would come to such settlements from time to time. A small town at your feet nestling against the beach. You pass through, stay for a short while then move on. They will not remember you unless you run beserk, shouting and screaming through their town. And an echo is not a lasting thing. It wanes to a speck of oblivion. When you take the road out, whether it is an hour or several hours later, you keep them in view until they are out of sight. Your passing through has barely been noticed. Your presence had changed nothing. There were times when I longed to be more than just dust in a wayward breeze.

The Carib Reserve lies between Castle Bruce and Marigot. This is where you will find the descendants of the people the Europeans found in the Caribbean islands when they came.

There are shops where you can buy their woven baskets and other handicrafts. Visitors come to the reserve specifically to see the Caribs. What must it feel like to be gawked at all the time? Theirs was the last bastion. This is their last bastion. They fought the white man for the right to remain in their own lands. My history book tells me Christopher Columbus *discovered* the West Indies. How can you *discover* islands which were already peopled, already thriving, already cultured? Spears against guns. The end of an era but it was far from being the last revolution. The wheel set in motion near Monsieur Thiebault's house was the same wheel which lay rusting among the moss and creepers of Tobago. Dormant yet still dominant in the vast crucifying concept of life and death. Its rotting form shudders away from the present having gained substance from the past. African, European, Carib, Arawak. I could not say how many of the people in the reserve were of pure Carib descent. Many had inter-married with other peoples. In the same way the rednecks of Barbados were betrayed by their features, the people of this region had the square, flat faces and short, squat build of their Amerindian ancestors.

I wanted to take photographs of two white huts built close to each other but the determined looks I was getting from a family nearby stopped me. The huts were circular with thatched roofs, an oblong opening for a door and two square holes for windows. I did not see anything else which compared. Could not help but wonder how close those ajoupas were to the sort of dwellings the Caribs may have lived in.

My eyes were shielded from the sun when I looked up to where the water cascaded, screaming as it fell from a great height. I am no judge of distance. How much further would the Caribs have leapt? Leapt to their deaths from Sauteurs in Grenada rather than be taken prisoner by the French. They leapt from that point on the cliff into the sea. Did they scream or were they silent? Did they shout their defiance, raging at a vengeful god, or did they go down without a sound? I believe they leapt without a word, not a whisper. The only sound was their bodies ripping through the wind and when they hit the water.

At the extreme southern tip of Dominica is a peninsula called Scotts Head. The road ends just before you get to it. This narrow strip of land has the Atlantic on one side and the Caribbean on the other. If you become desperate enough, you could walk out to it to feel the waters lap or roar on either side of your feet. I remained in the car to watch the two forces at play. Not far from Scotts Head is Carib Leap. Funnily enough, I did not find the landmark on the standard map of Dominica. It was the one issued by the tourist board which showed it. But then this was one of the islands they came to rather than the one they leapt from. When they were being driven from island to island, this was where they came to. Some say it was Dominica's mountainous terrain which stopped the Europeans from searching them out and completely annihilating them.

It would not have been possible for me to look down into those waters in Grenada without experiencing some sensation of vertigo. But I had gone as far as I could at Scotts Head and seen for the first time a visible interplay. The rage and the calm, separated only by a narrow carpet of land.

Nothing has changed. Nothing changes. The vow of silence was never broken.

The rain came after we had entered the Reserve. Heavy and torrential. I had watched them through rain and shine. Inscrutable faces which did not budge when cars slowed down to scrutinize them. They looked so placid going about their work, going about their work like anyone else.

Were these the warlike people who raised a fearless spear to destroy the enemy? I searched faces and hands weatherworn from fishing, looking for a throb from the pulse which sang of warriorhood.

The vow was never broken. They leapt to their deaths without a murmur. The only sound was the sudden shriek of wind being ripped like an invisible curtain.

We drove slowly through the Carib Reserve. I was like a tightrope walker edging my way along one of those eroded, rusty spokes. Blindfolded. If I fell, I would do my best to hang on. I had not set out to look for anything more profound than a basic understanding. Almost by accident, somehow, I could feel myself close to the hub. I was arriving. I was getting there. History had come alive, been lifted off the page into the shape of a reality. The spectres had been given some form of substance.

I had found it impossible to look down into those waters. They were too far below and the ghosts stacked too high. Concept of life and death. Death and life. And go down beneath the waters to come up again. Coming up. Rising still rising. Yet rising. Coming up from the sea – once our enemy.

Suck the air deep into your lungs. That last and final breath of death, of life. When you do down, come up again, exhaling gently. Controlled. Let it last through the years. Through the centuries. Forever.

They returned my look without a flicker of interest, those inscrutable Amerindian warriors. This time they had come home for ever. They returned my look without a flicker. A flicker. Nurture that almost invisible point of light from the eye of even the finest needle. Blow on it very quietly but determinedly. It will slowly glow, get brighter. What now? Once you have regained the fire, what do you do? Use it to burn a trail which will draw in the corners, the edges of time and history. Christopher Columbus did *not* discover the Caribbean. And the vow was never broken. The silence had been held.

We were in Russell's Landrover. The vehicle used in his

job. There were a number of them on the island, used by various aid organisations in helping the people to build roads and plant new trees. The word 'aid' can be interpreted according to one's needs or inclinations. While driving along, we would sometimes feel a bump or pull on the back of the vehicle and find someone had leapt on because he, she or they wanted to get to a place further along the road. The vehicle you are driving singles you out, putting you into a particular category. The Landrover said that Russell was not from the island. He was on the island for a specific purpose. The sense of things not being quite what they seemed or quite what you would expect, gained momentum. Russell was getting a lot of attention from the young women we met on the way. In a number of instances, I got the distinct impression they would have much pre-ferred it if I wasn't there. Clive explained it to me later.

'They see the boys in the Landrovers as the new marines. They have money. Probably marry one of them and get off the island.' At the same time, *our* passing through got a great deal of attention, on a different level. Dominica is an underdeveloped country. Even without hurricanes which come to devastate what she has achieved, like a number of other islands in the group, she is poor. We drove through Marigot without actually realizing we were there. We did not get any sense of town. This had nothing, nothing ostensibly to do with want or need. Nothing to do with the number of houses, shops, churches, schools, bars or commercial facilities. It was nothing to do with what it lacked and everything to do with something extra being offered. This did not only apply to Marigot and Castle Bruce but other areas. The people would stop whatever they were doing to look and keep on looking. I had only ever experienced this sort of curiosity in country districts. And yet, despite the attention, I still felt insignificant, almost invisible. My passing through had been scrutinized. Scrutinized but not noted. It was almost as if it had become habit. Something new had presented itself so they stopped what they were doing to turn their attention towards it. But how much of it did they actually see? Scrutinized yet somehow not noticed. At you, sometimes straight into your eyes. Eyes which follow until you are out of sight. Yet you sense your presence had stirred nothing. And I still longed to be more than just dust in a wayward breeze.

There was something else. As evening approached, a certain something manifested itself. Like the other islands, it started to get dark by six o'clock. However, it was the only island where I experienced the phenomenon of driving through a dimly lit settlement to find apparitions suddenly appearing in the headlights. They were being conjured up from the streets, from the pavements, in doorways. Sometimes, it looked as if the entire community was out in force. The people stood, sat, crouched, laughed in their twilight world. Such a shock to find them there. Every time it happened, it almost had me holding my breath in surprise. Reality begins with a question mark. Two funnels of light had projected certain images. What happened then? Were they sucked in, to be transformed once again into globules of darkness? Like a funnel which narrowed quickly, sharply, to disappear, I would turn to find the door had just as suddenly closed. Transparent. We passed through their lives, their world like ghosts.

We'd been told about a guest-house in Marigot. Found it, booked in and that evening went to join the people in their twilight world. They continued about their business in the growing darkness. Standing on the pavement, I watched them, to some extent, watching us.

Music reached us from somewhere in the pale evening. Ethereal? Not really. Reggae and calypso. If we followed our ears, we felt sure we'd find a disco.

No flashing lights, just an even darkness spread by the bulb above the bar. It was never crowded. At no time during the evening did it cater for more than a dozen people. They came and they went, perpetuating the transient quality of the evening. Some stayed for half an hour, sometimes less, sometimes longer. Others came to take their place. Later, I would recognize faces from earlier in the evening. There may have been other things happening. We never bothered to find out. We stayed, drank, danced and left when it closed. Only five permanent fixtures during the entire evening. The man at the door, the barman, the man with the music and us.

The other side of midnight. I could comprehend it more satisfactorily as we stepped into the night to walk the short distance to the guesthouse. No indecisive edge could twist a question into this. Darkness. Night, total and complete. And we now had it almost to ourselves.

My heart went out to the people when we came to Melville Hall. Their new and modern airport which once accommodated the larger aircraft. Destroyed in the hurricane, it was now just a shell. It had been set in beautiful grounds. An excellent way to begin your holiday. A fitting reception, to step out of the plane into such congenial surroundings. It is a mocking god who licks his serrated tongue into your sore. Just when you thought it was beginning to heal.

I had never seen sea urchins so close to the shore. We had come north to Calibishie. Row after row of them just below the water. You could not go into the sea while they were there. They held guard, almost daring you to take a chance. My thoughts went to Margo. She had stopped limping by the time we met up again. On her way home, she stopped over in Trinidad for a couple of days.

To get to the water, you would need to pick your way among them – very carefully. Russell did it. He eventually found a place to swim. I didn't go near. I sat and watched. Those black balls were like sentinels. What were they guarding? What did they *think* they were guarding? What the devil was going on?

'Our house is on a hill, you know. It overlooks the sea.' Well, there is truth and there is truth. There was a new and interesting kind of progress taking place. Large, expensive bungalows were being built on hills, though granted not hills as steep as those that property developers fear to tread. But like hills where the poor live, there was neither electricity nor running water. What they had, however, was potential. There were Dominicans who travelled home from England, Canada, America on holiday every year, every two years, to build houses they would eventually come back to. Every time they visited, a little would be added. When completed, all that remained was for electricity and water to be connected. They were certain that by the time they had finished building and were ready to return, supplies would have reached their hill. On other islands, I saw evidence of something I could best describe as pyramid psychology. To my mind, it made good practical sense.

Stake out your land and build one room. Live in it. As and when you can afford to, add more walls, floors and ceilings. Bit by bit, you were adding to that room to make it your home. The transition from wood to concrete was a major one. At any rate, it ensured permanence and durability.

Martin's house in St Lucia was being built along similar lines. Put some money by every pay day until you had the few hundred necessary for another spurt at your freedom and independence. Except, in his case, he continued to live in lodgings until the dream of that splendid home had been completed.

One of the things Russell and I did on reaching Portsmouth was to drop in on Clive. Later, the three of us paid a visit to Miss Ivy's. Miss Ivy's was a multi-faceted establishment which served as grocery, disco, bar and café. Peas and rice, beef stew, curry and such were on offer with a choice of salad, plantain, yam, dasheen or plain boiled rice.

It was a place full of atmosphere. Straight away you detected one or two little eccentricities.

'What you have today, Miss Ivy?'

'Like you blind or what?'

It wasn't quite the sort of reply you would expect from the person who would be serving you. The counter which separated you, the customer, from the goods and the person on the other side was a very long and narrow one. There were no signs to tell a newcomer where the café ended and the tables used for cards and dominoes began. You already knew that the section with alcohol and people holding glasses must be the bar. But was that vacant area in the centre for dancing? And those barrels in the corner. Presumably, still full of whatever was supposed to be in them. If you couldn't find somewhere to sit, would it be okay to perch on them without Miss Ivy clipping you round the ear?

The shop was a long, wooden, dingy place with three stone steps leading up to the main entrance. The foundations were so close to the ground, she may as well have saved her money. A not too strenuous leap was all it took customers who preferred to gain access via one of the other entrances. Customers arrived, already in full twitch as they walked up or bounded into Miss Ivy's. Anyone going past without stopping was probably on their way to the beach to pee or take a crap. Miss Ivy's was all there was in the alley. Beyond, just a stretch of shingle before you reached the sea.

It was a largely male domain. Husbands had been known to go missing for the entire day. One renegade female was at the bar drinking whisky glass for glass with the men. Apart from myself, the only other women to set foot in Miss Ivy's came to buy groceries. Even they were few and far between. It was mainly children sent out on errands. And one supposed that provided they didn't ask to be served with a double rum, she would have no objections to their presence for that little while. Were the children meant to report back? At least the wife knew where to find him – should she wish to. None were dragged out by the collar or dangling from an ear. At least, not during any of my visits.

Miss Ivy was tall, heavily jewelled, almost regal in her domain.

'No. I not blind, Miss Ivy. I just not sure what that fried thing is. Is fish, is chicken, is what?'

'You trying to say something 'bout my cooking?'

She moved away to serve someone standing at the far end of the counter, calling for a bar of soap. The food was on display behind a glass case. Just below the counter was a small two-ring cooker for anything which needed reheating. She dished it up on a paper plate. You took knife, fork, paper napkin, pepper sauce and went to sit at one of the small tables on your left (you soon got the hang of it!) if the dominoes players hadn't already beaten you to it. If they had, you could eat standing at the counter. There was nothing to stop you from wandering down to the other end of the counter. No physical restraint. But with arms and legs of two dancers flying in all directions, you probably wouldn't make it. If you survived that obstacle, an energetic glass might knock the plate out of your hand.

Miss Ivy greeted me like a long-lost friend.

'Well, girl, I say you dead.'

I had to take a quick look over my shoulder to make sure it was me she was talking to. Miss Ivy's was one of the places Clive had taken me during my stay in Portsmouth. He had introduced us.

'So, you from England.'

I believe I both nodded and smiled.

'My daughter badly want to go to England to study nursing, you know. Badly.'

She had fussed and flattered me while I ate, drank, jerked to the music and bought a couple of essential items. As Clive and I left she reminded me of a promise I had made earlier in the evening.

'You won't forget!'

'No, no.'

I had paid other visits to Miss Ivy's and on each occasion it had ended almost ritualistically.

'You won't forget!'

I would always affirm that I had not forgotten.

It had indeed been a little while since my last visit to Portsmouth. But 'dead'. Surely not. How about 'possibly no longer on the island'. 'Moved on to another, perhaps.' Had she asked Clive he would have been happy, no doubt, to put her straight.

There was a nice, warm, spontaneous, uninhibited atmosphere at Miss Ivy's. At times raucous to the brink of lawlessness. There were some loose floorboards along the centre of the shop. When the music of the alcohol began to take effect, one or two customers would take to prancing on them. Above the music, you could hear the twack, twack, twack of the boards. She didn't appear to mind. There seemed only one thing guaranteed to disturb her equilibrium.

'What that black thing in the stew beef?'

'What happen? Like your mother never tell you 'bout cloves?!!'

I had visited other places on the islands which offered a similar blend. None of them came close to rivalling Miss Ivy's for atmosphere. Her establishment offered a free-up. Free-up your body and your mind. Free-up your body and your mind for tomorrow you may –

There were beaches where the sands became the soil of the shrubs, plants and coconut trees long before they reached the beach. Fine and pale, they got paler yet as they came closer to the water. Suddenly, they turned grey. Ebb tide revealed a deeper grey like ashes. Ashes. Death with resurrection. Black sands.

I had stood on the runway in Point Saline and watched the road so wide, so long it stretched out of sight. Heard the echo of a sigh in the wind. Birth and death on the road.

Heard the echo of a sigh in the wind. Birth and death on the run –

I never asked but every now and then it would come into a conversation. Dark clouds across the horizons mirrored in eyes which pinpoint the starkness of the horror. The mirror glinted in my own understanding, painful stab on an intake of breath.

I had seen evidence of the hurricane. Sharp and vivid reminders. Houses, buildings, coconut groves. The airport at Melville Hall looked as if it had been ripped open. My thoughts had shot to Point Saline. Death and birth. Birth and death. Later, I would find it difficult to tell where one ended and the other began. Which came first. Which inspired the other. Which end of the spiral marked the beginning.

Birth and death on the runway. The road opens up. Virgin. Ready for the experience. Ready for the first feet to

248

trample the freshly laid tarmac. Ready for the onslaught of human feet, animals, cars, bicycles, lorries. Planes. Life. Death.

I had seen the Landrovers, had seen the workers. I had seen new roads in Dominica. Had watched the asphalt being spread, flattened, inching its way forward. Onwards. I had seen new roads being built. Unfolded, waiting for the experience. Had watched and still not been able to tell where life ended and death began. A different knowledge, a different understanding from the one I had known before. A difficult birth.

Free-up your body and your mind. Free-up your body and your mind for tomorrow you may –

'Cockroach? What cockroach? You see cockroach on my fish? Where it? Show me! Show me! You blasted liar!'

Incensed with rage, she had the customer by the collar. A party was now in full swing outside the shop.

As we were leaving Miss Ivy looked up from giving her customer what looked suspiciously like a butt. Her eyes glazed over for a few seconds.

'You won't forget?'

Habit. Now far too late for it to be broken. I turned to look at her with an expression of hurt indignation.

'How could I!'

Although, at that precise moment, I could not for the life of me remember what.

There were many things you took for granted. So many. I held my head in disbelief. I had to go over it again.

'You've got to be joking. Come on.'

Clive tried to keep his expression in place as he repeated what he had said earlier.

'That's right. Twice a week.'

Once again I held my head in disbelief.

'Mail is delivered to Portsmouth twice a week? Twice a week?'

The conversation was taking place on our way back to the Landrover after visiting Miss Ivy's. I had voiced my concern about a registered letter my mother had sent.

'I can't understand why it should be taking so long. It should have been here ages ago.'

'Yes, well, we only get deliveries twice a –'

I stopped to look over my shoulder. Perhaps, that was my mistake. I should have kept right on going without so much as a hint of a backward glance.

While in St Lucia, I found out I would not be allowed back in Trinidad unless I showed the immigration officials my return ticket back to London. I had not taken it with me. Two frantic phone calls to my mother. That night in St Lucia and another in Dominica. The second call confirmed it had been sent the day after I left St Lucia. Long enough, we both agreed, for it to have arrived. Even within the limitations of two deliveries a week to the only address I had at the time, Clive's in Portsmouth. No island was allowed to issue any holder of a non-Trinidadian passport with a one-way fare unless the person could show proof that their stay in Trinidad was only going to be a temporary one.

Until the ticket arrived, I could not book my return flight to Trinidad. I waited. Despite myself I continued to cast furtive glances over my shoulder.

I was staying with Russell in the house he was renting just outside Roseau. Every day from then on found me walking into the capital, to the sorting office. Twice a day. Every time they had mail coming in from abroad.

The clerk felt he knew what the problem was.

'It probably gone on to the Dominican Republic.'

'What?!'

'They does get our mail and sometimes we does get their mail.'

His face expressionless, he continued sorting through a pile of letters.

'Commonwealth of Dominica, you see. Unless you remember to put it on your letter, all sorts of things could happen.'

I stood looking at him for a full minute, attempting vain efforts to stop my stomach from making slow somersaults.

'You're just trying to cheer me up, aren't you?'

'Sorry?'

He still didn't look up from his work. He did nothing more than cock his head.

'Admit it. You're trying to put me in the right frame of mind.'

It was lost on him. Completely and utterly. Sarcasm was too subtle a weapon. Like water off a duck's back, it didn't even dent his armour.

Mean streets. I walked through Roseau in a daze. Everything was happening at once. Like a head-on collision. Something else. Snippets of a conversation I'd had with Russell when he returned from work the previous evening.

'When?'

'At the weekend.'

'But that doesn't give me any time at all.'

'What are we going to do?'

'What do you mean "we". I'm the one who's in shit.'

'I certainly don't want you to – '

'Look. It isn't your problem. It's mine. Okay?'

As things stood, regardless of what happened I would have to leave the house by the weekend. If the worst came to the worst I could stay in a guest-house. But I didn't really have enough money. I simply couldn't afford it.

Mean streets. Suddenly, everything was going wrong. At first it seemed as if some magnet was trying to hold me to the island. Then it felt as if when the collision took place, the magnet had been just as violently yanked away. Something was rocking my boat.

'Like someone working obeah on you, girl.'

A voice deep inside. The sower of superstitious seeds.

Mean streets. I had thought so on my first evening in the capital. I tried to remember in which sense. At the time, the word seemed apt. I tried hard not to let my current state of mind reinforce that first impression of Roseau.

Mean streets. Mean streets? Ah, yes, I had left the hotel in the cool of the early evening and gone for a walk.

Roseau reminded me of Port of Spain – strategically. Straight roads run vertically, horizontally, to intersect. You could almost play a game of noughts and crosses on an aerial map.

Mean streets? Roseau was small, limiting. Limited in the sense that she was not a commercial capital. I soon got a sense of being boxed in, not necessarily by those streets which crossed but because I once again sensed barriers, limitations. Most businesses had already closed for the day. Interesting architecture. Lots of wooden houses with balconies. Lots of shutters pulled down, shut. You looked up into faces which already had their eyes closed. And it was only just coming on to sunset. Trellis and ornate ironwork lent an interesting feature to the house I found myself looking up at. But surely I had been there before. Had already seen that house and its hanging baskets. I stood still to take stock before turning anti-clockwise in an attempt to centre my bearing. Yes, I had been there before. Even more recently than at first supposed. I had completed more than just the one circle. My judgement is sometimes clouded. I was retracing my footsteps without actually realizing it. There was more wood than concrete. Was it an illusion or was I once again doubling back on my footsteps? My sense of direction had become *pathetic*. I turned corners to find myself facing streets I had visited a little earlier. Dusty, dingy afternoon of stale sunshine where heatwaves no longer had the energy to rise. There were people leaning on balconies, sitting on doorsteps, on walls, chatting on street corners, strolling along the pavement. Always.

Trellis, wrought ironwork and wood. Sometimes only wood. Humble dwellings. Trellis, wrought ironwork and wood combined sometimes to give an impression of erstwhile grandeur. Sometimes. At other times a decaying colonial texture. On the whole, dark wood. Dark, disappointed wood.

'When the hurricane hit, everything went black. Was like night-time in the middle of the day.'

Is that how it was? Like night-time in the middle of the day?

I made for the waterfront, missed my turn and found myself walking towards a wall which separated the river from the city. From a distance there was nothing to give the game away. But looking over the wall, I could see the rubbish and filth which clung to the other side. Old tyres, tin cans, rags and more. Did some people empty rubbish there? It seemed that way at first glance. I certainly had no intention of looking any further. If I followed the wall – going in the right direction – even I couldn't get it wrong. It would, regardless, take me down to the bay. I went past the market place which led to Bay Street near the waterfront and went past the sorting office. But that was on my first evening.

From the sorting office, I now walked along Bay Street to the market place. My thoughts were in such turmoil it was only the sudden onslaught of sound which told me where I was. On better days, I would have stopped and walked through. There was usually something I needed. It was a fine market, regardless of my state of mind.

The old market was at the other end of Bay Street. This was a new indoor one but, like other islands, that really didn't say enough. I swear there must have been more people selling outside than on the inside. In the shade of the covered market, the women sat and sold their goods.

I felt I knew that part of Roseau well enough to walk it blindfolded. No matter how deep my preoccupation, the raw smell of fruit, vegetables, herbs and the babel of voices could not be straight-jacketed into any borders of alignment. Freedom. The noise rose to a crescendo then tailed off to be picked up a little further away where passengers waited to board the minibuses. Next to it was a stall which sold cooked foods and drinks. A snack to bridge the gap or to take with you if it was going to be a long journey. It offered a different sort of noise and hub, smell and sound from the market place. More cloistered, more contained. Like a river and its timid stream. Cooked food and passengers, a few chatting, most just waiting patiently to board the bus which would take them north.

It was all so academic, so precise, so mechanical. My feet took a right then left turn into Hillsborough, a street which offered a variety of shops and buildings including some government departments.

What a cock-up! What a complete and utter balls-up! If, as the prat at the sorting office had said, mail for the island could end up in the Dominican Republic, what on earth was I going to do? Firstly, they would not let me back into Trinidad. Secondly, I would not have my return ticket to get from Piarco to Heathrow. That was the less immediate of the two. Strange. Such turmoil. Such unease. Movement within a tight space caused the grooves to chip and wear away, shaping an uneven circle. Under any other heading it would still be erosion. Not to be allowed back into the country of your birth. How ironic.

If the islands were like stepping stones I could be caught in mid-stride, locked in an inertia. Even strong waves couldn't budge me. If my legs were spread wide when I keeled over, I would be like Guadeloupe. Every beach told a story. I had first seen it in Grenada. Beaches of black sand. Sulphur. And what volcanic wonder would spew from these uncertain thighs?

The bridge served its purpose. Did what it was meant to do. It saved me from falling as I walked through thin air in an attempt to get to the other side. Bridges are necessary practical things. The one I had to cross found me gazing down with the same longing. It took me out of myself to crash on to boulders. I always stopped to watch the women washing clothes in the river. The longing never left me. In this instance, I wished the bridge wasn't there. Odd. There was just the one. A lone figure below me, thigh deep among boulders, squeezed then wrung a piece of washing. About to spread it on a rock she seemed to freeze. Her back arched for an instant before turning her head quickly. She turned to look up at where I stood. Still. She stared but I do not think she saw me. Realizing there was nothing on the bridge for her to see, went back to her washing.

I had to cross a bridge which would take me to the other side. The bridge I crossed had already taken me to the other side. Already. There was a short cut which could get me to the house. I did not take it. I went the long way round, staying on the main road all the way.

Stop! Replay!

It didn't quite work out that way. But it may well have done. It took several more takes before it came right. Going back to the beginning at replay speed made the action look ridiculous. Walking backwards at break-ankle speed was never one of my strong points. The reality was even more of a farce.

It took four days for it to come right. Four days of nail-biting agony. And even then –

Both Clive and Russell came with me for support. This would be my last chance. In some form or fashion it would *have* to materialize that day. I took a deep breath before asking.

'Registered letter for Miss – '

He looked down his list.

'Yes.'

I may have whooped. At the least, a gasp of delight. Clive and Russell both voiced their relief.

'Gone on to Portsmouth.'

Stop! Repeat!

'What did you say?'

'Addressed to Portsmouth, so gone to Portsmouth.'

Action! Fast forward! – into infinity.

I would have preferred not to think about it.

No! Stop! Wreck the bloody frame and step out of the nightmare into some resemblance of anything which comes even vaguely close to reality.

I could hear Russell and Clive in the background. What they were saying was really of little importance. I took a deep breath to exhale words which came slowly.

'I have been coming here every day, twice a day, for the best part of a week. Every time I come, I ask you people about the same blasted letter, explaining the situation, explaining the problem and you asses have the audacity to tell me you sent my letter on to Portsmouth.'

There was a sort of explosion. Letters didn't exactly go flying through the air but what took place wasn't far short. Words darted through the room. Reasons. Excuses. Reasons. Excuses. Reasons. Excuses. Never apologies.

No need for a call for action. Or even re-action. My control had long since deserted me.

'What a bunch of inefficient wankers!'

Clive and Russell were both trying to calm me. They didn't stand a chance. There was now a full-scale row between myself and the man responsible. Everybody and everything else was excluded.

Stop! Freeze!

It had to happen. Even on the outside of the nightmare – outside? – there would need to be some external control.

An iron grip on my wrist held my arm motionless. I hadn't realized my hand was doubled into a fist drawn back, ready to strike out. Clive's was the restraining influence. Russell played his part. Words which soothed and made sense.

'Come on. Let's go to Portsmouth.'

I left it all behind. Words, the torrent, anger. But the mood remained. Every mile which left Roseau further behind should have presented a brighter perspective. But it didn't. Russell and I said little on the way. I voiced my feelings just the once.

'How much do you want to bet it's on its way back to Roseau right now.'

He gave a short laugh. Sharp and to the point.

'I'm not going to believe it until I have the damn thing in my hand.'

Clive had said he would telephone ahead to let the Portsmouth post office know what was going on.

Even as we walked up the steps I still had my doubts. The woman was polite, congenial.

'Ah, yes.'

She turned to walk into the next room. And seemed to be gone for an awfully long time. Russell and I were both silent, waiting for her. She came back with – an expression which – ? an empty – ?

'Will you sign for it, please?'

A slim, white package had appeared on the counter. I had not seen the woman's other hand. Only the one which was empty. The sight of my mother's handwriting split the chains. My signature on the page should have ensured my release.

'What's the matter?'

The portent was in my hand, unopened. Russell was trying to read my expression.

'What's today?'

Russell's reply brought bad news.

'I should have come yesterday.'

These were two uneven halves. I did not open the envelope until we were back in the Landrover. I knew then it would be all right. My mother had not sent the wrong ticket. As she assured me after another frantic phone call two evenings earlier, she had properly addressed it to the Commonwealth of Dominica. The other possible reason for the delay had immediately been ruled out.

'What's the matter?'

My reply to his question could only be equal, in part, to my own comprehension. I told him the truth.

'I don't know. I'm really not sure.'

The miles back to Roseau should have seemed shorter than the outward journey. It was not the case. The removal of that enormous obstacle had now given other doubts room in which to flourish. I held the portent against my stomach. The side on which my mother had written my name was pressed tightly against my skin. I used both hands. Strange butterfly spasms. I pressed the envelope even closer. My eyes were fixed on the road. Every mile which separated me from Portsmouth should have made it easier.

'What's the matter?'

This insistence continued to hammer at my door. When I pulled the envelope away all was quiet. I realized of course, all I may have done was applied the required amount of pressure needed to anaesthetize my stomach. Nevertheless, my reply shaped words into a form which united truth with logic.

'I should have come yesterday.'

Canefield Airport. All I was waiting for now was to board. I had arrived on the understanding that I would be on standby. While I was playing 'chase the ticket', multiple bookings had come in from Guadeloupe to Martinique. Dominica was piggy in the middle. The *remotest* of chances. What was more, the girl at the ticket office had assured me, the flight appeared to be overbooked. I told her I would take my chances.

So how come as soon as I checked in I was given my boarding pass?

This gap between checking-in and boarding was a strange hour. You were, in any case, in a state of limbo. The small waiting room, with its constant coming and going, did not allow much space for privacy. I probably didn't need any. I had already said my goodbyes. Clive on the previous evening when I dropped by the flat he used during his working week in Roseau. Russell, just minutes after my seat on the flight was confirmed. He was now preoccupied with more pressing matters and I welcomed the first chance in days to recharge my energy batteries.

I did not need the privacy of Canefield or any other waiting room. My thoughts ran between two vertical lines centred firmly on an object not that far into the distance.

The frantic beating of the drum had quelled to a monotonous throb. Dull but regular. The time and space between each pulse was predictable. In my own reading and deciphering of the message it was a dirge. My translation was not a literal one but the way my doubts rose to fill the gaps between notes left me very uneasy. The way the cadence of that name reinforced my doubts.

I had not forgotten. No.

'I should have come yesterday.'

There was something else I wanted to do in Portsmouth the weekend Russell and I toured the island, apart from visiting Clive. Sunday afternoon. Yes, there was a chance.

'Let's drive over to the wharf. I want to check someone out.'

They were there, loading up. Smiles and greetings all round. I asked for her by name trying to find the face among those of the other women.

'Where is she?'

The captain answered.

'Sick. Two weeks since.'

Sick? Two weeks since? That means she had not made the trip since we all travelled out together.

'Where does she live? How far away?'

Someone turned and pointed towards some distant hills. Too far a journey. Too steep a hill. That was an afterthought. My first instincts when I shielded my eyes to scan a nest of houses was to put my hands to my mouth and shout her name.

That was my initial reaction.

Too far a journey. Too steep a hill.

I said my goodbyes and walked away stepping around shadows being cast by boxes and sacks in the afternoon sun.

Had I travelled to Portsmouth a day earlier, I would have been able to meet the boat on its return from the next trip. She would surely have been well enough to join them that week. Wouldn't she?

Madelaine.

I had glimpsed the face I had least expected to see. It looked a good deal livelier and healthier than it had that Wednesday.

Madelaine.

There was now little doubt in my mind Madame Rico would outlive, would out-sell us all. If I returned to the island in ten years' time, she would still be crawling on board close to death for the return journey and resurrecting fresh as a lily in time for the outward trip.

Madelaine.

And how was it the bastards had got it wrong again? The plane was barely half-full!

In the tropics when a wind blows, you bask in its cool, soothing influence. I would stand still to enjoy the feel of its caress on my body. I used to be fairly certain about gentle daytime winds in the Caribbean. But there is a lot I used to be certain about which I have since needed to rethink and revalue.

I never thought my response to the mid-day breeze would be one of the things I would need to rethink and revalue.

It was of course, entirely my own fault. Who else could I blame? The sorting office in Castries, perhaps? A little too much like history repeating itself. In any case, they came into it only in so far as the second letter I sent him never arrived.

We had discussed the possibility of breaking my journey to spend a couple of days in St Lucia on my way back. My first letter had said I definitely wouldn't be able to do it. The second said I would, giving the date and time of flight.

I waited at Vigie Airport and waited and waited.

And it was an ill wind – but I would not find out about that until the following day. He was out of Castries for the day. The person at the other end of the telephone offered to come and pick me up.

It most definitely was an ill wind.

I had never paid more than fleeting visits to Martin's lodgings. On these instances we had only stopped to drop something off or collect something. On all but two occasions I had waited in the car.

I did not guess. I could not know. I would need to find out for myself.

By the time Martin's friends had picked me up at the airport and taken me back to their house, it was already after mid-day. Hot Caribbean afternoon where you long for a *sweet* breeze or the cool clear sea. Still afternoon. Little air in motion. The house was within walking distance of Vigie beach. Too late in the day to bump into Cecily Devereux. I certainly had no plans to pay the lady a visit. I grabbed my swimsuit and went down to the sea for the afternoon.

Christ! How could I have forgotten. It was Saturday.

Stand on one leg like a stork or bury your head in the sand. Either way there you were and there you would stay for a while. Everything has its own odour. The sea – weeds, fish – dead, shells, the rest. Whatever. Distinctive, at any rate. You couldn't escape it. Would you want to? There was an ill wind.

I found a spot and settled down for the rest of the afternoon, taking it all for granted. The cool balming breezes and everything else you would expect to find working to your advantage. Despite the noise, despite the crowd, despite all interferences I stayed there. Stayed until I felt it was time to go. I left, being wafted on my way by that last *sweet* breeze. I didn't know it, at the time, but for a little while it would be one of my last.

It was an ill wind.

When I returned I found Martin waiting. He had just got back.

It was an ill wind.

And how the devil didn't I detect it later when we dropped my things at his place before going boogieing? Or when we got back during the starlit hours of the next morning?

It was indeed an ill wind.

My mother would have said it served me right. I woke at a time when those who leave their homes suitably attired, bibles in armpits, had long since returned home. I would have got no sympathy from her.

Your sins will find you out.

Or something similar.

I'm not sure what woke me. Martin was putting in a seven-day week. It wasn't his leaving. Glancing at the clock I could see that must have been hours earlier.

I became instantly aware of something unfamiliar. Not just a bed I had never slept in before. Nothing to do with my immediate surroundings. Nothing at all. Everything to do with my immediate surroundings and that ill wind.

Each has its own. The sea — weeds, fish — dead, shells, the rest. Whatever. Distinct. I don't believe this! My imagination. Surely not! There it was again. White net. Bedroom curtains flapped in the open window. Wafting. Wafting. First just a tremble of net. Vague. Vague. A sudden strong gust of wind blew the curtains in. No sifting device this. No sieve which separates the desirable from the desired. The mesh was not of the quality where the question of choice was paramount. Selection did not come into it at all. In fact, the fine net was an aid to non-selection.

I leapt out of bed, dashed to the window and almost froze in my footsteps. Recovered. Rushing round the rooms I took a good look from each window. There weren't that many so I did not experience as much difficulty as at first supposed. The windows were on one side only. The house had been divided into two apartments by a thin wall, if the voices I could hear on the other side were anything to go by.

I was staying in what was, by definition, a *yard*. A group of dwellings in close proximity to each other shared common facilities. I was fascinated and at the same time repulsed. I already had my bearings. Now, I needed to take stock.

My thoughts immediately leapfrogged to Barbados. To that street. To those houses. What would it be like? What could it be like? I had asked myself the question when I was on the outside. I was asking myself now, as close as I was likely to get to the inside. For two days. For two days?

For two days. For just two days?

All your life. All their lives.

My thoughts darted back to Guadeloupe. Infinitely worse. Infinitely worse yet.

All their lives.

And for less than two days of yours? Christ, woman, day after tomorrow you catch an early flight. You decided to stay here to save on hotel bills. Like Martin you'll be using it as such. Gone first thing in the morning, back late at night. His sister and her boyfriend had invited me to Sunday lunch. I'd be out and about with them for the rest of the day, rendezvousing with Martin later. We already had plans for the evening.

I went back to the bedroom and fighting revulsion put my head out the window.

Was this where some came to worship? It stood almost in the centre of concrete relieved only by cracks in cement where weeds pushed their way through. A sort of shrine. It seemed to grow out of the base as if the three sides were an extension of the concrete surface. A place of marvel, of wonder. You take off your hat before you unhook wooden slats kept alert by nails. Concrete spread its grey uneven erosion as if the earth were a natural environment. It cracked and split its way to the guttering where green slime lay a gentle carpet for the effluence which foamed, spat then overflowed to seep into cracks or ran along the surface until stopped by more fissures.

Bow your head as you enter then close the door noiselessly behind you.

Someone came out to hang clothes on Martin's side of the yard. A fat, middle-aged woman whose pink dress took on a life of its own when she bent from the hip to take an article from the basket then stretched up to reach the clothes line. From time to time she turned to nod or shake her head as if carrying on a conversation with a person who stood outside the range of my vision.

I did not see anyone enter but I heard. Four pieces of corrugated iron with a spout above them. How had I escaped that the previous evening? Yes, of course. I had taken a shower at his friends' house when I got back from the beach.

My mind went semi-blank. Only certain realities filtered through as if part of my brain had taken a deep breath and having done so, rendered itself unconscious. Even the smell of cooking couldn't seriously rival it.

Never before so close. Never before in such close proximity. Never before. So close, it filled my sight and senses. I could not ignore it. Even when I turned away, back towards the wall which separated me from my neighbour, I could not escape. Even with my eyes closed its presence filled the room.

Difficult to say how long my thoughts remained bandaged. I suddenly found myself stepping out of the kitchen door, flannel and soap in hand, bath towel around me. The water flowed easily some of the time, the rest in jerks and spurts. Anyhow, I got there in the end.

I tried dressing as quickly as I could. Could feel it even as I did so, like a morse code. Erratic opening and closing of muscles.

Giant fists reached down knuckles first to knead and contort the pitch until it was soft, pliable, less resistant, warm then gooey as it began to stir. It moved to trap your feet in potholes which lay like empty sockets ravenous for any passing vision.

And when I could no longer escape, I reached up. I raised my hand to the shelf in the kitchen where he kept a version of the bible. Reverently descending the steps, I came to where the sun drained every ounce of moisture from the clothes on the washline before descending to the stone earth to soak up a recent circle of water around the shower. From there, it lay directly ahead. Entering, I kept my eyes closed and lowering myself on to the seat spent the next few minutes doing what they had been doing all their lives – I meditated above the perfumes of my neighbours' labour.

It was the biggest plane I had travelled in for weeks. Night-time flight on a Boeing 747 and my thoughts were racing onwards. A night-time flight, delayed by an hour. That was nothing. I had spent almost the entire day at Vigie Airport trying to get out.

St Lucia to Barbardos. Barbados to Trinidad.

Moored. The best part of a day at Vigie Airport. The plane had developed mechanical problems and had to turn back. The one which should have taken its place did not make it either. The passengers booked on the flight were taken in a minibus for a glorious lunch, some-where.

All except me.

Had come back nicely relaxed if not slightly intoxicated to be taken to the final departure lounge.

All except me.

And when the plane eventually arrived, were escorted courteously and apologetically to their seats.

All except me.

Million to one chance. Sweet Jesus, it was a million to one chance! What were the odds? I sat on the comfortable aircraft, my skin tingling, still smarting from the narrowness of escape. Escape. It had been close. It now seemed as if I had narrowly, only barely managed to squeeze sideways, through a space before the slab slid firmly, irrevocably in place.

A million to one chance! How was it possible? How was it possible that my name had been left off the passenger list? When the clerk first told me he could not find my name, I as good as called him a liar. I had gone over it with him. Slowly. Every name I passed on the way had left me a little weaker. There had been no mistake. My name had been left off the list. As far as they were concerned I did not exist. Felt it then, those spasms in my stomach like fists opening and closing at lightning speed. Looking down into the water and not finding your reflection.

Just head and neck on a shimmering silver platter. Decapitated. Just head and neck. When I inclined my head I could find no reflection. That was when I – that is when you – begin to doubt your identity. As far as they are concerned, you do not exist. And they hold the key which will get you from where you are to where you want to get to.

How was it possible? The first thing I did when I flew in from Dominica was to book the flight from St Lucia back to Trinidad, changing planes in Barbados. As soon as I left customs, I went straight to the reservations office to secure a seat on that Monday morning flight. It had been done before I turned my thoughts to Martin. To ask myself why he was so late. To ask myself why he was so very late. Somewhere along the line, the message had not got through.

The man kept moving his lips to form the word *standby*.

Standby. *Stand by*! So what the hell am I, for Christ's sake, an outcast on the periphery of their world?

I couldn't believe that after the trauma of Dominica I was still in danger of drowning. So now I was a bystander. Almost invisible, I looked on from the edge of a reality, deprived of privileges afforded the other passengers. A name at the bottom of a list. Separated from the others by three lines written in someone else's handwriting and a different colour ink.

I fell into a sort of shock. No man's land. I looked for a way out of the desert without contours. The numbness did not begin to wear off until I had boarded the plane and fastened my safety belt. I was the last. The very last to take my seat. Escape had been marginal. The passengers on the late afternoon flight had come and met us there. A bigger plane would be arriving to take us, to take all of them on to Barbados. I would not know until the very last minute if there would be room for me. At the very last minute, I was told there was.

When the numbness wore off, sensation came back. Having lost layers of skin, I smarted and tingled my way to Barbados. I had been warned that immunity was no longer guaranteed. I was not expecting any. And yet, apart from the flight from Barbados to Trinidad being delayed by an hour, I was continuing on my way.

A sigh of relief. Several sighs of relief. It should have ended there. The spent breath still held a little too much indignation, too much disgust to merely evaporate. It fuelled the ashes of a recent memory. Martin's face rose from the embers.

He had driven me to the airport on his way to work that morning.

'What's happening to the house? Thought you'd have taken me to see it. Haven't even talked about it.'

For a while he remained impassive.

'Problems.'

I had to prompt him.

'What sort of problems?'

His reply came in a hollow tone.

'With the bank.'

I had not entirely understood the system and how it worked. Did not realize he had taken a loan and was repaying it monthly. He was now anxious to press on with the house but the bank had refused him any more credit.

'What are you going to do?'

He didn't answer.

I closed my eyes again. I shut them tightly just as I had when he told me. The same fear. The same dread. The same worry. And I smarted and tingled my way from Barbados back to Trinidad.

What – what if – what if he didn't make it? The horror had me almost shaking with fright. A margin. A hair's breath separated the two.

Escape.

And it wasn't as if any of the rooms were yet completed. It wasn't even as if he could build around himself. Could watch the roots spread as the tree grew stronger. A sapling in the storm.

Escape.

Martin, you should have stuck to the old-fashioned way. Step by step by step. Leap and you may lose your footing. Miss and you could slip too far.

Escape.

Don't spend the rest of your life doing what they have been doing all their lives – meditating above the perfumes of your neighbours' labour. Don't spend the rest of your life inhaling your neighbour's shit.

*

I made a wish and looked up to find it had been granted. A starlit night. I was thinking about it. Thinking about stars against a midnight blue long before I saw them. Before I turned my eyes towards the heavens I was thinking of stars in the sky.

It had been close. So close. There was a sound which kept repeating in my head. Had been since Martin's face had wafted back down to become ashes. Strange. So strange. I felt so strange. Strange sound like a dull thud. Thud. Every time I heard it, I could not help but shudder. Closed. Sealed for ever. No crowbar could lift this one. I had slipped through the merest of gaps. Escape had been such a narrow one that, in squeezing through, it still felt as if I had left layers of skin behind. Thud. Layers. Thud. It was this perhaps which made me more vulnerable. More receptive.

Piarco Airport on a starlit night. And I was on the outside, bags at my feet. I glanced toward the taxi rank. Left it there for a while longer.

She was there in the shadows. I could sense her presence. Waiting. I must have called her. Was that what I did? In turning my thoughts towards her, I called her? There were stars in the sky. Mine or theirs?

No more onslaught of emotions. No more daggers ripping at my brain. Her presence like a cloak. Moving towards the taxi, I found myself listening to the still calm of layers which had now been replaced. Listening to the thud as it moved further into the distance. Until the sound was nothing more than a leaf drifting on to a sheet of cotton wool.

From the back seat, I watched the night, listening. No obstacles. No congestion. A clean, clear draught of air through the channels of thought. It felt as if I had come over the mountains.

I got out of the taxi, happy and relaxed.

I had telephoned my mother from Barbados. She was standing in the doorway, arms outstretched. Her features were obscured by the porch light. I dropped my bags and ran to greet her. Thud. The carpet was pulled sharply from behind. My heart faltered. Thud. My hands fell to my side. Thud. It was not my mother. Thud. I did not know this – Thud. Yes, I did. It looked like Aunt Ru – Thud. No, it wasn't. It was – Thud. No. It looked more like Hel – Thud. Or could it be Madela – No. Was it Miss Ivy?

'What's the matter?'

The carpet stopped moving.

'Aren't you pleased to see me?'

A violent shake of the carpet sent me tumbling on to my mother's portal.

'You look as if you've seen a ghost.'

My mother's voice.

Relief had me hugging her tightly.

'Yes. Ghosts.'

It was after midnight. My mother had gone to bed. I was on my own and sensed danger. Every minute brought it closer. In less than three days I would be once again at Piarco Airport. That flight would take me back to the U.K.

There was a task I had to perform. It could not wait. It had now become imperative. Moving quickly to the drawer I took out the cloth and unrolled it.

Footprints wore along the length where dirt and grime clung. Under that surface were two other layers. The foundation was bland and regular but the erratic patches of colour had now blanched back to nothing, drained by a weave, hungry. Hungry. Hungry for the wealth of experience.

See. The sea. The sea – of faces. Ghosts. They grew paler by the minute, fading with the coming morning.

She was now so close, I was wearing a second skin. Difficult to separate my will from hers and say the impatience was not my own.

Go on! Go on!

Bring the colour back. Give it life. Give it energy. Let it sparkle against any glimmer of light. Gold in the daytime. Silver by night.

Don't go!

Stab.

Stay!

Stab.

Incantation begins to draw blood. The ritual continued. Unspoken. Broken only by the steel point as it cut through.

Stay!

Stab.

Picking up her needle, I had already started to sew.